D1549666

REFEREN͡ DEPARTMENT

WAR ON DISEASE

War on Disease

A HISTORY OF THE LISTER INSTITUTE

HARRIETTE CHICK

MARGARET HUME

MARJORIE MACFARLANE

ANDRE DEUTSCH

First published in Great Britain in 1971
by André Deutsch Limited
105 Great Russell Street London WC1

Printed in Great Britain
by Ebenezer Baylis and Son Ltd
The Trinity Press, Worcester, and London

ISBN 0 233 96220 4

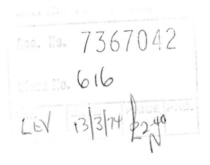

Foreword

BY SIR LINDOR BROWN, C.B.E., F.R.S.

The Governing Body welcomes the publication of this history of the Lister Institute. The authors themselves worked for many years in its laboratories — Dame Harriette Chick from 1906 until 1946; Margaret Hume, whose death before the completion of this work is deeply deplored, from 1916 until 1961; and Marjorie Macfarlane from 1926 to 1965. Their combined experience spans therefore nearly all of the Institute's existence, and much of what they write is within their personal knowledge.

This is not a definitive history of the Institute, for the minutiae of its affairs and its work would fill a large volume. It tells the story of its foundation by a group of Victorians of great public spirit, who were determined that Britain should have an institute for medical research comparable with the Institut Pasteur in Paris; of its splendid endowment by the first Earl of Iveagh, which set it on its feet at the turn of the nineteenth century; and of the classic researches that followed. It tells of a triumphant struggle to maintain its existence by the efforts of its production laboratories, and of the benefactors who have helped to further its researches. Among these benefactors, the Guinness family and Company are outstanding in the continuity of their interest and help; it is for this reason that the authors dedicate their work to the memory of the second Earl of Iveagh, whose last benefaction to the Institute was a generous gift to make possible the writing of this history.

It is in a sense the tale of a microcosm, but of one which reflects the changing problems and the changing climate of a larger world. The layman and the medical scientist may well find interest in this account of an Institute once unique in Britain and always part of its social and medical history.

June 4, 1970   *G. L. Brown*

Contents

1*

List of Plates

List of Plates

Dedicated to the Memory

of

Rupert Edward Cecil Lee Guinness

K.G., C.B., C.M.G., F.R.S.

Second Earl of Iveagh

Preface

On July 21, 1891, the Institute was incorporated as 'The British Institute of Preventive Medicine'. Within a few years its name had been changed twice; first in 1898 to the 'Jenner Institute of Preventive Medicine' and later to the 'Lister Institute of Preventive Medicine', in honour of the illustrious surgeon and pioneer of medical research who had been one of its founders. It was as the Lister Institute that it became world famous, celebrating the seventy-fifth anniversary of its foundation in 1966. Nevertheless its first name was as appropriate as any, for both its founding and its nature are rather characteristically British.

The Institute was conceived in 1889 at a tea party after a committee which had just decided *not* to form a centre similar to the Pasteur Institute in Paris. It was brought to birth by a small band of distinguished men, already leading arduous professional lives. To get laboratories for experimental work they had not only to raise funds but to fight official timidity about and public antipathy to vivisection.

The Institute had two main aims: to undertake fundamental scientific research into the causes, prevention and treatment of disease in man and animals; and to prepare and supply special protective and curative materials, such as vaccines and antitoxins. It had therefore a slightly anomalous position. On the one hand, it was an academic research institute, hungry for endowment to pursue research; and on the other a production laboratory, expected to augment the income for research by the profits on its sales, and at the same time to be open for students of any country to study its methods. With the same British capacity for detachment which enables a man to be a private banker in the morning and a Governor of the Bank of England in the afternoon, the Institute retains its dual status.

A certain amateurism about the demands of good business

14   *Preface*

reflects the status of the Institute's workers. At first and for many years their financial reward was meagre; though often enough their personal austerity was as much inherent as it was imposed. To them, the Institute was not merely a place where they were employed but a way of life, a habit of thought. Through their work the Institute quickly gained authority at the beginning of this century, with official bodies, such as the India Office, the Colonial Office and the Local Government Board, asking for its co-operation in problems affecting the public health. The value of its service can be gauged by the official recognition of the necessity for such an institute in 1911, when a provision of the National Insurance Act directed the Government to set up a National Institute for Medical Research. The proposal that the Lister Institute should become the nucleus of a National Institute was discussed but was eventually defeated by the members of the Institute. In 1914 the Medical Research Committee (later the Medical Research Council) set up the National Institute for Medical Research, now at Mill Hill. The Lister pursued its separate existence but at all times with friendly co-operation and often in joint enterprise with the Medical Research Council.

For more than twenty years, therefore, the Lister Institute was the only institute of its kind in the country, ranking internationally with the Pasteur Institute in Paris and the Rockefeller Institute in New York. Research students and more experienced workers came from home and abroad, and it was a haven also for medical scientists on leave from foreign service. 'Of course I worked at the Lister,' said H. J. Bensted, who after thirty years in the Royal Army Medical Corps became Director of the Public Health Laboratories at Colindale, 'everyone in my generation worked there at some time or other; we boxed and coxed out of the Battersea Park flats.' The size of the building in Chelsea, though possibly fortuitous, was admirable for the fostering of research. The top floor had a fine library and the Director's flat, the basement had various services and a workshop. The four intervening floors, less than fifty yards in length, with no sharp divisions between departments, housed people engaged in bacteriology, immunology, virology, physiology, biochemistry, cancer research and other diverse activities. The ease of opportunity for the cross fertilization of ideas, for the exchange of expert information and for the formation of lasting friendships were and, according to a recent visitor, still are unique. The Institute became a kind of club, rigid in standards, informal in manner; a little puzzling to strangers, remembered nostalgically by its guests, held in pride and an often exasperated affection by its more permanent residents. In that atmosphere, the tradition of the Institute was forged. The whole was greater than its parts.

The history of the Institute is like the symbol of Aescapulius, the serpent of learning coiled round a shaft, here the shaft of time; or, more topically, like the helices of protein and nucleic acids. Along the axis of time run the continuing affairs of the Institute, its constitution, administration and finances; its relationship with bodies such as the University, the Medical Research Council and other foundations; the chronicle of its changing buildings and staff. Around this axis twists the rope of the work done in the Institute, a rope made of many fibres. In 1953, C. J. Martin, its first Director, recalling the early work of the Institute, wrote: 'Studies ranged from epidemiology of plague to the coagulation of protein by heat or alcohol, from the cause of *purpura haemorrhagica* to the synthesis of vitamin B_1, from the biology of virus infection to the statistical study of cancer incidence, from the mechanism of the disinfection process to the prevention of scurvy and beriberi, from the fermentation of sugar by yeast to the domestic habits of the body louse.'

Yet the studies were not as haphazard as that catalogue might suggest. The rope of learning is continuous, and though some fibres have been short, others are as long as the rope, and many are cross-linked. Since one of the aims of the Institute was the study of the causes of disease, microbiology has been a major theme, beginning with bacteriology and going on to include virology and protozoology; here, in addition to systematic investigations of specific disease and specific immunological remedies, one may trace the connection between Ledingham's pioneer work on vaccinia virus and the present day preparation of smallpox vaccine; or between Arkwright's fundamental discovery of bacterial variation and the present studies on immunochemistry and bacterial genetics. The classical work of Chick and Martin on heat coagulation of protein, which began as a bacteriological study of disinfectant action, had repercussions on the purification of antitoxins in the Serum Department and was a stone in the foundation of the Biophysics Laboratory built thirty years later.

The Institute was one of the cradles of biochemistry in Britain, and studies on the metabolism of carbohydrates and fats have been continuous since its foundation. The work of Harden and Young on the mechanism of alcoholic fermentation is a keystone in our knowledge of intermediary metabolism in animals, plants and micro-organisms; and there is a fascinating linkage between this work and that of the Nutrition Department on deficiency diseases, culminating later in the synthesis of vitamins.

This book does not attempt to chronicle all the work carried out in the Institute since its foundation. In selecting material, it has seemed important to set down most fully the history of early years from the records and memories available to us. The work of our colleagues is published in scientific journals; and since we are by profession scientists rather than historians we beg their indulgence for omissions and shortcomings in a history which essentially they have made.

The plan adopted has been to interpose accounts of some pioneer studies and of the people engaged in them between chapters dealing with the Institute as a body. It will be seen how sometimes an enquiry is begun by the threats of pestilence or war; and how particular lines may alternate between dormancy and fruition as the limits of older techniques are reached and new ones evolved from contemporary progress in other fields.

This chronicle of the Institute extends approximately over seven decades. The first decade covers the years in Bloomsbury and the brief priod as the Jenner Institute; then come the three decades under Charles Martin, broken by the First World War; the next two decades, first with John Ledingham and then with Alan Drury as Director, include the greater upheaval of the Second World War; the seventh decade, under Ashley Miles, continues now into the eighth.

In his biography of Lord Lister, written in 1917, Godlee wrote of the Institute: 'No one can predict the ultimate fate of an Institution which, in its short life, has seen many changes, but it would not be a rash prophecy that, if it should ever lose its independence, it would in time almost cease to be a memorial to Lister, as it has already almost ceased to be a memorial to Jenner.' *Si monumentum requiris, circumspice.* For many years the Institute was unique, and as such, a period piece. The fact that it is no longer unique is a measure of its success and of the wisdom of its founders. That it should change is inevitable, for the ability to change is the mark of continuing vitality.

We acknowledge most gratefully the help we have received in writing this history of the Lister Institute. Particularly we thank Sir

Ashley Miles for his patient help in bringing it to fruition. We are indebted to Dr Alfred Byrne for his detailed researches, especially into the foundation of the Institute and its earlier years; to the late Douglas McClean for much information garnered from the older staff at Elstree; and to many of the scientific staff, past and present, for accounts of their work and their reminiscences. Part of the early material is drawn from two short memoirs previously published, one in 1949 by Sir Alan Drury in the *Proceedings of the Royal Society*, and the other in 1949 by one of us (H.C.) in *Endeavour*.

We are grateful to the following for permission to reproduce pictures. Cambridge University Press for the photographs of plague research in Bombay; The Chemical Society for the portrait of Sir Henry Roscoe; Gordon Fraser Gallery Ltd for the photograph of the Institute at Chelsea; Messrs Arthur Guinness Son and Co for the photograph of the second Earl of Iveagh; The National Portrait Gallery for the photograph of Lord Lister's Portrait Bust; The Radio Times and Hulton Picture Library for the photograph of the first Earl of Iveagh; and The Royal Society for the photograph of Sir Joseph Arkwright.

We are grateful to Macmillan and Co Ltd for permission to quote the letter of the Empress Frederica of Russia from Godlee's *Life of Lord Lister* (1930).

Finally, we wish to thank Miss Barbara Prideaux and Mrs Pamela Greene most warmly for their invaluable help in the preparation of the script.

H.C.
M.G.M.

1. The Pioneers

During the fifteen years before the Institute was founded, exciting and momentous events had been taking place in the new field of systematic bacteriology. In Berlin, a former country physician, Dr Robert Koch, had worked out a simple way of preparing microbes for examination under the microscope, and in a dozen laboratories one important bateriological discovery followed another in quick succession once the new method became known. Koch's procedure simplified the study of bacteria; and another original technique for cultivating them in a pure state, which he announced soon afterwards, helped to explain many mysteries that had been puzzling scientists for centuries.

In August 1881, a historic meeting took place in the Physiological Laboratory of King's College, London, at which Koch demonstrated his culture technique to scientists and doctors attending the Seventh International Medical Congress. For the demonstration, he had on the bench before him a sterilized glass slide covered with his new solid culture medium made of gelatine and meat extract. A glass bell-jar covered the slide to exclude organisms circulating in the air. Koch began by passing a piece of platinum wire through the flame of a Bunsen gas-burner. He dipped one end of the wire thus sterilized into a glass vessel teeming with assorted bacteria. Then, raising the bell-jar for a moment, he lightly stroked the surface of the jelly medium with the contaminated wire before replacing the cover.

The demonstration was continued by showing a second slide coated with the medium, which had been similarly treated the day before and placed in an incubator. Dots stippled the tracks he had made on the shining surface, where colonies of various organisms had begun to grow. The German scientist again ran the wire through the flame, and uncovered the slide on which the bacteria were growing. With the end of the wire he carefully picked up one colony, derived from a single microbe, swiftly transplanted it into a test-tube containing more of the same medium and plugged the tube with sterilized cotton wool. To show the assembled doctors what would happen after a further twenty-four hours' incubation, he passed round a series of test-tubes for inspection. Each contained a culture of a single species. It was thus that the first demonstrably pure culture of a bacterium was obtained.

Watching the demonstration were two men whose names were to become immortal. One was the French chemist, Louis Pasteur, who had long been teaching that living microbes were a cause of disease. He had reached that conclusion from his investigation of the fermentation changes occurring in wine and beer, from studies on disease of silkworms and, later, from observations on the process of putrefaction. By his side was the great London surgeon and experimenter, Joseph Lister, whose practical application of what was still being called 'the germ theory of disease' had given the world the life-saving boon of antiseptic surgery. Pasteur had no love for the Germans. There had been a bitter exchange of views between himself and the Principal of the Medical Faculty in the University of Bonn ten years before, when the Frenchman had returned his honorary medical diploma as a protest against the German bombardment of Paris during the war of 1870. This, however, was no time for rancour. When the demonstration was over he picked up one of the test-tubes and examined its contents closely. Lister heard him say to Koch: 'C'est un grand progrès, monsieur.'

Events soon confirmed the verdict. Before the end of the nineteenth century the agents responsible for fourteen different diseases had been identified, including the germs of tuberculosis, tetanus, typhoid and diphtheria. Moreover, the fundamental work of Pasteur on the prevention of fowl cholera led to the establishment of the principles of immunization against disease. Pasteur grew the organism causing fowl cholera in a medium of chicken broth, and repeatedly transferred the bacterial culture from one flask of medium to another over a period of months. He finally obtained a strain of 'attenuated' or enfeebled organisms which were no longer capable of causing the disease. Yet if a chicken was first inoculated with these harmless microbes and later injected with the normal virulent variety, it proved to be immune to fowl cholera.

Pasteur, a great chemist without formal medical training, spent the rest of his days applying this principle of 'attenuation' to the development of methods for immunization against other diseases; of these the work on rabies (hydrophobia) is perhaps the most famous, and particularly relevant to the founding of the Lister Institute. Pasteur found that when the spinal cord taken from a rabbit that had died after inoculation with rabies was hung up in clean dry air, the virulence of the infecting agent or 'virus' present in extracts of the dried cord diminished with the passage of time until finally it disappeared. By varying the period of drying of the cords it was possible to obtain extracts with falling degrees of infective potency. Pasteur then injected dogs with extracts of these cords, starting with a non-virulent specimen and gradually increasing the degree of virulence; at the end of the course of injections he found that the dogs were completely immune to the disease. In 1885 he first applied the treatment to a human being, when he gave it to a nine-year-old Alsatian boy, Joseph Meister, who on his way to school had received fourteen bites from a mad dog. The boy did not develop rabies.

The success of this immunization against a fearful and invariably fatal disease was soon confirmed. In gratitude for what Pasteur had done for man and animals, and for his great scientific services to the wine and silk trades, the French Government in 1888 helped to found the Institut Pasteur in Paris. Its first function was to provide treatment for those threatened with rabies, but research on other diseases soon developed.

In 1888 Roux and Yersin showed there that the deadly nature of diphtheria, rampant then throughout Europe, was due to a soluble toxin elaborated by the diptheria bacillus. Two years later, in Berlin, the German pathologist, von Behring, and the Japanese bacteriologist Kitasato discovered that a filtered culture of tetanus bacilli likewise contained a toxin. When this filtrate was injected in small doses into rabbits and mice, the animals became immune to any ill effects of tetanus microbes. Their blood serum, the clear fluid remaining after the red cells had been separated by coagulation, was antitoxic; removed from the body, it could neutralize tetanus toxin in a test-tube. From this observation arose the concept that inoculation with a foreign substance, the 'antigen', could induce an animal to develop in its blood serum an 'antibody', which could specifically neutralize that particular antigen, but not others. The animal becomes immune to a particular disease after inoculation with a particular bacterial antigen.

Shortly afterwards, von Behring announced the discovery of an antitoxin against diphtheria, analogus to that against tetanus. It was a short step from these animal experiments to the possibility of treating people with the blood serum of animals containing artificially induced antibodies. One of the first persons to be treated was a child with diphtheria, who was injected with anti-diphtheritic horse serum (diphtheria antitoxin) by Dr Geissler in a Berlin clinic on Christmas night, 1891.

Within a few months forty institutes for treatment modelled on the Pasteur Institute had been set up in other countries, and in Berlin an Institute for Infectious Diseases was built for Koch. Although our knowledge of immunity had started in Britain, with Jenner's discovery that inoculation with cowpox protected against smallpox, Britain had no centre for treatment or for the kind of experimental studies in the new bacteriology that were yielding such a rich harvest on the Continent. Yet surgeon-bacteriologists such as Lister and Ogston had certainly made notable contributions in their work on the prevention of surgical infection, and the medical schools had not lagged in other aspects.

Indeed Britain was leading the world in the practice of preventive medicine in a wide sense. The efforts of a long line of humanitarians — including Bentham, Southwood Smith, Chadwick and Simon — had resulted ultimately in many legislative reforms of the appalling sanitary situations created by the Industrial Revolution, and in other measures such as compulsory vaccination against smallpox. In 1875 a Public Health Act had imposed upon every area the duty of appointing a Medical Officer of Health. It became necessary to train people for these posts, and a consequence of this Act which is relevant to the history of the Lister Institute was the foundation in 1886 of the College of State Medicine, with which the Institute was later amalgamated. But in 1889 any one in Britain bitten by a rabid dog still had to go to Paris for preventive treatment against rabies.

The first Briton to receive the anti-rabies treatment, four months after the boy Meister had been successfully inoculated, was an Oswestry physician, Dr John Hughes, who departed hot-foot to Paris after being bitten by his own rabid dog. Many others had followed him, for rabies was common enough among the dogs which roamed the streets of cities. For instance, in the year 1885, thirty-nine people in and around London died from hydrophobia after being bitten and in the first six months of 1889, forty people bitten by rabid dogs went from Britain to Paris for treatment, bringing the total in four years to 214. In every case treatment had been given free of charge.

On July 1, 1889, the Lord Mayor of London, Sir James Whitehead, invited a carefully chosen group of scientists, veterinarians, doctors and dog lovers to a meeting in the Egyptian Hall of the Mansion House to discuss the problem. The Lord Mayor was a business man as he repeatedly said. It was as a business man and not as a scientist, he explained, that he had gone over to Paris one Sunday morning six weeks earlier to inspect the records of cases treated at the Pasteur Institute. What he had learned there gave him the idea of collecting money to send Pasteur as a present. If enough funds could be raised, some could be used to enable poor patients to go to Paris when treatment was imperative. No one present dissented from this recommendation, for by now there was unanimous agreement in Britain about the value of Pasteur's inoculation treatment against rabies.

Three years previously the Member of Parliament for South Manchester, Sir Henry Roscoe, F.R.S., had suggested to Joseph Chamberlain, who was then President of the Local Government Board, that Pasteur's claim ought to be assessed by a group of British scientists. Chamberlain agreed. Roscoe, a former pupil of Bunsen at Heidelberg, was himself a chemist of distinction occupying the Chair of Chemistry at Owen's College, Manchester and was largely responsible for the expansion of that college into the present university. He was made one of the investigating commission, which included Lister, T. Lauder Brunton, the London physician, and John Burdon Sanderson, the Oxford Professor of Physiology, as well as the surgeon James Paget. The secretary was the pioneer neurosurgeon, Victor Horsley, who was at that time Professor-Superintendent of the Brown Animal Sanatory Institute in Wandsworth Road, London.

The Commission weighed the results of anti-rabies inoculation on French and British patients, while Horsley himself conducted confirmatory experiments on animals. It was fifteen months before they expressed themselves as satisfied. All six members of the commission attended the Mansion House meeting to affirm their faith in Pasteur's treatment. All six were soon to play more important parts in championing the cause of medical research nearer home.

With the official verdict in favour of Pasteur's method, it was almost inevitable that the idea of a Pasteur Institute for Britain should arise. There had been considerable talk about that possibility during the weeks before the Lord Mayor called his meeting. Indeed, he had taken the precaution of asking Pasteur whether he could name a suitable director for such an institute if it came into being. Pasteur suggested a medical graduate, named Marc Armand Ruffer. Ruffer, who was the thirty-year-old son of a French nobleman and a German mother, had studied under Pasteur and taken his medical degree at University College, London.

There were, however, powerful forces against the proposal to establish a rabies treatment station for Britain. Many of the newspapers were actively opposed to the principle of using animals for medical research and Pasteur was under constant fire for his 'cruelty to animals'. When the Mansion House meeting was first mooted, Sir E. Ray Lankester, then Professor of Comparative Anatomy at University College, London, had suggested to the Lord Mayor that it would be necessary to have a 'strong posse of police' to guard the entrance and to order the stewards to deny admission to anyone who had not received an invitation.

Fortunately there was no trouble but equally there was no enthusiasm for the idea of a Pasteur Institute in Britain. Paget, as one of the delegates from the Royal Society, spoke enthusiastically about Pasteur and his achievements, and about the good results being obtained in Moscow, Odessa and Warsaw, but he did not mention England. Roscoe read a letter from Pasteur himself suggesting that, as England had already got rid of wolves, she could stamp out rabies by the administrative control of dogs. Lister expressed his admiration of the 'generous philanthropy of M. Pasteur' in supporting a suggestion for stamping out the disease, which, if successful, would make his own method superfluous in this country. Horsley was present as a representative of the Society for the Prevention of Hydrophobia. He too insisted that rabies could be eradicated if the Government would introduce a bill ordering the simultaneous muzzling of every dog in the British Isles, with quarantine of a suitable length for all dogs imported. Another Royal Society nominee, Sir Michael Foster, mentioned enviously that French scientists were allowed to pursue their investigations 'without trammel and molestation'; the concept of a Pasteur Institute in Britain, however, was out of the question, since scientists engaged on animal studies were 'put upon a criminal footing and are allowed only to pursue their investigations on ticket of leave'.

Advised, presumably, by the scientists, the Lord Mayor expressed himself opposed in principle to the setting up of such an institute. As a business man, he estimated that out of a possible sixty cases a year of threatened rabies calling for treatment, about one half would be unable to pay for themselves. If £25 were allowed to cover travel and accommodation in Paris for two people for a fortnight, the total cost would amount to £750 a year. That sum would not go far towards running a similar institute at home. Besides, the establishment of a British institute might interfere with the measures for stamping out rabies which the Government would soon be asked to sponsor.

Sir Ray Lankester agreed. With Paris only eight hours from London it would, he felt, be 'out of proportion and somewhat absurd' to start a similar institution in London by means of private subscriptions. He looked forward to the time when London would have an institute for studying diseases of parasitic or bacterial origin, but that could be done only by the Government. Discoveries like those of Pasteur, he asserted, could be expected only with the aid of grants from the public purse. 'We cannot by private subscription maintain an institution for scientific research,' he said. 'It has been tried. It cannot be done. It is simply out of the question.'

How wrong Ray Lankester was then, and ultimately perhaps how right, will be seen in these pages. For the moment, business sense prevailed and a Committee was set up to raise money for a gift to Pasteur and the financing of travel to Paris of patients for treatment. Four months later, on November 6, 1889, Sir James Whitehead entertained the members of this Committee in the Lord Mayor's parlour. They had collected £3,200, of which £2,000 was to be sent to the Pasteur Institute; the rest was to help indigent persons bitten by rabid dogs to travel to the Continent for treatment. The Committee's work was done, and Sir James regretted they would not meet again.

During tea, however, Charles Smart Roy, then Professor of Pathology at Cambridge, urged the others not to abandon the notion of creating an anti-rabies station in Britain like the one in Paris, though not perhaps so elaborate as the centre recently established in St Petersburg. Roy was staunchly backed by Dr Sidney Turner, who owed his presence there to the fact that he was a dog-fancier and the secretary of the Mastiff Club. So effectively did the two argue the case with Lister, Horsley, Roscoe and the rest, that the

members of the disbanded committee immediately re-formed themselves into another committee, to find out how practicable a British
Institute might be. In spite of the dissident views he had publicly
expressed a few months before, the Lord Mayor agreed to become
chairman of the new committee. Armand Ruffer was made the
honorary secretary and Roy and Turner were asked to put the
project down on paper.

They reported in a few weeks. In the light of present-day familiarity
with the part played by microbes in the causation of disease, the
need for their preamble to a report made to a committee consisting
mainly of doctors and scientists, must seem remarkable. Scientific
men, it read, have discovered that many serious and fatal diseases of
man and animals are due to 'small living beings' called micro-
organisms, microbes, or germs, introduced into the system. These
micro-organisms have been found also to give rise to suppurations,
high fevers and 'many of the dangers frequently found following
surgical operations and wounds from other causes'.

Fight against the germs of disease would be the main purpose of
the proposed new institute. That, said the report, could be done by
learning how to destroy the microbes themselves, and by using the
discoveries of Jenner and Pasteur to vaccinate and inoculate people
against diseases. As a beginning, the 'Jenner-Pasteur Institute for the
Prevention of Infective Diseases', as the new centre might be called,
would make, administer and distribute materials for inoculation
against diseases like rabies and anthrax. The scientists working in the
Institute's laboratories would also try to discover more about the
nature of disease-producing organisms, so that the community
might be better protected against them.

Cambridge was proposed as the most suitable place, because the
new establishment could be affiliated with Roy's Department of
Pathology, which at that time was the best equipped of its kind in
England. Adequate staff would be close at hand. London was only
seventy-five minutes away by rail.

The proposals of Roy and Turner were well received by the committee of twenty-one, which then became an executive body determined to translate them into fact. The original idea of associating
the names of Jenner and Pasteur with the project was dropped,
though why is not clear. In searching for a descriptive title for the
Institute, epithets such as 'microbic', 'microbiological', and even
'bacillological' were considered and discarded. Turner has left a note

saying that there was some talk of calling the new establishment a Bacteriological Institute, only 'bacteriological' was rather a 'mouthful'; the public, he thought, would not have heard of the word, much less have understood what it meant. 'Preventive Medicine would appeal more directly to the public being a term to show we intend to *prevent* disease rather than merely *study* it.' The Committee finally decided that the new centre should be called 'The British Institute of Preventive Medicine', and should concern itself primarily with research into the cause of disease in man and animals, with treatment as a secondary consideration.

Before asking the public for money, the organizers thought it prudent to sound opinion in wider scientific and medical circles. The Council of the Senate of the University of Cambridge welcomed the idea of a new institute within the precincts of the University. The Royal Society 'learned with satisfaction' of the project and hoped at some future time to be able to add more material support. The British Medical Association offered to pay one fifth of the first year's running costs, up to £300. Thus encouraged, the organizing committee, led by Lister after Whitehead's resignation through ill health, went into action.

2. A Medical Research Institute for Britain

The problems facing the organizers of the new Institute were manifold. They had to get money and — what was almost as difficult — a licence for animal experiments. They had to define the scope and the administration of this new kind of enterprise, decide on a site and consider plans for a permanent building; and in the meantime they needed a nucleus of scientists to start work in temporary quarters.

They began with a public appeal for funds. The list of private subscribers was headed, with a cheque for £2,000, by the German industrial chemist Ludwig Mond, who with J. T. Brunner was to establish in Cheshire in 1926 the largest alkali works in the world, later united with Nobel Industries and other companies to form Imperial Chemical Industries. The Dukes of Westminster and Devonshire, the Earl of Derby and Lord Rothschild each contributed £1,000; Ruffer's mother also gave £1,000 and the First Earl of Iveagh £250. Amongst other contributors the Clothworkers Company gave £100, and the Guiana branch of the British Medical Association collected £18. The only hospital to appear on the list was the Central London Throat and Ear Hospital, which gave two guineas.

Money was slow in coming in. The project only looked like taking shape when the organizers gained the sympathetic ear of the trustees of a Mr Richard Berridge, an Irishman who had changed his name from MacCarthy. He had left two-thirds of his £300,000 estate for 'advancing the sanitary and economic sciences'. The Berridge trustees promised £20,000 if the founders of the Institute could themselves raise £40,000 for land and buildings. It was also stipulated that the Institute should be in London, not Cambridge. The Committee wrangled for several meetings over the change in location but ultimately agreed to build in London.

At this stage the Committee began a move to incorporate the proposed institute into a limited liability company. They applied for a licence to the President of the Board of Trade, Sir Michael Hicks Beach, and asked that the word 'limited' should be omitted from the proposed company's name, because they thought the term might repel subscribers by suggesting that the establishment was trading for gain.

When news of the application got about, animal lovers throughout the country rose in wrath. No less than thirty memorials signed by over 4,000 people reached the office of the Board of Trade warning Sir Michael that the objects of the Institute clearly pointed to experiments on living animals. The petitioners urged that the registration licence should be refused altogether, or else that such experiments should be excluded from the Institute's activities. Hicks Beach refused the licence. He later confessed that he had been afraid that by complying he might have got into trouble with the Home Office. The Cruelty to Animals Act of 1876 had made animal experiments illegal except with the sanction of the Home Office. He also wished to avoid showing anything like official approval of vivisection; it is not hard to see the dilemma of a Minister faced with a popular outcry. He was repeatedly asked, both formally and personally, to change his mind, but he remained obdurate until after he had met a deputation in June 1891 at the Victoria Hotel in Northumberland Avenue.

That remarkable meeting was attended by some 270 of the country's leading doctors and scientists and other influential persons, including the Duke of Westminster, the Earl of Derby, Everett Millais of the *Fancier's Gazette* and a member of the Basset Hound Club, and Walter Gilbey, the noted horse breeder and agriculturist. The presence of such popular sportsmen leads one to wonder whether some more august sympathy was being discreetly exercised. The Prince of Wales had opened the Medical Congress in 1881, and on one of his visits to Paris had gone to see Pasteur's work for himself. He had received in December 1890, a letter from his sister, the Empress Frederick of Germany, which is quoted in Sir Rickman Godlee's biography of Lord Lister. It runs in part:

'I do so want to call your attention to a matter which has long been on my mind, though of course it is no business of mine. Had our beloved Father been alive I am sure he would have taken it up. I refer to the question of a Bacteriological Institution for England. It makes me mad when I think that Englishmen have not had a chance of pursuing these vital questions of Science, these investigations and experiments, in England, and are obliged to go to Germany and France to study Bacteriology. We ought to have a "Versuchs-Station" in England, where every opportunity should be afforded for studying these great questions of the day, half physical, half chemical, half pathology. I know the Vivisection Act rather interferes with this, but still perhaps an Amendment might be passed for such an Institution, leaving the Act in force for the rest of the country in general.

'Could you not forward and suggest such a plan? . . . '

The Empress's letter was sent to Sir Lyon Playfair, and by him to Roscoe, who replied explaining the exact position with regard to the proposed Institute for Preventive Medicine and adding: 'I quite agree with the remarks of H. Majesty that our Government ought to take a prominent part in the foundation of such a national Institute, and I cannot but think that the interest which the Empress and H.R.H. the Prince of Wales show in these questions will compel the Government to take some steps . . . and that before long we shall see the foundation of an Institute worthy of our country.'

Hicks Beach capitulated to the impressive deputation, though he insisted that, in order to protect the Board of Trade from the wrath of the Home Office, a clause should be inserted in the Memorandum of Association making it clear that in issuing a licence for incorporation he was in no way condoning the practice of vivisection.

The British Institute of Preventive Medicine was legally incorporated on July 25, 1891. A few days later Roscoe had the satisfaction of announcing the formation of the Institute to the Tenth International Congress of Medicine then meeting in London, in the presence of Koch, Roux and other notable men.

The chief aims of the Institute as set out in the Memorandum of Association were:

1. To study, investigate, discover and improve the means of preventing and curing infective diseases of man and animals.

2. To provide instruction and education in Preventive Medicine to Medical Officers of Health, Medical Practitioners, Veterinary Surgeons and advanced Students.

3. To prepare and supply to those requiring them such special protective and curative materials as have already been found or shall

in future be found of value in the prevention and treatment of infectious diseases.

4. To treat persons suffering with infective diseases or threatened with them, in buildings of the Institute or elsewhere.

The signatories to the Memorandum were Lister, Roscoe, Turner and Roy — the driving forces in the venture — together with Sir George Humphrey, Professor of Surgery at Cambridge, Everett Millais, the surgeon William Watson Cheyne, and Sir Thomas Spencer Wells, immortalized in surgery by the artery forceps he invented. Lister was the first Chairman, and Roscoe the first Treasurer, of the Institute, and a Council of seventeen members controlled the affairs.

The task of collecting money went on. As part of a drive to obtain enough to meet the terms of the Berridge offer, Mr George Cooper, later the Institute's Secretary, was sent round from door to door, to explain the aims of the Institute and to collect what he could. His first call was on Dr John Williams of Brook Street. After a few minutes' conversation the doctor wrote a cheque for £100. Other successful practitioners were not so well disposed towards the new-fangled notion of preventing disease instead of treating it. One of the most fashionable doctors of the day, physician extraordinary to the Queen, and a council member of the College of State Medicine, told Cooper warmly that what was really needed was not preventive medicine but a 'good healthy epidemic', and showed him empty-handed to the door.

More than any other of the City Companies, the Worshipful Company of Grocers had in the past shown their interest in promoting science, by giving scholarships and prizes for original scientific work. A special memorial asking for help was addressed to the Grocers' Hall. The request was at first refused. Fortunately, it happened that the Master of the Company was Mr John Kingdon, a prominent surgeon and a friend of Lister, so that Lister was able to ask personally for help. In October 1893 the Company agreed to give the Institute £10,000 with the proviso that the organizers should succeed in raising £20,000 in addition to the Berridge offer, and should obtain a suitable building site.

By October 1893, donations and subscriptions, without any conditions attached, amounted only to about £12,000. It would seem, however, that the Berridge trustees were not inclined to insist on their

2

original stipulation that £40,000 should be raised because, at that
stage, a search for a building site was begun. It was not necessary to
look long, because the Duke of Westminster capped his earlier gift
of £1,000 by offering to sell a fine site on his estate for £6,000. The
Institute's expert valued it at £10,000. It was on the Embankment at
Chelsea Bridge, across the road from the gardens of the Royal
Hospital, where the red-coated veterans of past wars lived out their
lives in calm and comfort. The offer was accepted with alacrity. The
deal was concluded in December 1893 and a building committee was
set up.

A month earlier there had been a further stroke of good fortune.
The Berridge trustees, with the consent of the Attorney General,
offered a further £25,000, provided the Institute spent that sum on
investigating a method introduced by a Frenchman, M. Hermite, for
disinfecting sewage and 'other kindred objects' by means of electro-
lysed sea-water. A specification, drawn up for the benefit of the
Berridge Trustees, suggested that the project would take at least
five years and, with the costs of building and equipping special
laboratories and paying the suggested staff, would cost more than the
sum to be provided; a satisfactory agreement was, however, reached.

Meanwhile the planners had been going ahead with a scheme
which would make it possible to begin research at once and also get
over the difficulties to be expected if an application for a licence to
perform experiments on animals was made directly. This scheme was
to amalgamate the Institute with the College of State Medicine,
which possessed both the coveted licence and laboratory accommodation.

The College of State Medicine, like the Institute with which it was
to merge, owed its existence to the enterprise and pioneering spirit of
a group of scientifically minded men anxious to advance a branch of
British Medicine. On March 6, 1886, this group met in the offices of
the Volunteer Medical Association at 26 King William Street, off the
Strand. They were progressive thinkers who, realizing the importance
of preventive medicine for public health, were disturbed at the limited
facilities which existed for training doctors in that specialty. By that
time there were 1,200 medical officers of health employed by the
Local Government Board; hardly fifty had a registrable qualification
in public health.

The College, a private non-profitmaking concern, was created to
help fill this gap. Postgraduate students were prepared for a diploma

in public health. Public lectures on sanitary science were delivered in a theatre in Jermyn Street and a diploma was issued to successful candidates, although the College was not officially recognized. In 1887 the College of State Medicine was incorporated. The Honorary Secretary was Surgeon-General W. R. Cornish, and Roscoe was a member of the Council, which also included Ludwig Mond.

At first the College consisted only of two rooms lent by the Volunteer Medical Association. Two and a half years passed before there was any question of rent being paid. Then it was agreed that it should be £15 a year. In those modest surroundings Dr Edward Klein, F.R.S., a lecturer in advanced bacteriology at St Bartholomew's Hospital, taught half a dozen doctors. The Professor of Hygiene and Public Health was Dr William Smith, who gave the classes practical instruction in his own private chemical laboratory at 74 Great Russell Street. In conjunction with the Volunteer Medical Association, lectures and demonstrations were given in first aid, stretcher drill and the management of military casualties.

Things remained on that scale until the end of 1888, when Klein and Smith began to complain about the difficulties of working in such cramped conditions and asked for more suitable quarters in which to work.

At the time the College had only £70 in the bank, but that did not daunt its founders. They told Klein, Smith and Cornish to look about for better quarters, and in a couple of months they were handed a report on a house at 101 Great Russell Street. As the premises seemed suitable, the Berridge Trustees were asked for funds and promised £1,000. An eight-year lease of the house at £90 a year was taken from the Bedford estate; at the same time the vestry of Holborn reduced the rateable value from £120 to £84.

The old house was far from fitted to become a teaching establishment; girders had to be inserted to carry the weight of the laboratories and the bulging walls had to be strengthened. By the time the rooms had been converted and equipped as chemical and pathological laboratories, and the offices and library furnished, there was only about £200 left of the Berridge gift.

All presents were welcome. In the minutes of a Committee Meeting of the period, there is acknowledgement of electric lamps from the Denham Light Co and from Messrs Siemens. From Messrs Doulton came 'one of their newest pattern flush water closets'. On May 2, 1888, with the paint barely dry on its walls, the College of

State Medicine's new building was thrown open to any medical practitioners desiring instruction in public health and allied subjects.

The College lasted for five years, and for a time attained a mild degree of prosperity. In 1890, the Prince of Wales consented to become its president. Two years later, the Berridge trustees added a further £4,000 to their original gift. By that time, the College had thirty-seven fellows and eighty associates; forty-eight students were attending the classes and, according to a claim by the Honorary Secretary, a further twelve advanced students were carrying on original research under the direction of the professors.

That state of affairs, however, did not last. For, with a lead from the General Medical Council, the medical schools of University College and King's College in London and others in the provinces had followed the example set by the College of State Medicine and had themselves started to teach public health.

In 1891 Klein resigned, Smith went to King's College, and the chair of hygiene and public health was taken over by the medical officer of health for St Marylebone, Dr Wynter Blyth. Dr Allen Macfadyen, an Edinburgh medical graduate, holding a Grocers' Research Scholarship, who had studied in Berne and Munich, came in Klein's place, with a salary of £50 a year and about £40 from students' fees. The number of students fell and the College got into low water financially. Roscoe, who was on the Council of both the College and the new British Institute of Preventive Medicine and familiar with the problems of both foundations, began negotiations with the governors of the College in December 1892; seven months later they accepted the idea of a union.

Accordingly, in December 1893, the British Institute of Preventive Medicine and the College of State Medicine were amalgamated. The Council of the Institute was increased to twenty-four, to include Ludwig Mond and six other representatives from the College. It was agreed that the name of the College should be included as a sub-title for one year. Blyth and Macfadyen were given £50 in gratitude for their services to the College, and it was agreed that Macfadyen should remain as bacteriologist and lecturer in the British Institute.

At last the pioneers who planned to align Britain with the rest of the world in medical research had laboratories and a licence for experiments.

3. Beginnings in Bloomsbury

The building of the College of State Medicine at 101 Great Russell Street was less impressive than its name. It was a stucco-fronted dwelling of three storeys and eleven rooms, in which the bedrooms had been converted into laboratories; a studio had become the class-room and the kitchen provided quarters for animals.

Pasteur's protégé, Armand Ruffer, then only thirty-two years old, was made interim Director of the Institute during its temporary abode in Bloomsbury. His appointment was for three years at £200 a year; the smallness of his salary could hardly have worried him as he was a man of means. Ruffer, Macfadyen and a chemist, Joseph Lunt, also from the College, constituted the core of the staff. There was also a smart lad of fifteen named William Whittingham getting twelve shillings a week as a laboratory attendant, who slept in the basement. He got a rise of two shillings when the Institute was established. Whittingham remained in the service of the Institute until 1932, ruling over the media kitchen in the basement at Chelsea. The staff of four themselves cleaned and restocked the old building and were ready to begin work in February 1894.

Lunt had been working with Roscoe on the best method of sewage disposal, and it is of interest that a paper presented to the Royal Society of London on the bacteriological aspects of the problem shows an apparatus for photographing bacteria, in which the source of illumination was a domestic paraffin lamp. With their experience of sewage research, Roscoe and Lunt were well equipped to colla-borate in examining the Hermite process, for which two rooms at Great Russell Street, designated the chemical laboratory, were set aside in compliance with the terms of the Berridge trustees. It did not take long, however, for Roscoe and Lunt to demonstrate that the chlorine liberated in the water by electrolysis had not the magic qualities claimed by M. Hermite, and the method was never adopted in Britain.

Attracted by the laboratory facilities, several investigators who had worked at London hospitals and elsewhere immediately asked to undertake research at the British Institute, to which they became attached as honorary assistants. There was nothing especially noteworthy about the first studies undertaken. Macfadyen who was described as Professor of Bacteriology was perhaps more successful as a teacher than as a scientist, and Ruffer's attention was soon to be distracted from the investigator's bench by a far more stirring contact with clinical medicine.

It may be of historical interest, though, to record the problems that engaged those early workers. By April 1894, a certain Dr Dempster was ready to publish his observations on the behaviour in soil of Koch's cholera bacillus and the bacillus of typhoid fever. Macfadyen was investigating the biology of an infecting agent found in ringworm; in collaboration with Dr Blaxhall he was identifying in soil, sewage and elsewhere, organisms which survive at abnormally high temperatures, which they called 'thermophilic bacteria'. Dr H. G. Plimmer, who had earlier collaborated with Ruffer in studying curious protozoon-like bodies found inside cells of certain malignant tumours, was trying to discover if they might be a cause of cancer. Chemical and bacteriological analyses of different kinds of ice cream were being performed by Mr Colwell. Dr Thomson was beginning an investigation of the bacteriology of the nose. The 'toxines of erysipelas' were to be produced and then tested in cases of sarcoma. Dr Russell Wells was about to test on bacteria the action of extracts from various body organs. Mr J. E. Barnard had just begun to give instruction to the students in the art of microphotography.

At Macfadyen's instigation, a bacteriological museum was established for the benefit of brewers, doctors and chemists; Blaxhall and Plimmer were the honorary curators. At the annual meeting of the British Medical Association at Bristol in August 1894, they exhibited the Institute's collection of over a hundred bacteria both disease-producing and harmless, and 'it excited considerable interest'.

The most important activity of the first year of the Institute, however, was the beginning of the Serum Department. It was in August 1894, that Ruffer discussed the diphtheria situation in Britain with Roscoe and Lister, two trustee members of the Council.

It was truly appalling. The previous year had been the worst on record; 3,265 people, most of them young children, had died from the disease. During the thirteen weeks before Ruffer approached Roscoe and Lister, there had been 598 further deaths from diphtheria in Britain. In 1893 the first published report had come from Germany about the treatment of diphtheria with Behring's new antitoxin. Ruffer described how the German claims, that blood serum from immunized horses could reduce the death rate in children, were supported by the latest reports from Dr Roux at the Pasteur Institute. He was told to go ahead with whatever he had in mind.

Ruffer had obtained a piebald pony called 'Tom', and since only small animals could be kept in the transformed kitchen at Great Russell Street, he arranged for Tom to be stabled at the 'Brown'. The Brown Animal Sanatory Institution (which was destroyed during an air raid in the Second World War) had been established in Wandsworth by the University of London with a bequest from an eccentric Irishman, Thomas Brown. Mr Brown had left something over £20,000 to establish within one mile of Westminster, Southwark or Dublin, a centre for investigating and curing 'maladies of Quadrupeds and Birds useful to man'. He added the bizarre condition that, if the Institution should be discontinued for any reason, the money should go to establish, at Dublin University, three or more chairs in Welsh, 'Sclavonic', Russian, Persian, Chinese, Coptic or Sanscrit.

In 1894, Charles Scott Sherrington, the great neurophysiologist, was Professor-Superintendent of the Institution. Ruffer went to the Brown Institution with a vessel of toxin which he had obtained from cultures of diphtheria bacilli. With the assistance of Sherrington he injected Tom with the first small dose of toxin. Further injections followed in gradually increasing doses at intervals of some days. Then, when the animal's resistance to diphtheria was believed to be at a peak, it was bled. The blood was allowed to coagulate and the clear golden serum was carefully decanted from the clotted red cells. Tom's serum contained the first therapeutic diphtheria antitoxin to be made in Britain. One of Tom's hooves is still preserved at the present Institute; on the mount is an incription commemorating the event.

At the next Council meeting, Ruffer reported on the effectiveness of the serum in animal experiments. With the pathologist Almroth Wright, from the Army Medical College at Netley, as a witness, he had inoculated four guinea-pigs with lethal doses of diphtheria microbes. One animal left untreated died in eighteen hours. The other three which had been injected also with a few drops of Tom's serum remained alive and well. Ruffer added that a second horse was already being immunized and that he had prepared enough toxin to start on a further dozen horses at an hour's notice.

While Tom was still being immunized, a dramatic midnight scene occurred at the Brown, which Ruffer did not report at the Council meeting. It was Sherrington himself who first made clinical use of British-made diphtheria antitoxin, in order to save the life of his nephew, and his own account of the event could hardly be bettered:

'Ruffer and I had been injecting the horse — our *first* horse — only a short time. We were badly in the dark as to the dosage to employ, and how quickly to repeat the increasing injections. We had from it a serum partly effective in guinea pigs. Then, on a Saturday evening, about seven o'clock, came a bolt from the blue. A wire from my brother-in-law in Sussex. "George has diphtheria. Can you come?" George, a boy of seven, was the only child. The house, an old Georgian house, three miles out of Lewes, set back in a combe under a chalk down. There was no train that night. I did not at first give thought to the horse, and, when I did, regretfully supposed it could not yet be ripe for use. However, I took a cab to find Ruffer. No telephone or taxi in those days — '93 or '94. Ruffer was dining out. I pursued him and got a word with him. He said "By all means you can use the horse, but it is not yet ripe for trial." Then by lantern-light at "The Brown" I bled the horse into a two litre flask duly sterilized and plugged with sterile wool. I left the blood in ice for it to settle. After sterilizing smaller flasks, and pipettes and some needle-syringes I drove home, to return at midnight and decant the serum, etc.

'By the Sunday morning train I reached Lewes. Dr Fawsett of Lewes — he had a brother on the staff at Guy's — was waiting in a dog-cart at the station. I joined him carrying my awkward package of flasks, etc. He said nothing as I packed them in, but, when I had climbed up beside him, he looked down and said, "You can do what you like with the boy. He will not be alive at tea time." We drove out to the old house; a bright frosty morning. Tragedy was over the place, the servants scared and silent. The boy was very weak, breathing with difficulty; he did not seem to know me. Fawsett and I injected the serum. The syringes were small and we emptied them time and again. The Doctor left. I sat with the boy. Early in the afternoon the boy seemed to me clearly better. At three o'clock I sent a messenger to the Doctor to say so. Thence forward progress was uninterrupted. On Tuesday I returned to London, and sought out Ruffer. His reaction was that we must tell Lister about it. The great surgeon (not Lord Lister then) had visitors, some Continental surgeons, to dinner. "You must tell my guests about it," he said, and insisted — so we told them in the drawing-room, at Park Crescent. The boy had a severe paralysis for a time. He grew to be six feet tall and had a commission in the First World War.'

When Ruffer had finished the description of his guinea-pig tests, the Council ordered him to begin making the serum for stricken children without delay. They told him to buy six horses which could be stabled for a weekly payment of twelve shillings a head at a farm called 'The Poplars', tenanted by a Mr Sivell, at Sudbury, near Harrow. Enough serum to treat 100 children was to be prepared and sent, free of charge, to the Eastern Hospital, Homerton, with further supplies for the patients of the Hospital for Sick Children, in Great Ormond Street.

Word of Ruffer's experiments had evidently got about, because at the same Council meeting a letter was read from the pharmaceutical firm of Burroughs and Wellcome offering to act as sole agents for all the antitoxin against diphtheria and tetanus that could be produced, as well as to handle the Institute's output of mallein for testing horses for glanders. The offer was declined and the agency was later given to Allen and Hanburys. One condition of sale was that the diphtheria antitoxin should be used only in the United Kingdom or in the Colonies.

Ruffer was authorized to buy a further fifty horses for serum production. They too were kept at the Poplars, which was the property of Dr William Perkin, the famous chemist whose accidental synthesis of mauveine started the great industry of the aniline dyes. On payment of £800 compensation to Sivell, a lease was taken of the farm at £150 a year. Tom Sivell was a man much thought of by farmers in the district because he had once ridden in the Grand National. He later became caretaker of the farm and he and his family shared some of the rooms with the resident medical director. The two next generations of the Sivell family remained attached to the Institute.

The thrilling news of the new cure for diphtheria was soon in all the newspapers. It has a strong emotional appeal and the Institute decided to invite contributions towards an 'antitoxin fund'. Only about £1,200 was subscribed, mainly by the London City Companies; that money was used to buy more horses and to build a laboratory at Sudbury. When it was realized that there was a great risk of the serum becoming contaminated with bacteria from the air in the course of preparation, a special room was constructed where the danger could be reduced to a minimum.

Towards the end of 1894 anti-diphtheria serum was being supplied to hospitals controlled by the Metropolitan Asylums Board. Word soon came back that use of the serum was halving the death rate from diphtheria, which was then about thirty per cent. Moreover, all the evidence suggested that when serum was administered at the first appearance of suspicious signs, it could reduce the mortality still further.

Dr Bertram Hunt was appointed at a salary of £150 a year as assistant bacteriologist in charge of producing anti-diphtheria and anti-tetanus serum. Macfadyen acquired also, for two pounds a week, the services of another assistant, Dr Richard Hewlett. When the Sudbury project was beginning to go smoothly, Ruffer, whose appointment as director was still only temporary, thought it was time to put relations with the Institute on a more secure footing. His way of doing so was to offer the Council his resignation which he did in March 1895. The move gained him his point, and shortly afterwards he was appointed the Institute's first director. A clause was included enabling either side to terminate the arrangement with six months' notice.

In July of the same year, Ruffer went to bed with a headache and a sore throat. A swab was taken from his throat and a culture made from the bacteria present. Among them, the microscope revealed the presence of the curved, clubbed, striated killer, first described by Klebs and Loeffler. Ruffer had diphtheria. He was the first of the Institute's staff to contract a grave illness from the organisms with which he was working. Shortly afterwards, Plimmer too became infected. Both were promptly given the Institute's antitoxin and both recovered. Ruffer developed a severe post-diphtheritic paralysis that kept him away from work for six months. In February 1896, without giving any reason, he resigned from the posts of Secretary and Director of the Institute. Beyond a polite expression of regret, the Council accepted his resignation without any recorded comment, waiving the six months' period of notice. Ruffer went to live in

Egypt and in a few months was appointed professor of bacteriology at the Medical School of Cairo, where he proved an immense success. Two years later, he was created president of the Sanitary, Maritime and Quarantine Council of Egypt. He became the leading authority on public health in that country and published some interesting pathological studies on mummies, showing that arterial disease was as common several thousand years ago in Egypt as it is here today. He was knighted in 1916.

Ruffer was a commissioner of the British Red Cross Society. During the First World War, he went to Salonika at the request of the provisional Greek Government to reorganize the sanitary services. The ship on which he was returning to Egypt was torpedoed by the Germans, and Marc Armand Ruffer was lost.

With the departure of Ruffer from England in 1896, Macfadyen was made honorary Secretary of the Institute and, a year later, its Director for a period of two years. There were several other changes in the staff of the Institute in Bloomsbury, which was thriving, and at Sudbury, which was not doing at all well. In 1895 Bertram Hunt, the assistant bacteriologist, left and Dr William Bulloch took his place. He began with a salary of three pounds a week, later raised to four pounds, and had sleeping quarters in the old farmhouse at Sudbury. Bulloch was the first of many promising young workers who spent some of their early years at the Institute before proceeding to distinguish themselves elsewhere in medical science. He left the Institute in 1897 to become lecturer and later professor in bacteriology at the London Hospital, and his place was taken by a thirty-four-year-old medical graduate from Aberdeen, George Dean, who had studied in Berlin and Vienna before becoming assistant to the Professor of Pathology at Aberdeen. In 1897 the chemist, Joseph Lunt, took a post as assistant in physics to Her Majesty's Astronomer at the Cape of Good Hope. His place at the Water Laboratory was taken by Arthur Harden, a young chemist with the degree of M.Sc. from Owen's College, Manchester, who was later to prove one of the most distinguished members of the Institute's staff.

During 1897, the year in which both Dean and Harden joined the staff, the Institute issued the first volume of its transactions. Published by Macmillan, the 163-page book contains nine papers, all but one of them concerned with bacteriology. Bulloch contributed the first paper, a study of the variation in virulence shown by *Streptococcus pyogenes*, a common pus-producing organism. One of his conclusions was that 'an animal immunised against a streptococcus from a case of erysipelas is also immune against a streptococcus from an abscess'.

The year 1897 was the last complete one to be spent in the neighbourhood of the British Museum. How things then stood may be gathered from annual reports issued by Macfadyen and Roscoe. Macfadyen pointed out proudly that there were eighty students working at the Institute, a sixty per cent increase on the previous year. They had come from nine countries including America, Africa and China, and among them were ten women. The nucleus of a library had been created. Diagnostic tests were being made for thirty hospitals and other public institutions, and there was reason to believe that the Clinical Investigation Department would become self-supporting when its existence was more widely known. Macfadyen's section of the report related that, in addition to the staff, there had been nine research workers at the Institute; six of whom were former pupils.

Roscoe's report was less rosy. The money from the Berridge trustees and the Grocers' Company had been received together with £3,500 which had been the funds of the College of State Medicine, bringing the Institute's capital up to nearly £70,000. By the time the building at Chelsea, now ready for occupation, could be paid for and furnished, there would, however, be only about £33,700 left, giving an income of about £1,000 a year, which would barely suffice for the upkeep of the new establishment.

Sudbury was experiencing heavy weather. The staff had been cut to a minimum and although the price of diphtheria antitoxin had been raised, its sale and that of other curative sera could not be made to pay. In the previous year there had been a loss of over £2,000. It was regretfully concluded that if Sudbury continued to be so costly, the work planned for the scientists at Chelsea would have to depend on income derived from students' fees and diagnostic tests. In short, the prospects were in accordance with the gloomiest of Ray Lankester's earlier prognostications.

That then, was the state of affairs when the Council met and separated at 101 Great Russell Street for the last time, on March 29, 1898.

4. The Jenner Institute and the Iveagh Benefaction

While the British Institute of Preventive Medicine, the origin of which was due to the fear of hydrophobia, was making medical history in this country by the preparation of diphtheria antitoxin at Sudbury, its new home on the Embankment was taking shape. There was also in train a series of events which, curiously enough, also originated in the prevalence of rabies, and which led to two changes in name and to a dramatic change in fortune.

There had been strong opposition from people living in the neighbourhood to the erection of the new building in Chelsea. Goaded by the anti-vivisectionists, a thousand residents had signed their names to a petition asking the Home Secretary, H. H. Asquith, to veto the building himself or advise them how that could be done by someone else.

Soon after the site had been bought in 1893, a deputation led by three M.P.s and a member of the Chelsea vestry, all ardent opponents of animal experiments, met the Home Secretary to state their objections. They were a woolly-headed lot and must have had an uncomfortable time under Asquith's searching interrogation. Their main argument was that the Institute would be a source of danger to the public health because any of its employees living nearby, and patients coming there for inoculation, would bring infection to the district. There were many doctors, they claimed, who would agree with the reality of this risk. Chelsea Embankment and the Grosvenor Road were favourite Sunday evening promenades and the price of houses was rising. If the building were allowed, it would inevitably have the effect of lowering the value of neighbouring property. In fact, the only residential property close to the building site consisted of five blocks of industrial dwellings.

Mr Asquith listened attentively, but he was clearly more interested in hard facts than unsupported speculations. He asked the petitioners what proof they had that the building and its activities would be insanitary and a public danger. They had none. Had they any medical men prepared to say that the erection and use of a building of this sort would be a source of danger in the neighbourhood? They had not. Then, showing how poorly briefed the leaders had been, he told them that he had no power in the world to stop the erection of the building; nor had they. The deputation withdrew.

That, however, was only the beginning of the organized opposition to the new Institute. Heartened by brass bands, banner-bearing crowds held meetings in the district to denounce the British 'Pasteur Institute'. Nowadays, the misnomer might be taken by British scientists as a compliment. At that time, however, the name of Pasteur was invoked to add the final touch of horror, since it stank in the nostrils of everyone who believed the false reports, circulated by his opponents, of diabolical cruelty in Pastuer's laboratory.

In 1896 a petition carrying 8,000 attested signatures was sent to the Home Secretary at the time, Sir Matthew White Ridley, asking him not to permit the transfer of the licence for animal experiments from 101 Great Russell Street to the new building at Chelsea. In a brief and evasive reply Ridley explained that he had not yet been asked to effect the transfer. A deputation claiming to 'represent a million working men' asked for an audience, to join their voices in the general protest. They were, however, refused. Two years later, the largest petition in fifty-nine years, signed by 183,607 of 'the people of Chelsea' again asked Sir Matthew to withhold his assent to the transfer. Undeterred by these formidable figures, he announced that he could not see any reason for doing so, but added cautiously that if scientists wanted to perform painful experiments at the Institute they would, of course, first have to apply for appropriate licences.

At the outset, the Institute's Council had evidently been interested to discover the true feelings of the neighbours about the building project because they had sent a Mr Whalley round to canvass the views of the tenants in Chelsea Gardens, the nearest block of flats. The tattered remains of his report show that he got a poor reception from most of the fifty residents whom he succeeded in interviewing. They were mainly 'of the female sex' and almost unanimously opposed to the new building, on the ground that they objected to experiments on animals. Only Miss MacGregor at No. 5 favoured

THE PROPOSED PASTEUR INSTITUTE

A PARADE & MASS MEETING

WILL BE HELD ON

SUNDAY, APRIL 29TH.,

To Protest against the Erection of the proposed Institute of Preventive Medicine (so called)

ON THE

CHELSEA EMBANKMENT

(NEAR CHELSEA BRIDGE),

The Procession will start from the Pimlico Radical Club, Sussex Street, at 1 o'clock sharp, and will meet on the Old Pimlico Pier at 3.30 p.m. when addresses will be given by the following Ladies and Gentlemen :—

W. EVERITT (Chairman).

C. A. SMART (President Chelsea Labour League.)

MISS JESSIE CRAIGEN.

F. LONGMAN (West London Anti Vaccination League.)

H. CORRY. C. FITZPATRICK.

H. LITSTEY. ARTHUR WESTCOTT.

Working Men attend and Protest against the Erection of this Institute.

W. AUSTIN, PRINTER, 82, COLLEGE STREET, CHELSEA, S.W.

Handbill issued by those opposing the Institute (1894)

the use of 'animals for the good of man'. Another supporter was Miss Ramsay at No. 7 who shrewdly observed that the Duke of Westminster was hardly likely to sell the site for a purpose calculated to depreciate the rest of his property.

Many disliked the idea because they expected that it would entail unsavoury smells in the vicinity. When the proprietress of the dress-making establishment at No. 92 heard from Whalley that vivisection might take place, she summoned her seamstresses and cried 'turn him out, girls'. The occupants of one block of eight flats were pre-pared to 'strike' by leaving, if the Institute were allowed. Not every-body knew what all the bother was about. One woman, who said indignantly 'a nice thing to have dogs howling all night long', had been under the impression they were going to build a dogs' home. Nor did everybody care. The jocose tenant who said he personally did not mind if a lunatic asylum were being built next door, was eagerly asked by Whalley:

'Then you are in favour of the Institute?'

'No,' was the reply, 'I am leaving next week.'

Along the street, in Chelsea barracks, the soldiers took a materialistic view of the affair. When Whalley paid a visit to the guard room, they 'expressed total indifference' to the building project. But they would, they assured him, be able to supply him with an unlimited number of animals 'for a consideration'.

A building committee had been set up in 1893. Though unmoved by the hostility shown by the public towards the project, it operated with as little ostentation as possible. Mr Alfred Waterhouse, R.A., was chosen as the architect. He protested that he had not the specialized knowledge for such an unusual commission, but made up for his lack of experience by asking for a loan of their plans from the Institutes in Berlin, Breslau, Vienna, Munich and St Petersburg. Later, his son Paul, with Armand Ruffer, visited the laboratories in Paris, Berlin and Munich to gain first-hand information about the layout and the type of equipment that would be required to furnish the completed building.

The foundations were laid by the autumn of 1894. Progress was slower than had been expected because of seepage from the river, which entailed a considerable amount of pumping, and twenty-nine concrete piers had to be sunk. Upon them a concrete raft was laid, for which the cost was £6,611, more than had been paid for the site.

The first portion of the new Institute was ready for occupation by

June 1898. Furnished and equipped, it cost in all somewhat over £36,000. A further addition, which completed the building, was finished in 1910. The whole is constructed of red brick and Ham stone, a combination not previously seen in London. Among the deputation to Mr Asquith had been a Mr Paul, who in speaking of the building he was attempting to prevent, said: 'It must be an eyesore to thousands of people, and I cannot help thinking it will make an impression on children which will last all their lifetime.'

When the first stage of the building was completed in 1898 all that was lacking to make it a going concern was hard cash.

In the year that Ruffer left the Institute in Bloomsbury, a meeting took place at St George's Hospital at Hyde Park Corner in London, which was to involve the Institute in a change of name and a good deal of trouble, without proportionate reward. St George's was proud of its one-time pupil Edward Jenner, the Gloucestershire village doctor, who as a preventive against smallpox had introduced vaccination with the lymph of a cow infected with cowpox. It was in 1796 that Jenner had tested its protective value by inoculating, with material from a smallpox patient, a trembling and terrified boy named Phipps, whom he had previously vaccinated. The boy escaped the smallpox.

To commemorate the centenary of that critical hour in the life of Jenner — and of young Phipps — the Board of Governors of St George's Hospital held a meeting on December 7, 1896, to 'promote a worthy memorial to one whose work has been of incalculable benefit to the whole human race'. Lister, by then a peer and President of the Royal Society, was voted into the chair.

A public subscription was opened in the following March. The funds raised were to be devoted to research at the British Institute of Preventive Medicine; the researches were to be 'of some national utility' with which Jenner's name would be linked. Lister agreed that if sufficient money were raised to put the Institute in a satisfactory financial position the name of the Institute would be altered in Jenner's favour. If the public were less generous it was proposed to establish a Jenner professorship of bacteriology or a Jenner research studentship or both.

As it proved, the name of Jenner no longer held any appeal for the British public. During her lifetime, the Empress Catherine of Russia had ordered that the first Russian child to be vaccinated should be

christened 'Vaccinoff', and when, after the peace of Amiens, Jenner
interceded with Napoleon for the release of English soldiers, the
Emperor said 'To such a man we can refuse nothing.' At home,
however, his memory was less revered and Jenner's statue had been
bundled off from Trafalgar Square to the comparative obscurity of
Kensington Gardens. A more immediate and popular appeal which
eclipsed that destined to commemorate Jenner was launched early in
1897 by the Prince of Wales to celebrate sixty years of Queen
Victoria's reign, and in the first four months over £130,000 was
raised for what is now known as King Edward's Hospital Fund for
London.

The sponsors of the Jenner Memorial Fund had in mind a figure
of £100,000. When the Fund closed after two years the total sum
raised for the Institute was £5,770, and of that, Lord Iveagh had
given £5,000, the Duke of Westminster £600 and Lord Lister £100.
Apart from the amount absorbed in collectors' expenses the contribution from the normally warm-hearted British public amounted to
about £70. In the end the money was used to found a Jenner
Memorial studentship in bacteriology. In spite of the smallness of the
sum collected, the Council of the British Institute in July 1898
altered its name to 'The Jenner Institute of Preventive Medicine'.

Soon after the change of name, a Mr Marshall served notice on the
Institute threatening the members of the Council with an injunction
if they should make smallpox vaccine from calf lymph and sell it
under the name of the Jenner Institute. It appeared that Mr Marshall
was the manager of a small business in Battersea which, under the
trade name of 'The Jenner Institute for Calf Lymph', was making
and selling smallpox vaccine. He insisted that any orders for calf
lymph which were directed to the Institute should be sent across the
river to his firm.

As the Institute had at that time no intention of making calf
lymph for sale, the Council agreed not to prepare it as long as they
kept the name of the Jenner Institute. In 1901, however, there was an
epidemic of smallpox in Britain, during which, according to the
Institute's records, inferior calf lymph was sold, to the discredit of
the Institute. Confusion arose also from the fact that some of the
lymph being prepared by Government staff for issue to the public
vaccinators was actually made in laboratories leased by the Institute
to the Local Government Board.

The similarity in name of the Battersea firm and the new Institute caused orders for one to be delivered to the other. There were serious doubts about the reliability of the lymph made by some English firms, and private doctors became dependent on German, French and American sources for their supplies. For all these reasons, and because they themselves were being pressed to make calf lymph, the Council of the Institute decided to change their policy.

They secretly commissioned Mr Frederick Hanbury of Allen and Hanburys to negotiate on their behalf with Mr Marshall to buy the name, goodwill and premises of the Battersea establishment. Mr Marshall proved an elusive negotiator. He agreed verbally to sell for £6,000 but later, when he heard who were behind the purchase, he raised his demand to £8,500. Finally, he declared that he did not wish to part with his business at all.

At that stage the Institute felt that the only way to avoid further confusion would be to change the name of the Institute. One way of paying tribute to its distinguished chairman and of keeping faith with the Jenner Memorial Committee would be to name itself the 'Lister-Jenner Institute of Preventive Medicine'. Mr Marshall was consulted on this suggestion. He put his foot firmly down by vetoing any combination of names that included the word 'Jenner'. The law moreover was on his side. He had no objection to the name 'Lister'. But Lister himself, who had demurred at the proposed honour, pointed out that if Jenner's name were omitted the subscribers to his memorial would be morally entitled to have their money back. The Memorial Committee, however, did not think that necessary. Consequently, in 1903 the name of the Institute was altered to 'The Lister Institute of Preventive Medicine', and so it has remained.

The existence of the Institute as the Jenner Institute was brief and for the most part uneasy; almost its only tangible memorial is the branding iron that is still used today at Chelsea to put the letters 'J.I.P.M.' on brooms and brushes. But it was as the Jenner Institute — at a time when, with an assured income of only £1,000 a year, it seemed impossible for the work to go forward — that the Institute was set on its feet by a munificent gift from the first Earl of Iveagh.

In a novel the circumstances of this gift might seem somewhat contrived. Jim Jackson was a middle-aged man who tended the heavy cart horses used for the building of Elveden Hall, the Suffolk seat of Lord Iveagh. He was setting off for work one February morning in 1896 when his dog began to follow at his heels. When he bade the dog return home, it refused to go. He turned to cuff the animal; to his astonishment it rounded on him and buried its teeth in the palm of his hand.

While Jackson was having the wound dressed he mentioned his dog's peculiar behaviour to the local medical man, Dr Walter Trotter, whose fears that the animal might be rabid were at once aroused. The doctor had only just received a circular from the Board of Agriculture advising that all dog bites should be treated immediately as potential rabies and emphasizing that, even in circumstances only faintly suspicious, treatment should never be deferred while awaiting a laboratory verdict on the dog's condition.

When the matter was reported to Lord Iveagh instructions were given to pack James Jackson off at once to Cambridge or to London, if necessary, to have anti-rabies treatment; but there was, in fact, no such treatment to be had in the whole of Britain. Instead, accompanied by Dr Trotter, Jackson was sent post-haste to Professor Pasteur. Between visits to the Rue Dutot for his daily injections he had the rare experience of seeing the sights of Paris at his master's expense. He lived to the age of eighty-nine for, although the dog that bit him was proved to be rabid, Jackson did not contract the disease.

A few weeks before Jackson was bitten, Lord Iveagh had confided to his private secretary, Mr Jacob Luard Pattisson, that he was thinking of giving a sizable sum of money to promote some worthy public cause in Dublin and another, not necessarily of a like nature, in London. When he learned as a result of Jackson's experience that there was no centre in Britain corresponding with the Pasteur Institute in Paris, he began to wonder whether his gift should go to an establishment of that kind. Lord Iveagh had in fact contributed to the original fund for the British Institute. He made enquiries and learned of the new building going up in Chelsea. In January 1898, Pattisson arranged with the director, Macfadyen, to visit the Institute. He was accompanied by Iveagh's son, the Hon. Rupert Guinness (later the second Earl) who was already greatly interested in medical and agricultural research. The visitors gave no indication of the reason for their visit nor did they drop any hint of Lord Iveagh's intentions.

Four months later, Iveagh went to Paris, taking Pattisson with him. Together with an official from the British Embassy they called by appointment at the Pasteur Institute, where they were received by

Dr Roux, who had become the Director after Pasteur's death. The French scientist explained the activities of the Institute and turned up the case-report of the Elveden groom. He expressed polite satisfaction at hearing that Jackson had escaped hydrophobia.

On their return home Pattisson visited Dr Thorne of the Local Government Board to discuss in confidence what Iveagh had in mind, and to ask Thorne what he thought of the idea. The advice given was that the Institute had been well planned, and was in good hands, but was crippled for lack of money. Thorne suggested it would be better to endow the establishment at Chelsea than to build a new institute elsewhere.

It is not certain what rumours may have reached Lord Lister. He did not know Lord Iveagh personally but knew that he had contributed to the original fund; so he enquired if he might call to ask for help towards the Jenner Memorial fund. Pattisson was present at the meeting as 'someone who was interested in the Institute'. Lister told him later that he received such a heckling about the aims and objects of the new Institute, that he expected nothing. He was all the more delighted next morning when a cheque for £5,000 arrived by the post.

On that occasion, Iveagh did not disclose his larger intention, in order to avoid impeding the flow of public money. Lister told him that he had been promised several large donations towards the target of £100,000. By November, however, it had become evident that the public had no desire to contribute to the Jenner Memorial Fund; so Iveagh told Lister and Roscoe, in confidence, what he proposed to offer to the Institute, and stated the conditions he expected in return.

On December 23, 1898, every newspaper of note throughout the British Isles with the exception of *The Star*, which strongly supported antivivisection, was jubilant in announcing the news of Lord Iveagh's magnificent Christmas box of £500,000 to the nation. Half was given to help the poor of Dublin: the other half — £250,000 — was given to the newly completed Institute in Chelsea, on condition that a change in administration was accepted. By that time membership of the Council had been increased to twenty-seven, in order to include the Duke of Westminster and two representatives of the Grocers' Company. Iveagh agreed that the Council should continue, but stipulated that direct control of the Institute should pass from it to a committee of seven trustees, later termed the Governing Body. Three members of the new body were to be appointed by himself or his representatives, three were to be appointed by the Council and one was to be nominated by the Royal Society. Iveagh asked for a decision within a few days.

The Council had no difficulty in accepting these terms, even though there was no time to consult the Grocers' Company over forfeiting their direct say in the running of the Institute. The Company was mildly annoyed at the time but magnanimous enough not to press their grievance; they have nominated two representatives on the Council ever since.

Lister, as the representative of the Royal Society, became the first Chairman of the new Governing Body. Roscoe, Professor Burdon Sanderson and Dr Rose Bradford were appointed to the Governing Body by the Council. Iveagh nominated Lord Rayleigh, Jacob Pattisson and himself.

Lord Iveagh's gift assured to the Institute a yearly income of over £7,000, enough to complete the building, to raise the salaries of the underpaid staff, and to create scholarships for promising workers. With the income expected from the sale of sera and vaccines, the financial future of the Institute in 1899 seemed assured.

The dog's bite was indeed well-timed. In 1897 Mr Walter Long, the Secretary of the Board of Agriculture, courageously enforced the unpopular orders making the muzzling of dogs compulsory and imposing a six months' quarantine on all dogs imported into the United Kingdom. As Pasteur and Horsley had predicted, rabies was stamped out within two years; since 1898 there have only been two deaths from hydrophobia contracted in Britain.

It is relevant to describe here the mechanism of government of the Institute as it stood amended after the Iveagh benefaction. The Institute is incorporated as a company, limited by guarantee but authorized to omit the word 'limited'. It is subject to company law, and since 1962 has also been registered as a charity under the Charities Act 1960. The subscribers who signed the original 'Memorandum of Association' form a body called 'The Members of the Institute'. They receive no dividend, but are equivalent to shareholders in any public company. A report with audited accounts is presented to them at an Annual General Meeting; and, most important, any proposal by the Governing Body which alters the aims or scope of the Institute as set out in the Memorandum must be submitted to their vote.

The number of Members is maintained by invitations from the

Governing Body to suitable persons interested in the Institute, including from time to time senior members of the scientific staff. The Members, as a body, have another important right, to elect a number of persons to the Council of the Institute; the maximum number at first was twelve.

There are also statutory representatives on the Council from various bodies, which include the Royal Society, the Grocers' Company, the Royal Colleges of Surgeons and of Physicians and the Universities of Cambridge, Edinburgh, London and Dublin. The Council is advisory, but its most important function is, as we have seen, to elect three persons, usually distinguished in medicine or science, to the Governing Body.

The Governing Body, which elects its own Chairman and Treasurer, is responsible for the policy and finances of the Institute and for the appointment of the scientific staff. The Director of the Institute is responsible to the Governing Body for the general direction of the work and for the day-to-day administration. The heads of departments are responsible in their turn to the Director.

The government of the Institute is therefore not a self-perpetuating oligarchy, but a hierarchy in which the lowest tier, the Members of the Institute, has some control over the actions or policy of the Governing Body. Until 1949, when the constitution of the Governing Body was amended, the Director was not *ex officio* a member of the Governing Body, but its servant.

5. Early Days in Sudbury and Chelsea

All the material essentials for the successful pursuit of medical research and tuition were embodied in the partially completed building by Chelsea Bridge which first opened its doors in May 1898. Bright, spacious and lofty laboratories, with teak work-benches and pine-block floors, were equipped with the most up-to-date apparatus of the day. In the basement one room was maintained at body temperature for the cultivation of bacteria; another was designed and fitted for making culture media and, in a third, chilled by a cold storage installation, materials could be kept at and below freezing point. An apparatus in the basement warmed and ventilated the building by circulating hot air through shafts in the walls, from which the warm air emerged through gratings in the rooms and corridors. How modern it appeared to its director, Macfadyen, can be inferred from passages in the brochure which he wrote for the public. 'The whole block of buildings is lighted electrically, the current being taken from the mains of the local company. The entire current can be cut off from each floor of the building by means of switches placed in the corridors. The Institute has been placed on the Central Telephone Exchange and the Messenger Boy Service, while the various departments are connected by means of an inter-communicating telephone.'

But for fruitful research men are more important than buildings, and discernment more valuable than apparatus. Wide fields lay open for exploration, but the members of the staff still had to choose specific problems for their own experimental work and there was no tradition of research to uphold them. Moreover they had to teach the students enrolled for the courses in bacteriology, hygiene, chemistry and physics, and carry out the routine work of a diagnostic laboratory. By 1899, the Institute was examining specimens of all kinds for

eighteen Public Health Authorities in the London area, the bacteriological work being done in the bacteriology department under the
director, Macfadyen, and the water analyses in the water laboratory
under Arthur Harden. The fees from the students and from the
diagnostic work were important, for every penny of income was
needed.

It is not surprising therefore that in the first few years of the
Institute's life in Chelsea a number of projects were begun and
abandoned, and that the studies undertaken arose for the most part
ad hoc from the state of public health. The great thing was that they
began; and out of some of them at least there emerged fundamental
lines of enquiry and ideas that are still being pursued today. We shall
be examining some of these projects in this chapter.

The preparation and supply of materials for the prevention or
treatment of infectious diseases was one of the main aims of the
Institute at its foundation. This was of course of great benefit to the
public, for the pharmaceutical industry as we know it today was in its
infancy. The public was expected to pay for the materials, and it was
hoped in this way to support the other activities of the Institute. At
the serum laboratory at Sudbury, George Dean, the bacteriologist
in charge since 1897, had a very difficult job. There was a constant
demand for both diphtheria and tetanus antitoxins, production of
which entailed the preparation of toxins from the bacterial cultures,
the immunization of horses over a long period to get a serum of high
potency, and the processing of the serum to make it safe for clinical
use. Dean had to put a product on the market while continually
adjusting the technical processes of its production.

On the scientific side the results were admirable. He obtained
highly potent diphtheria antitoxin by using a strain of the bacillus
the toxin of which was five times stronger than any previously
produced. The great Frankfurt investigator, Paul Ehrlich, who tested
the efficacy of the serum on laboratory animals, pronounced it to be
of quite exceptional quality, and of a strength which hitherto had
rarely been reached. The costing of the technical processes, under-
standably, was not so admirable. The price of the antitoxin was
raised twice, but in spite of this the serum department still lost
money.

In August 1902, the serum department had to seek new quarters.
The Great Central Railway, pressed for space, had bought the lease

of the Sudbury farm for £1,500. The freehold of a small estate, Queensberry Lodge, near Elstree in Hertfordshire, was bought by the Institute for £8,100 and the unit was transferred there.

Diphtheria was also a topic of current importance in the bacteriology department at Chelsea. Dr Williams and a surgeon, A. G. R. Foulerton, were trying to solve the riddle of individuals who, though apparently healthy themselves, harbour the diphtheria bacillus and carry the disease to others. A little earlier Max Neisser, the German bacteriologist, had described a new stain for diphtheria bacilli, which would distinguish them from harmless, 'diphtheroid' organisms often found in the healthy throat. Dr Hewlett was assessing the reliability of Neisser's method, and Dr Tew was investigating diphtheria in cats.

Other topics of clinical interest were trachoma and tuberculosis. Dr Lawson was studying the bacteriology of the normal eye in the hope of elucidating the cause of the blinding disease known as trachoma which afflicted many British school children. It is a pity that no record of his observations survive for comparison with present work in the Institute on that disease. The 'white plague', tuberculosis, was treated with tuberculin, a product of the tubercle bacillus, and horses suffering from glanders were hopefully treated with the analogous product of the *Bacillus mallei*, known as mallein. For some years the sale of tuberculin and mallein brought a small but steady income to the Institute; both methods of treatment were later abandoned, though the materials are still in use for diagnostic tests.

As early as 1896, Macfadyen had mooted the idea of a laboratory for industrial bacteriology, a suggestion inspired by the important research on yeast and fermentation which was then taking place on the Continent. Lister apparently approved of the notion and asked the Institute's solicitor whether a laboratory for the study of fermentation would be in accord with the terms of the new constitution which had just been agreed upon with Lord Iveagh. The aims of the Institute had been considerably extended and included the study of food and drink, so the lawyers solemnly decreed that 'inasmuch as the purity and good quality of Beer and other articles of consumption have an important bearing on our health, Zymotechnical instruction and investigation fall within the province of the Institute's work'. Lord Iveagh, being a Guinness, was unlikely to object to the project.

A laboratory named after Emil Christian Hansen, the great Danish fermentation chemist, was opened in the year after the Institute moved to Chelsea. For the benefit of students a working model of Hansen's apparatus for cultivating pure yeast on an industrial scale was installed. Dr G. Harris Morris, an expert on fungi, was put in charge of the laboratory. Its purpose was to aid the activities of brewers, chemists and agriculturalists interested in the phenomena of fermentation. Instruction in the microbiology of fermentation was expected to attract students who would otherwise have to go abroad for tuition. Only five students, however, attended classes in the first year and still fewer in the second.

The Hansen laboratory was closed in 1901, presumably through lack of students. Similarly, since some of the London medical schools had begun to teach bacteriology and hygiene, the number of pupils seeking tuition in these subjects at the Institute steadily declined. No attempts were made to attract more, so the teaching activities of those two departments also ended in 1901.

A more academic idea of Macfadyen's was a series of studies on the freezing and grinding of bacteria made by himself, Morris, and Sydney Rowland, a young medical graduate who had joined the staff as an assistant bacteriologist in 1898. Rowland was a lively character who had tried his hand at journalism under the eye of his uncle, Ernest Hart, the editor of the *British Medical Journal*, as well as becoming a specialist in the use of X-rays, before coming to the Institute.

It had already been shown that seeds subjected to extreme cold did not lose their power to germinate, and Macfadyen wondered whether the same principle applied to bacteria. Initial experiments showed that yeast cells which had been mixed with liquid air at a temperature of 90°C below freezing point multiplied normally when they were again thawed. Various disease-producing bacteria could also survive exposure to the temperature of liquid air, and even of liquid hydrogen at −250°C, for a period of six months. In those conditions there was neither life nor death but 'suspended animation'. A luminous organism, *Bacillus phosphorescens*, proved an interesting tool for investigating so strange a state. Watery emulsions of the microbe ceased to emit light when cooled to the temperature of liquid air but began to glow when warmed once more. Rowland devised an apparatus for grinding frozen bacteria. When it was used to disintegrate the living luminous bacilli the glow died away, showing that the power to emit phosphorescent light was a property of the intact living cell.

With this freezing and grinding technique, Macfadyen and Rowland set out to discover whether the typhoid bacillus contained a toxin. There was ample clinical evidence of the microbe's pathogenicity but no one had so far succeeded in isolating a toxin from filtrates of typhoid cultures. It appeared that the toxic agent must be inside the organism — that it was an *endo*toxin' in contrast to an *exo*toxin', such as that of the tetanus or of the diphtheria bacillus, which is liberated in soluble form into the culture medium. Their technique lent itself admirably to a study of the typhoid bacillus, which could be broken up without the addition of abrasive materials. By this method they separated from the bodies of typhoid bacilli an opalescent extract which proved fatal on inoculation into experimental guinea-pigs. It proved to be about as lethal to monkeys as the entire living bacillus. Moreover, the blood serum of monkeys or goats previously inoculated with less than lethal doses of the extract protected smaller animals injected either with typhoid organisms or with the extract itself. In short, injecting the cell extract into goats or monkeys produced a serum which was both antitoxic and antiinfective. The observation was taken as evidence that the typhoid bacillus contains an endotoxin.

Macfadyen continued to use Rowland's method of grinding frozen bacteria to make extracts from the organisms of cholera, Malta fever and plague. His object was to use the cell extracts, in preference to whole bacteria, for inducing immunity against infectious diseases. At this stage of the research the Governing Body became alarmed at the possibility of spreading cholera and typhoid bacilli about the premises at Chelsea. Subsequent events justified their concern.

Another noteworthy enterprise in the Institute was the opening of a photographic laboratory equipped for taking pictures of objects under the microscope. Several new features are described in an article on 'A New Photomicrographic Apparatus' by Joseph Edwin Barnard, which appeared in the second volume of the Institute's Proceedings. Barnard was an amateur microscopist whose father was the head of the prosperous firm of Walter Barnard and Son, Hatters in Jermyn Street. Young Barnard put in his mornings at the shop and worked at the Institute without pay. Besides such routine duties as preparing photographic records and compiling a cabinet of lantern slides to be used for illustrating lectures, he began to do scientific research.

His first experiments were designed to find which light rays are most efficient in killing bacteria. Light from several sources was split up by means of a spectroscope and the killing capacity of the different wavelengths tested. From those studies he was apparently the first to show that the lethal effect on bacteria of the light from a carbon arc is due to the radiations beyond the violet end of the visible spectrum and that the same ultraviolet rays are mainly responsible for the tissue reaction of severe sunburn which follows exposure to light containing these rays.

Barnard's later interest in ultraviolet radiation probably dated from those early investigations. In 1904 he left the Institute and later went to the National Institute of Medical Research, where he won renown in the investigation of ultramicroscopic viruses for whose study he developed the ultraviolet microscope. He was elected a Fellow of the Royal Society in 1924 and for three periods was president of the Royal Microscopical Society before he died, still a hatter, in 1949 at the age of seventy-nine.

In 1901, after the closure of the Hansen laboratory, a new department for the study of pathological chemistry was established. Dr S. G. Hedin, a medical graduate from the University of Lund in Sweden, was put in charge. Hedin was interested in enzymes, the catalytic agents formed in cells which carry out the various chemical processes of the organism. His studies dealt mainly with the contents of extracts which had been expressed from various animal organs by Rowland. Hedin found several protein-splitting enzymes in the extracts; the work continued for some years, giving useful information but no spectacular results.

Two members of the staff in Hedin's department were already able investigators and struck more fruitful lines. Dr J. B. Leathes was engaged in a study of the fats present in different body organs. It was well known at the time that the carbohydrates in our diet are built up into fats somewhere within the body. Leathes made the important discovery that the liver is the place where that occurs. He became known as an authority on the metabolism of fats and soon attracted a number of students to that field. He had later a distinguished career as Professor of Pathological Chemistry in the Faculty of Medicine at

Toronto and then as Professor of Physiology at the University of Sheffield. He became a Fellow of the Royal Society in 1911.

The name of the second assistant in Hedin's laboratory is commemorated in the hypochlorite antiseptic called 'Dakin's Solution'. Henry Dakin came, already with a considerable reputation, from J. B. Cohen's famous school of chemistry at Leeds to work at the Institute with the aid of an 1851 Exhibition Scholarship. He made some important studies on the mechanism of enzyme action and on the physiological activity of substances related to adrenaline, one of the hormones or chemical messengers secreted by the adrenal gland. One of his researches led to a method of synthesizing adrenaline, the first hormone to be made in a laboratory; unfortunately just as Dakin was about to publish this important work, he discovered that some German workers had discovered and patented a synthesis of adrenaline the year before.

Dakin left the Institute in 1905 to work with Dr Christian Herter, a wealthy New York scientist who used the upper storeys of his house on Madison Avenue as a private research laboratory. On Herter's death Dakin took charge of the laboratory and there did much elegant and famous biochemical work. During the First World War he worked in France on the treatment of infected wounds and devised the hypochlorite solution which bears his name. Under his direction the Cunard liner, *Aquitania*, was converted into a hospital ship in which the hypochlorite used for dressings was obtained by continuous electrolysis of sea water. It is interesting to recall that a first task of the water laboratory at the Institute had been to examine the claim of the French chemist, M. Hermite, that sewage could be disinfected by electrolysis of sea water.

The water laboratory, like the bacteriology department, was a main department of the Institute at Chelsea, busy with analyses for the public health authorities. Here Arthur Harden at Macfadyen's suggestion began to investigate the fermentation of sugars by intestinal bacteria.

The object was to determine the varieties of the coliform bacilli occurring in nature, so as to make easier the identification of these bacilli in the specimens sent for examination. Harden gave a wider scope to the research. He identified all the products of the bacterial decomposition of various sugars and determined their relative amounts. To Harden, a chemist trained mainly, in the fashion of his time, in analytical methods, this precise accounting was a normal and indeed his only weapon; its application to bacteriology was revolutionary. But the bacteriologists did not understand, and few chemists were interested. It was thirty years before this original, classic work, published in 1899 and 1901, was appreciated as a pioneer contribution to our knowledge of bacterial metabolism.

A transient enterprise in the early days of the Institute was a laboratory for special research on cancer, set up in the autumn of 1902 in charge of Dr H. G. Plimmer with Dr A. Paine as his assistant. Expenses were borne partly by the funds of the Institute and partly by a donation from Lord Iveagh. An assessment of radium bromide for the treatment of advanced cancer showed that the compound was of no value. A contemporary claim by a German worker, that bodies to be seen with the microscope inside certain malignant cells were the parasitic cause of cancer, was tested experimentally but not confirmed. Plimmer, however, seemed less interested in cancer than in the organism causing a tropical disease of horses and cattle, known as nagana, and in the microbes concerned with monkey malaria and sleeping sickness. In 1904, he asked to be allowed to resign. Paine went elsewhere and the work on cancer came to an end.

Macfadyen had been appointed honorary Secretary of the Institute in 1896, and a year later its Director for a period of two years. It must have become increasingly apparent that he was not the right man for the post, for in 1900 the Governing Body announced that 'in the conditions of the altered circumstances of the Institute the present engagement of the Director of the Institute be determined and that for the present no Director be appointed'. Macfadyen was given charge of the bacteriology department and also received a salary as secretary to the Institute, exercising supervision and control over the administrative work. The head of each department was made directly responsible to the Governing Body.

In 1903 the Governing Body implemented a decision which had been reached at the end of 1901. Macfadyen's secretarial and administrative duties were terminated to enable him to concentrate on his laboratory work. It was advertised that 'a gentleman of scientific eminence' was required for the post of Director of the Institute, at a salary of £1,000 a year.

Among the nine applicants for the post were names which, if not already well known in the scientific world, were soon to become famous. They included Surgeon Colonel David Bruce, the bacteriologist who discovered the bacillus of Malta fever; Dr Leonard Hill, the distinguished physiologist; Professor Waldemar Haffkine, the Russian bacteriologist who had been one of Pasteur's assistants and had founded the Indian Government Research Institute in Bombay; and Dr Almroth Wright who, while Professor of Pathology at the Army Medical School at Netley, had witnessed Ruffer's early experiments with anti-diphtheria serum.

From so distinguished a field the gentleman chosen was Charles James Martin, Professor of Physiology at the University of Melbourne.

6. 'A Gentleman of Scientific Eminence'

The man who contributed most to the successful development of the Lister Institute laid the foundations of his scientific training one day in 1881 with a minor transaction over a bookseller's box of cheap oddments in the Charing Cross Road. Charles Martin was a boy of sixteen when he decided to invest in a secondhand copy of *A Hundred Experiments in Chemistry for a Shilling*, from the books offered at twopence apiece. He had reason to think twice before parting with his money as his weekly wage from the British Life Assurance Company came only to thirteen shillings and sixpence. He had gone there as a junior clerk at the age of fifteen because both his father and his step-brother were actuaries in the Company and Josiah Martin had decided that Charles should follow the same calling.

Charles, however, had the romantic idea of becoming a doctor rather than an actuary. His ambition to be a medical scientist owed much to a boyish admiration for his uncle, Dr Francis Buckell, who had a country practice near Romsey in Hampshire. On holidays from school, he often stayed with his uncle and doubtless his enthusiasm to adopt a medical career was fired by his experiences driving with the doctor on his rounds in a pony trap.

At first there was strong opposition in the family to the boy's idea of becoming a doctor. Eventually his father decided to put him to the test by agreeing that if he succeeded in passing the matriculation examination of London University he could leave the City and begin to study medicine. That meant attending evening classes at Birkbeck College and King's College, London, including an intensive study of elementary chemistry. In his spare time he therefore withdrew to an outhouse in the garden of the Martins' Georgian house in Dalston Lane, Hackney. His twopenny textbook lay before him as, with the help of a few cheap chemicals, some simply contrived apparatus and

3

a considerable amount of determination, he plodded through the hundred prescribed experiments. He matriculated at seventeen and left the family home to become a medical student at St Thomas's Hospital.

Three years later he took the B.Sc. degree with honours in physiology, winning the university gold medal and a scholarship of £50 a year for two years, which took him to Leipzig to study physiology under Carl Ludwig, whom he described as his 'physiological hero'. He had been there only six months when he accepted an offer from Professor G. F. Yeo, who had been impressed with Martin's quality when examining him for his degree, to come to King's College as demonstrator in biology and physiology and as evening lecturer in comparative anatomy. In the time left after the performance of those duties, Martin continued his medical studies, and graduated in medicine in 1889. Two years later he left King's College to take a similar but better paid post, which had just been vacated by Almroth Wright, in the physiological department of the newly established medical school in the University of Sydney.

During his twelve years in Australia, first in Sydney and later in Melbourne, where he held the Chair of Physiology, Martin showed his ability as both teacher and investigator. His versatility as an investigator appeared soon after his arrival in Australia and, in accordance with his nature throughout his scientific life, his curiosity was aroused by any urgent or exciting problem found close at hand. He was always as much concerned with the fundamental principles involved as with any practical application that might emerge.

His first important research was made on snakes' venom, more especially that of the Australian black snake. He explained the variable effects of its bite by separating from the venom two distinct poisons, one a nerve poison causing paralysis of the respiratory system and the other a blood-clotting enzyme. The separation was achieved by the use of his gelatine ultra-filter which was an ordinary Pasteur-Chamberlain candle as used for filtering microbes from fluids, impregnated with gelatine, an apparatus which was destined to play a useful and honourable role, particularly in one historic instance later at Chelsea. The gelatine made the filter more selective so that the small molecules of neurotoxin passed through its pores while the larger molecules of the enzyme failed to do so. The nature of the snake's bite therefore determined the action of the venom, which if introduced directly into the blood stream would kill swiftly by blood clotting, but if injected into skin or muscle would induce respiratory failure because the more readily diffusible neurotoxin would reach the nervous system first.

In work on immunity to snake venom Martin and his Australian colleagues showed that, although the effects of the bites of different snakes might be indistinguishable from one another, the antibodies produced in serum of horses injected with any one venom was specific for that particular snake.

In this conclusion Martin came into collision with the French bacteriologist, Albert Calmette, who maintained that the antitoxin he had obtained with cobra venom would be able to counteract the venom of any other snake with similar action. There was a more general controversy in which Calmette was supported by his German colleague, Edouard Buchner. They maintained that the neutralization of bacterial toxins and snake venoms by the appropriate antisera could only take place within the living body, and involved some vitalist operation. Martin and his team showed, however, that the neutralization of snake poison by its specific antitoxin occurred readily in a test-tube. Similar controversies occurred later where vitalist theories were combated by the results of reseaches at the Lister Institute.

Martin's studies on the mechanisms controlling heat production and heat loss by man and animals were begun in Australia and revived repeatedly throughout his scientific life. The first subjects investigated were the primitive half-mammals indigenous to Australia, the spiny anteater, and the duck-billed platypus. These strange creatures, possessing no sweat gland, or very few, could only withstand rise in external temperature by reducing heat output in their own bodies, and this only to a very limited extent, so that a very high external temperature caused death from heat apoplexy. Martin concluded that in the lower animals regulation of internal temperature was originally made by reducing the production of internal heat. In higher animals and man, as Martin showed later, internal heat production varies little, whatever the climate, and body temperature is kept steady by heat loss — a wasteful arrangement but one that works satisfactorily.

By 1901, Martin had become accepted as an outstanding investigator and at the age of thirty-five he was elected to the Fellowship of the Royal Society. He was no less successful as a teacher. He made a valuable and lasting contribution to the progress of medical education in Australia, which was then in its formative years. The 'Martin spirit' is still quoted more than half a century afterwards, and in 1951 the debt owed to him by medical education in Australia was acknowledged in an impressive manner. The National Health and Medical Research Council of Australia founded two Sir Charles Martin Fellowships in Medical Science 'to be awarded periodically to young Australians, to give them overseas experience'.

Charles Martin left Australia and came to Chelsea in October 1903. One of his early tasks was to organize the field and laboratory work on plague epidemiology in India, described in Chapter 10. That duty took him to India for several months in 1905, and again in 1908. Another enterprise of a field nature was a visit in 1912 to Angola in Portuguese South West Africa, when he accompanied the geologist Professor J. W. Gregory in a survey of the Banquela plateau as a possible National Jewish Home. The expedition, made largely on foot and thus entirely to Martin's taste, was sent by the Jewish Territorial Organization under agreement with the Portuguese Government. Martin's share was to study and report on the health aspects of the area, more especially as to the presence of the tsetse fly, sleeping sickness and other diseases of man and animals. The region, 4,000–6,000 feet above sea level, was found to have a fine climate and to be unusually free from tropical disease. No practical result followed the expedition's findings, as Jewish sentiment towards Palestine was too strong; but it is interesting to imagine the change in world affairs that might have followed a more favourable reception.

Martin's interest in the science of nutrition and his own contributions to that subject are described in other chapters. In later years and throughout his scientific life he worked at the question of internal heat regulation in man and the problems of physical work under conditions of tropical heat and humidity. Those subjects linked naturally with his Australian work on heat regulation and, according to his usual preference, the experiments were made on himself. They had a practical aim, for Martin was shortly to give the presidential address at the Sydney Meeting of the Pan Pacific Congress held in Australia in 1923, when the prospects of using white labour in the mines and tropical regions of that Continent were to be discussed. With characteristic ingenuity he arranged a small thermostatically heated room with a steam vent to control the moisture in the air. In that chamber he took exercise on a stationary bicycle, a 'brake ergometer', of his own design. Wearing only thin running pants he could work without distress even when the temperature was 101 °F, so long as the atmosphere was dry. If, however, he continued working in a damp atmosphere at the same temperature, his respiration, pulse and temperature rose, and palpitations forced him to stop.

Atmospheric moisture was thus of the greatest importance in limiting physical effort at high temperatures. Clothing interfered with the loss of heat by evaporation and so caused danger from rise of body temperature. These experiments were described in the Croonian lectures on 'Thermal Adjustment of Man and Animals to External Conditions' which Martin delivered to the Royal College of Physicians in 1930. He then concluded that 'the obstacle to work in hot climates is, for the European, as much a social as a physiological one. It is clothing. The coolie works with his nice brown body exposed and covered with sweat, and is jolly, whereas the white man distressfully labours in a hyperthermic condition, straining his heart to work a refrigerating plant which he has rendered inefficient because his sense of dignity forbids him to expose his skin.'

In 1923 Martin made use of the great changes of temperature and moisture during the voyage to the Australian Congress, to find out how his own rate of metabolism varied with the external temperature. He was allowed to equip his cabin as a laboratory by courtesy of the shipping company and maintained a constant régime of food and exercise while measuring his basal metabolism first thing every morning before stirring from bed. The morning temperature ranged from 62 to 90 °F but, even on the hottest day, his basal metabolic rate did not drop more than by twelve per cent, showing how little less was the heat he produced.

Later, when back in Chelsea, Martin and three volunteers exposed themselves to severe cooling immediately after a night's rest in a warm bed. The basal metabolism was not raised by more than nine to seventeen per cent unless shivering occurred, when at once the metabolic rate rose by as much as thirty per cent.

The influence of direct summer sunshine on body temperature was investigated on the roof of the Institute. Martin designed an apparatus to measure electrically the total energy of direct sunshine and the fraction reflected from an exposed surface. He tested various materials as well as the skin of the backs of fair, dark and coloured men. The proportion of energy absorbed was calculated by subtracting the amount of energy reflected from the total impinging on the surface. About sixty per cent was absorbed by an ordinary European skin and forty per cent was lost by reflection. The proportion absorbed by a dark-skinned Indian was about eighty per cent. As Martin pointed out, that result explains why well-tanned children at an Alpine Sanatorium can run about in the snow with a temperature below freezing point, if they are in direct sunshine and there is no wind.

Like almost every male member of the Institute's staff Martin did military service in the First World War. Again working on his favourite experimental animal, himself, he found a practical application for some of his investigations. He interested himself in the clothing of the troops and the protection afforded by their headgear. His sergeant has related how on one grilling day when stationed at Rouen, Colonel Martin decided to investigate the degree of ventilation offered by the hats worn by the Australian Army. He ordered holes to be punched at different levels in his regulation hat. Standard maximum and minimum thermometers were inserted while his sergeant measured the velocity of the wind recorded on the anemometer and read the wet and dry bulb thermometers.

In the summer of 1915 Martin joined the medical service of the Imperial Australian Forces and, with the rank of major, was appointed pathologist to No. 3 Australian General Hospital established at Mudros on the island of Lemnos, which was the base for the Gallipoli campaign. With his faculty for making something out of nothing he soon improvised a good working laboratory that could offer a sound diagnostic service for the hospitals on the island, which contained as many as 10,000 beds. He devised an acetylene generating plant out of oil drums and odds and ends which he found 'worked beautifully' and provided points for lighting, Bunsen burners, a blowpipe for glassblowing and a lamp for microscope work, with everything 'just as convenient as gas'.

Most of the troops reaching the hospital where he worked had been vaccinated against typhoid fever. Nevertheless many Australian soldiers were coming to the Mudros hospitals with a diagnosis of enteric fever. The mystery was solved when Martin tested the blood of 350 enteric patients for evidence of infection with the related organisms of paratyphoid A and paratyphoid B. In only seven cases did the serum give a reaction with the typhoid bacillus; in all the others it reacted to one or other of the paratyphoid organisms. Martin immediately notified the Director of Medical Services of the

Commonwealth Forces, asking that future anti-typhoid vaccines should contain also the two paratyphoid organisms. The advice was acted upon, so that Australian troops received the added protection of what is now known as T.A.B. vaccination, before it was approved and provided for their British comrades.

Martin's advice was sought also on the treatment and control of cholera in the Eastern Desert among the forces engaged in the Palestine campaign. His plan which was adopted was to set up 'diarrhoea camps' with temporary field laboratories attached. Serious cases of suspected infection could be diagnosed and treated on the spot instead of being sent back to base. The scheme prevented the disaster which would have followed the spread of infection across the Suez Canal into the crowded civilian population of Egypt. The sufferers got prompt treatment and mild cases could be returned to their units in a relatively short time.

Early in 1917 Martin was recalled to England to advise on cerebro-spinal fever which had broken out among troops coming from Australia. Many of the administrative staff at Australian Head-quarters were found to be carriers of the causative microbe. On Martin's advice a central pathological laboratory for the London Command of the Australian Imperial Force was set up at the Lister Institute for study and diagnosis of the different strains of the organism and the control of carriers.

Martin's service to the Australian Army Medical Corps was greatly valued. How greatly can be seen from the many grateful references to his work and influence contained in the official history of the Corps written by A. G. Butler. Martin was twice mentioned in dispatches and received the award of the C.M.G. for his contribution to the war effort before he was demobilized in the autumn of 1918 and returned to Chelsea.

When Charles Martin retired from the directorship of the Lister Institute in 1930, at the statutory age of sixty-five, three years after being knighted, his days as a working scientist were by no means done. Australia still had need of his help and called him again. For about three years he was Director of the Institute of Animal Nutrition in the University of Adelaide. That Institute's present impor-tance owed much to the impetus it received from Martin's guidance. He was made Professor of Biochemistry and General Physiology at the University, which also awarded him an honorary doctorate of science.

Returning to England, he settled in Cambridge at Roebuck House, an interesting old house and formerly the Roebuck coaching inn, with a fine garden and lawns stretching down to the river. Many years earlier, when strolling along the south bank towards the 'Pike and Eel' at Chesterton ferry with a former Institute worker, J. B. Leathes, he had declared that he would wish to end his days in the attractive house on the opposite bank, which indeed he did.

His retirement there was only nominal, for the Australian Government once again sought his services. He was soon engrossed in laboratory and field investigations at Cambridge and at a rabbit-infested island, Skokholm, off the coast of Pembrokeshire. The work was undertaken in 1934 on behalf of the Australian Council of Scientific and Industrial Research. Wild rabbits had long been a serious plague and cause of economic loss to Australia and Martin's experiments were designed to discover how the virus of myxomatosis could be successfully used to mitigate the plague. The strain of virus was sent to Australia in 1936, but it was not until 1950 that attempts to start an epizootic were successful.

The Second World War raised topical problems in nutrition which brought him back to work with some of his old pupils at his side, when the Division of Nutrition was evacuated to his home at Roebuck House, Chesterton.

In addition to an unusual intellectual endowment, Charles Martin possessed a fine memory and a great knowledge of physiology, which he regarded as the essential basis for medical research. His collected papers reveal a remarkable diversity of interests ranging from physiology, biochemistry and biophysics to nutrition and bacteriology, apart from the studies on snake venom and the monotremes which had established his reputation before he came to the Lister Institute.

Martin was an unselfish Director and, although only a small fraction of the researches published from the Institute during his directorship bear his name, there were very few that had not the benefit of his inspiration and help. He was seemingly without personal ambition, only anxious for a job to be well done, and unconcerned where the credit went. He was critical and could at times be harsh and wounding, but his verbal surgery was usually beneficial and in the end its value and friendly intention were appreciated. He did not suffer fools gladly and had little patience with pomposity or insincerity.

Martin had a gift for discovering special talents in his staff and could encourage their development without interfering with their freedom. Being skilful with his hands and an accomplished maker of apparatus, he had great feeling for the work of the skilled maintenance staff, and the carpenters and engineers were among some of his warmest friends.

His scientific interests and curiosity about recent developments remained keen and unimpaired for many years after his final retirement from the bench, in spite of physical weakness. He died in Cambridge in 1955, in his ninetieth year.

7. The First Decade of Martin's Directorate

Martin arrived from Australia in October 1903, to become the first Director of the Lister Institute of Preventive Medicine, with laboratories in Chelsea and Elstree. In 1904, Lord Lister resigned his position of Chairman of the Governing Body because of increasing ill-health, and in recognition of his great services was elected President of the Institute. Sir Henry Roscoe succeeded him as Chairman.

Martin found himself in charge of six departments, a staff of fourteen scientists, four research students, some half-dozen guest workers and a dozen or so laboratory assistants. Five of the departments — bacteriology, chemistry, pathological chemistry, cancer research and photography — were housed in the building at Chelsea, which at the time consisted only of the southern half of the present building. Some of the rooms were rented by the Local Government Board for the preparation of anti-smallpox vaccine (calf lymph) until their new laboratories at Colindale were ready. The sixth department of the Institute, for the preparation of antitoxin, was at Queensberry Lodge, Elstree, where George Dean was bacteriologist in charge, with Charles Todd and George Petrie as assistant bacteriologists. Todd left in 1904 to join the Egyptian Health Service, and Alfred MacConkey took his place.

In 1904, J. E. Barnard and H. G. Plimmer also left the Institute and the cancer research and photography departments were closed. The following year some important rearrangements were begun, which arose out of a letter from Lord Iveagh to Sir Henry Roscoe. Iveagh observed that seven years had passed since the Institute had been thoroughly equipped for scientific research and it seemed an opportune time to review the progress that had been made. He had gained the impression from some of his scientific friends that the

Institute was not making the best of its opportunities; he had also gathered that the standard of work being turned out by the staff as a whole had been disappointing. Martin and George Dean were cited as 'brilliant exceptions', but as to some of the others, he wrote, 'a lack of confidence in their ability is hardly concealed'. He therefore suggested that the scientific members of the Governing Body should review the activities of the staff to see if any changes in personnel or in the system of research should be made.

An investigating committee examined the material published by the various departments and agreed that results in general had not come up to expectation. They found no fault with the conduct of the antitoxin department and noted with pleasure recent signs of increasing activity in the chemical laboratory. But they were disappointed with the output from the department of pathological chemistry and criticized the bacteriology department, where, they said, the work was not conducted in such a way as to attract investigators to the laboratories.

Macfadyen's appointment as head of the department of bacteriology was terminated as a result of this report. Three years earlier the grinding procees for extraction of antigens from live bacteria had led to some apprehension. He himself had contracted typhoid, and the Institute's second mechanic, Ansell, and a young bacteriologist, Dr Louis Jenner, who joined the staff in 1902, had both died of it. Macfadyen left the Institute in May, 1906, with some reluctance and a retiring allowance of three years' salary. He continued his work at King's College and in the Wellcome Institute, and succeeded in obtaining highly toxic substances from the organisms of typhoid fever, cholera, plague and Malta fever. He reported in the *British Medical Journal* an important modification of his method for extraction which had 'rendered the grinding process devoid of danger'. But a few months later he became infected with the organisms of typhoid and Malta fever with which he was working and died in March 1907, at the age of forty-six. He died before his time, and perhaps he had lived before it too; for he had good ideas, which have since been developed by others, but with the knowledge and techniques available to him they never quite reached fruition.

George Dean came from Elstree in 1905 to take charge of the bacteriology department at Chelsea, bringing with him an assistant, John Ledingham; in the following year Joseph Arkwright came to the Institute. In 1908, when Dean went to the Chair of Bacteriology at

Aberdeen, Ledingham became head of the department and remained so until 1931, when he became Director of the Institute. MacConkey was put in charge at Elstree, with George Petrie as assistant, and at the same time the production of smallpox vaccine, for the use of private doctors, was begun at Elstree in the charge of Dr Alan Green, who had previously been in the service of the Local Government Board.

Hedin's appointment as head of the department of pathological chemistry was also terminated in 1905. Leathes, however, who held an appointment at St Thomas's Hospital, continued to work in the laboratories until he went to Toronto in 1907; thereupon the two chemical laboratories were fused in a new department of biochemistry, under Harden.

The criticisms of the investigating committee were no doubt beneficial and the rearrangement at Chelsea into three main departments, bacteriology, biochemistry and experimental pathology, the last Martin's own department, was to hold for many years. But in 1906 the Institute was, in fact, already humming with activity and within six years of Martin's appointment, the number of guest workers had risen from six to thirty.

In 1905, the Lister Institute was admitted as a school of the University of London. In the following year, the Colonial Office, aware of the effects of diseases such as malaria and sleeping sickness caused by protozoa, and of the vital need for research, offered to endow a chair of protozoology, and the suggestion that a department should be equipped at Chelsea to accommodate the new professor and his staff was welcomed by the University authorities. E. A. Minchin, who was Jodrell Professor of Zoology at University College, London, was appointed to the Chair, with J. D. Thomson and H. M. Woodcock as assistants. The department of protozoology had to provide systematic teaching as well as to conduct research. Their course of lectures and demonstrations to members of the Royal Army Medical Corps and of the Colonial and Indian Medical Services was one of the few in this subject at that time.

Minchin was already a well-known authority in other branches of zoology, notably the sponges, but while at the Institute he devoted his entire energies to the unicellular forms of animal life, the protozoa. With his assistant, Thomson, he studied the life cycle of the protozoon *Trypanosoma lewisi*, which is parasitic in the blood of wild rats and is transmitted from one rat to another by fleas. Minchin worked out in minute detail the highly complicated life cycle, which takes place entirely in the animal and insect hosts; the study was a model of its kind and still stands unchallenged. Minchin's work was a triumph over ill-health, for he suffered from a *spina bifida*, which precluded him from many activities and led to his early death.

In 1909, Muriel Robertson, a graduate of Glasgow University, whose zest was to add spice to the Institute for many years, joined Minchin's department as junior assistant. She had worked in the zoology laboratory at Glasgow, as a Carnegie Fellow, on the life cycle of trypanosomes found in the blood of sea fish and other cold-blooded creatures. The idea of an intermediate host was not widely accepted at the time, but it was suspected that in this case leeches might transmit the trypanosomes from fish to fish. Muriel Robertson found a friendly fishmonger on the Isle of Rothesay who allowed her to set up her microscope at the back of his shop. There, fishermen returning from lifting their night lines brought 'the young leddy from Glasgow' live leeches detached from freshly caught skate. In the gut of the leeches trypanosomes were moving about. Uninfected leeches reared in the laboratory were made to feed on skate infected with the typanosomes; soon trypanosomes were seen multiplying in the crop of the leech, which was thus incriminated as the intermediate host.

Muriel Robertson then went to Colombo, where she showed that the trypanosome inhabiting an aquatic tortoise was also acquired through the agency of a fresh-water leech. On her arrival at the Lister Institute she made a study of the life cycle of trypanosomes that had been observed by Petrie to inhabit the goldfish in the pond at Queensberry Lodge; here again the intermediate host proved to be a leech. These experiences gave Muriel Robertson a knowledge of trypanosomes and of field work that equipped her for an adventurous study of sleeping sickness in Africa.

Trypanosomiasis has been a great destroyer of life in Tropical Africa. It is primarily a blood infection, but in the later stages the central nervous system is attacked and ultimately the sleepy state develops from which the disease takes its popular name. Before sleeping sickness was recognized as a distinct disease, a fatal illness of cattle, called by the Africans nagana, was well known. In 1894 Sir David Bruce first detected trypanosomes in the blood of cattle with that disease: while working in Zululand he established that a species of biting fly belonging to the genus *Glossina*, called tsetse by the Africans, was the agent carrying the disease from one animal to another. Bruce and other workers subsequently established the life history of the trypanosomes which inhabit man, domestic cattle and wild game.

In 1911, the Colonial Office offered Muriel Robertson a temporary appointment to study the life cycle of the trypanosomes in the tsetse fly. With Martin's approval, she set off for Mpumu, a hill village in Uganda where Bruce had earlier been stationed, with his wife as laboratory assistant, after his studies in Zululand. There she lived and worked for eighteen months with one white colleague but no white technical help.

Later, when she was based on Kampala, Muriel Robertson went on safari, travelling by bicycle, to study the distribution of the tsetse fly and to examine the herds of the Baganda chiefs for the presence of trypanosomes. When, after a ceremonial exchange of courtesies, she obtained permission from a chief to examine his cattle, she looked at a sample of blood under her microscope which was respectfully known as 'the iron of wisdom'. It was a curious fact that animals in whose blood the trypanosomes could be seen moving among the red corpuscles generally seemed healthy; by the time they appeared sick, the organisms had usually migrated from the blood to the tissue spaces. It was hard to make the chiefs believe that healthy-looking animals were already fatally infected, but an invitation to look down the microscope proved more convincing than prolonged explanation. One chief, asked what he saw, answered 'Niabo [my mother], I see red stones and a little fish.'

It took three years to complete the investigation, which apart from its scientific value was a quite remarkable exploit for a young woman. When Muriel Robertson returned to the Lister Institute, the First World War was imminent and the activities of the department were soon to change. Minchin was in failing health and died in 1915. The male workers were soon engaged in war work away from the Institute, and Muriel Robertson turned to the urgent problems of the bacteriology of wound infections. After Minchin's death, the department of protozoology ceased to exist and was never formally reconstituted.

Another pioneering contribution to experimental medicine and epidemiology was the creation in 1909 of a department of statistics, which though ephemeral itself was of great significance. Dr Major Greenwood, a young medical graduate working at the London Hospital under Professor Leonard Hill, had been trained to use mathematics in the measurement of biological phenomena by Professor Karl Pearson at University College, the pioneer in this field. Greenwood's use of mathematical statistics to assess the validity of experimental findings led him into a controversy with Sir Almroth Wright over the margin of error in Wright's estimation of the famous 'Opsonic Index', from which Wright emerged without gain in prestige. Martin saw the immense potentialities of statistical methods in medical research and invited Greenwood to form the nucleus of a department of medical statistics in Chelsea.

In the next few years, many of the errors that beset scientists too ready to draw conclusions from inadequate or unreliable data were uncovered by Greenwood. Together with the distinguished statistician George Udny Yule, who was an honorary consultant to the Institute, he did much to set the standards for assessing the value of prophylaxis or treatment of disease. In 1919, Greenwood left the Institute to go to the newly created Ministry of Health as its first senior statistical officer. In 1927, he was appointed to the Chair of Epidemiology and Medical Statistics at the London School of Hygiene and Tropical Medicine; this post was later combined with that of Director in the Medical Research Council's Unit of Medical Statistics. The pioneer department of statistics at the Institute closed when Greenwood left in 1919.

Although after the reorganization of the Institute in 1906, the main departments no longer had regular teaching duties, a considerable amount of routine work was carried out, such as the examination of disinfectants, samples of water and milk and pathological specimens. In the bacteriology department for instance during 1912 more than 3,000 samples of milk were examined for tubercle bacilli at the request of the London County Council. The examination of diphtheria swabs and the testing of milk samples for tubercle infection indeed continued until the outbreak of war in 1939. The bacteriology department was also responsible for the preparation of various vaccines. These duties in themselves entailed much research on methods and the microbial causes of disease, which eventually led Ledingham into virology and Arkwright into studies on bacterial variation. During the decade, H. R. Dean, J. Henderson Smith and E. E. Atkin were among the assistant bacteriologists in the department.

In the biochemistry department, Harden and his colleague Young, in a series of epoch-making researches, were vigorously pursuing the function of phosphate and of a co-enzyme in the fermentation of sugar by yeast juice; and Leathes, with H. S. Raper, Hugh McLean, Percival Hartley and later Ida Smedley, was doing equally remarkable work on fat metabolism. In 1906, Harriette Chick, at Martin's suggestion, began to investigate the process of disinfection by chemicals and heat, which led to pioneer work in collaboration with Martin on the nature of proteins. Under Martin's general aegis, a team led by J. B. S. Haldane worked on compressed air sickness. The Institute also took a leading part in the work of the Plague Commission.

In 1910, the second part of the Institute's building in Chelsea was completed; this included a small lecture theatre and more laboratories, and a flat for the Director on the top floor. A year later, the Governing Body acquired the premises known as the Studios, adjoining the building at Chelsea, for the future expansion of the activities of the Institute.

Soon afterwards, Arthur Bacot the entomologist, who had been working voluntarily at the Institute in his spare time, was appointed to the staff, and Evelyn Ashley Cooper and Casimir Funk at Martin's suggestion began a study on beri-beri, the first of a series of nutritional researches which was to continue in the Institute for forty years. In 1913, W. J. Young left the Institute to become biochemist to the Australian Institute of Tropical Medicine at Townsville; he later became the first professor of biochemistry in the University of Melbourne. Young's place as assistant in the biochemistry department was taken by Robert Robison, a thirty-year-old lecturer in chemistry at University College, Nottingham.

A group photograph of the scientific staff taken in 1907 shows a galaxy of talent. In the stiff collars and formal clothes of the period, they probably appear more solemn than was their wont, for none of them was over thirty-five years old. Few being less than twenty-five years old, they were a well-knit band of mature men and women at the peak of their activity. The Governing Body had reason to be pleased, and the annual report for 1913 reported the continued development and progress in all the activities of the Institute.

Plate 1:
No. 101 Great Russell Street: The British Institute of Preventive Medicine

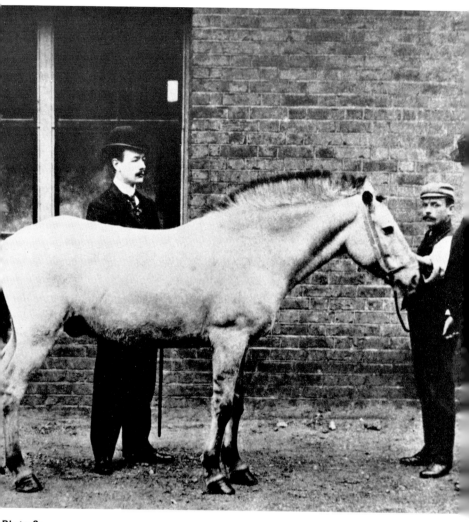

Plate 2:
The immunized pony 'Tom' with Charles Sherrington (*behind*) and Armand Ruffer (*right*)

ate 3: Sir Charles Martin, Director, 1903–1930. *From a drawing by A. J. Murch*

Plate 5: (*above*)
Rupert Edward Cecil Lee Guinness, K.G.
2nd Earl of Iveagh

Plate 4: (*left*)
Rupert Cecil Guinness. 1st Earl of Iveagh

In the next five chapters of this history a fuller account is given of the Elstree laboratories and of the classic researches — on proteins, on carbohydrate metabolism, on plague and on 'divers' palsy' — which were carried out in the Institute during this decade.

8. The Elstree Laboratories

The original nucleus of the Lister Institute at Elstree was Queensberry Lodge, a charming unpretentious eight-roomed house built in 1880, with twenty-eight acres of land, situated about two miles from Elstree village in Hertfordshire. The estate was bought for £8,100 in 1902, when the Serum Laboratory had to move from Sudbury. It had been used previously by a Mr Moseley for breeding and training hackney and carriage horses, and had stabling and quarters for a stableman. Albert Riggs, who was technician in the serum department for forty-eight years, has recorded the impression he got on the day he applied, at the age of seventeen, for the job of laboratory assistant at a wage of twelve shillings a week:

'At six o'clock on a lovely August morning in 1903, I first saw the Lister Institute, or as it was then known locally "Queensberry Lodge", and now whenever it comes to my mind, I see it as I saw it then, the lovely tree-lined drive, the green fields, the trim hedges, the old house with its rustic porch in front, the stables with their eighteen horses and whistling stablemen, and the calm peace that reigned over everything.'

Even in the 1960's, the estate is a rural oasis, although it is only fifteen miles from Charing Cross and scarcely half a mile from the M1 motorway. Lying in the sector between the old London and North Western Railway through Watford and the Great Central line from Marylebone to St Albans, its lack of easy public transport for commuters saved the district from early development. The Institute lies secluded between two reservoirs and, although many new laboratories are now scattered over the green fields, the impression in approaching Queensberry Lodge today is much the same as in 1903.

The first new structure was the serum laboratory, with single-storey offices built on to the side of the house, and the technical laboratories and packing rooms extending behind them. The bacteriologist in charge, George Dean, who put a shilling piece in the hand of young Riggs as engagement money, was a strict disciplinarian, but as Riggs put it, his was a happy ship. Dean had an artificial leg that prevented his taking part in outdoor games, but he encouraged his staff to do so during their leisure hours by having a football ground laid out in one field and a quoits pitch in another. A small golf course was marked out round the estate for the use of the staff in the evenings. The doctor was particularly gratified when his men beat the 'scientists' of Chelsea at football by ten goals to none.

Queensberry Lodge itself was used at first for the production of smallpox vaccine; two bedrooms were fitted up as laboratories, and a third as an office for Dr Alan Green, who came there from Chelsea. As assistants he was allotted Billy Sivell, a son of the former tenant of the farm at Sudbury, and a small boy to help with the care of the animals, and the packing and cleaning. In 1903 a new building for making smallpox vaccine, later used for bacterial vaccines, was built on the far corner of the estate, isolated from the serum laboratory by a couple of fields. For nearly forty years Queensberry Lodge was used partly as a residence to accommodate bachelor staff and temporary guest workers, with a housekeeper in charge. When W. T. J. Morgan went to Elstree in 1928, he lived in the house with his family, and so did B. C. J. G. Knight until 1943. Since then the rooms have been used for laboratories or offices.

In 1906 the Yersin block of laboratories and stables was built for work on plague, again well isolated from the serum laboratory. More stabling and cottages for the stablemen were added in 1910 to cope with the expanding activity of the serum department, and some isolated huts were built for the culture of the pathogenic bacteria used for the immunization of horses. In the following year a larger building with improved facilities was built for the production of smallpox vaccine. A house adjacent to the estate, now called Lister Lodge, was acquired in 1902 as a residence for the bacteriologist in charge. Except for the erection of a biochemical laboratory in 1933 the establishment at Elstree then remained much the same until 1945.

In 1904, Dean's assistant, Dr Charles Todd, left the Institute and a year later, when Dean himself went to be head of the bacteriological department at Chelsea, Dr Alfred MacConkey took his place as bacteriologist in charge. In the annals of bacteriology, MacConkey's name is associated with a special medium for cultivating bacteria, which proved to have a wide application and great usefulness in the recognition of organisms causing intestinal disorders. In the history of the Institute, however, MacConkey figures as the man whose mission it was to make the serum department pay, for he received a directive to this effect from Sir Henry Roscoe, the Chairman of the Governing Body. In his efforts to do this, MacConkey wasted no time on half measures. Games during the lunch hour were discouraged, for the reason that they dissipated energy that could more usefully be devoted to serum production. The men were forbidden to ask for early leave to play in football or cricket matches. If an employee appeared on a Monday morning with an injury acquired while disporting himself over the weekend, MacConkey was liable to remind him that a man could not serve sport and the Institute as well. In the stables there was no more singing or whistling at work.

His policy of stringent economy allowed no time for research, other than that directly bearing on the more efficient production of therapeutic sera. Any apparatus not essential for that purpose was loaded on to the float used for transporting calves for the vaccine laboratory, and sent back to Chelsea. MacConkey discharged the clerk, Mr Jones, and took over the office work himself. There was no central heating in the laboratories and, in the economy drive, fires were fuelled with small coal and slack. MacConkey was not above setting traps to catch those assistant that he had decided to dismiss, and those members of the subordinate staff that he trusted were encouraged to report on the behaviour of others.

There can be little doubt that MacConkey was a natural dictator with some peculiar traits, and not an easy colleague. Early in the First World War, several of the Chelsea scientific staff were sent to Elstree to help in the urgent preparation of tetanus antitoxin. They found the atmosphere so intolerable that they protested to Martin, the Director. MacConkey was not a man to suffer criticism; the protesters were soon informed that their services were no longer required in the serum department, and they were returned to Chelsea. Alan Green eventually found MacConkey so difficult that in 1915 he succeeded in putting a substantial distance between them by getting the smallpox vaccine laboratory moved to Cornwall.

There was one member of the staff, George Petrie, who tolerated the MacConkey discipline; he continued with his own work and kept out of the way as much as he could, though he had to endure being treated like a schoolboy. Petrie had arranged to spend some afternoons at Chelsea to study biochemical methods in Robison's laboratory. MacConkey refused permission for leave; however permission to get a hair-cut in working hours was forthcoming, so Petrie became an addict to the barber.

It has to be remembered however that, both scientifically and as a business man, MacConkey had a stiff job and did it successfully. He had to produce antisera, such as those against tetanus and diphtheria, which would be safe for injection into human beings. Production work of this kind is subject to the regulations of the Therapeutic Substances Act and is a heavy responsibility. At the same time he had to make the production economic, and consider the preparation of other immunological products to extend the range offered for sale. Under his régime the serum department began to make a substantial contribution to the revenue of the Institute, and did splendid work in the First World War to meet the demands of the Services. MacConkey retired in 1926, and subsequently the legends of those of his staff who survived became somewhat hallowed by retrospective admiration for a 'character'. The Institute was indeed fortunate in the long and faithful services of the technical staff of the serum department, who in their turn became 'characters' also and within their own sphere just as autocratic. Amongst these were Riggs, who became chief technician, J. Gooder, responsible for the preparation of the bacterial cultures for the toxins, A. Ling, an ex-Guardsman of gigantic proportions who assayed the finished antisera, and J. Crawley, the head stableman for many years, who during his army service in the Veterinary Corps had acquired the knack of tending camels as well as horses.

MacConkey was succeeded in 1926 by his assistant, George Petrie, who had returned to Elstree in 1919 after eight years work on plague in India, China and Egypt, and war service in the R.A.M.C. Petrie was by temperament a recluse, kind but shy, and in his opinions and decisions excessively cautious even for a Scot; so that other people were often baffled about his intentions, particularly when he was driving a motor car. He was a good naturalist, with keen powers of observation, and became a recognized authority on the production and standardization of antisera. Petrie investigated many bacteriological and immunological problems, and with his colleagues W. T. J.

Morgan, who joined the serum department as biochemist in 1929, and Douglas McClean, who went there in 1931 as assistant bacteriologist, a happy period of fruitful research as well as production ensued at Elstree.

During the early years at Elstree the most important product was diphtheria antitoxin. Toxin produced in cultures of the diphtheria bacillus was injected at spaced intervals of time into horses, which were bled later in much the same way as was done by Sherrington with Tom, the first pony to be immunized. Some of the horses at Elstree were superannuated carriage horses presented by their doctor owners, but most of them had spent their active years clip-clopping through the streets of London drawing omnibuses. The bus horses often gave a particularly high yield of antitoxin because their harness galls and chronic sores had previously become infected with the diphtheria bacillus in the large stables used by the bus companies; they had thus acquired a basal immunity which was readily boosted by the injections of toxin.

Next in importance came the preparation of tetanus antitoxin. The value of injecting tetanus antitoxin is well established for those who have suffered an injury perhaps trivial in itself, but liable to be infected with the tetanus bacillus from dirt or manured soil. The problem in the serum laboratory was to avoid risk to the horse during immunization. A safe method was evolved by using tetanus toxoid, a filtrate from the culture of tetanus bacilli treated to inactivate the toxin as a poison without destroying its immunizing power. The need for tetanus antitoxin became acute during the First World War. At the beginning of the war, Martin realized that tetanus would be a likely infection of wounds received by men fighting in the heavily manured fields of France and Flanders. Within a few weeks he had organized a supply of tested and standardized antitoxin sufficient to protect every wounded soldier in the British Expeditionary Force. The Medical Department of the War Office did not at once accept the offer of this antitoxin for, still impressed by the prevalence of typhoid and dysentery in the South African War, they concentrated on that risk and did not anticipate the danger of tetanus. It required the tragic death of wounded soldiers in hospital to alter the official regulations; but when the order was given for every wounded man to receive a prophylactic dose of tetanus antitoxin at the earliest possible moment, the material was ready and waiting. By May 1915, more than 120,000 doses of antitoxin had been sent from Elstree to the Medical Departments of the Army and Navy.

Between the wars, the method of protecting against tetanus gradually changed. In the Second World War, the forces were actively immunized by tetanus toxoid, but in the British Army it was still customary for a wounded man to receive a dose of antitoxin to give immediate protection.

A rather unusual antiserum prepared at Elstree was one to counteract the effect of scorpion stings, which were very common in Egypt. Dr Charles Todd, who had joined the Egyptian Health Service when he left the Institute, arranged in 1909 with the authorities that the serum department should prepare the antiserum and sell it to them, as it was not feasible to make it locally. The scorpion's poison is contained in the terminal segments of its body, so scorpion tails were sent from Egypt and from them venom was extracted and injected into horses. Orders from Egypt for the antiserum increased until 1922, after which the yearly demand remained constant at about 80,000 doses. It appears that village headmen and local barbers as well as doctors used it to treat persons who had been stung. After the Suez Canal dispute in 1956, orders from Egypt ceased, but a steady trade with India and other Asian countries is still maintained.

Other antisera prepared were those used in the treatment of dysentery, pneumonia and meningitis, and of infections caused by streptococci and staphylococci. These antisera were made for many years, but the demand was fated to disappear with the discovery in 1935 of the sulphonamide group of drugs, and later of penicillin and other antibiotics, which have revolutionized medical treatment of infections. The need of antitoxins for these diseases gradually dwindled. Until the Second World War, the main products of the serum department continued to be diphtheria antitoxin, tetanus antitoxin, and later anti-gas gangrene serum.

The other important production at Elstree was that of smallpox vaccine. Vaccination against smallpox by inoculating Jenner's fluid from blister on the skin of a cow infected with cowpox is the oldest form of artificial immunization against disease. The part played by the cow (Latin *vacca*) accounts for the word vaccine, although nowadays the term is not confined to smallpox vaccine but is used widely for a number of microbial immunizing agents.

During the first nine years at Elstree, like everyone else making smallpox vaccine, Green used calves. These were inoculated with the seed lymph from previous animals, and after a few days the animals were killed and the skin removed; the lymph containing the vaccinia virus was harvested from the blisters on the skin. This lymph was treated to remove contaminating bacteria and distributed in ampoules to the vaccinators. During the First World War, it was difficult to get calves, so Green used sheep and found the vaccine from them just as effective as calf lymph. Unlike calves, sheep are not liable to tuberculosis and are easier to keep clean. Consequently the Institute has ever since used them for production of smallpox vaccine.

In 1915, difficulties with MacConkey prompted Green to make a remarkable proposal to the Governing Body to which, even more remarkably, they agreed. He suggested that his department, with himself in charge, should be moved to Cornwall. He claimed that 'the damp cold on the Herts clay in winter was distinctly prejudicial to the production of the best quality lymph'. While conceding that the winter climate of West Cornwall was also damp, it was, he urged, *warmly* moist, a condition which he considered favourable for lymph production. In the letter in which he proposed the move, he added that, being subject to attacks of pleurisy, he personally would welcome the change to the warm winter climate of Cornwall.

The laboratory moved first to temporary premises at Hayle. Later, with financial assistance from the Institute, Green bought a large private residence at Marazion. One wing was used for laboratories, another as living quarters, and the rear of the house was consecrated as a Roman Catholic chapel. Battlements on the house lent support to its name of Acton Castle. There Green divided his time between producing a satisfactory smallpox vaccine and living the life of a country gentleman. During his sojourn of twenty-one years at a distance of 280 miles from the parent institute, his scientific contributions to bacteriology were slight, but the financial success of the department did not suffer from the change in location. When Green retired in 1935, the department returned to Elstree and was placed in the charge of Douglas McClean. By that time, Ledingham and his colleagues were actively investigating the nature of viruses in general and the vaccinia virus in particular. This led to improved methods for the preparation and storage of vaccina virus for smallpox vaccination; these are described in a later chapter.

9. Disinfection and the Heat Coagulation of Proteins

In the young science of bacteriology the principles underlying the process of disinfection were not understood and there was no reliable technique for testing the claims made for the efficiency of disinfectants. The general view was that when disinfectant acted on a population of bacteria of one kind, the members of the population all died suddenly at about the same time. This idea prevailed despite the demonstration in 1897 by the German workers Krönig and Paul that disinfection does not take place abruptly but is a process in which most of the bacteria die at first and the numbers surviving get gradually smaller and smaller as disinfection proceeds.

The Lister Institute was receiving samples of disinfectants sent by the Chief Government Chemist on behalf of the Office of Works and other Government departments, to have their efficacy tested by bacteriological methods. To clear up the confusion in methods, Harriette Chick, at Martin's suggestion, embarked in 1906 on a long study of the fundamental principles involved in the process of disinfection. This proved to be a classic contribution to bacteriology.

Harriette Chick had graduated in science from University College, London, and then turned her attention to bacteriology. Her researches, which included one on the function of green algae in polluted waters, had gained her a doctorate in science at the University of London. With the help of an 1851 Exhibition, she had worked at the Hygienic Institutes of Vienna and Munich under Professor Max Gruber, whose school was one of the earliest in the field of bacteriology, and at Liverpool under Professor Rupert Boyce. At the suggestion of Charles Sherrington, who was then Professor of Physiology in the new Thompson-Yates laboratories at Liverpool, Harriette Chick applied in 1905 for the Jenner Memorial Research Studentship at the Lister Institute. As soon as her application became known, two members of the scientific staff implored the Director not to commit the folly of appointing a woman to the staff. She was, nevertheless, appointed to the Studentship and soon accepted on terms of equality and friendship by the apprehensive males.

Harriette Chick remained on the Lister Institute staff until her retirement, when she became an Honorary Member of the staff. During the First World War she turned from bacteriology to studies in nutrition, which are described in a later chapter. For her distinguished work in this field, which continued long after her official retirement, she was created D.B.E. in 1949.

Harriette Chick investigated first the course of disinfection with different classes of disinfectant and different types of bacteria. In a typical experiment carbolic acid killed anthrax spores in a manner resembling the course of a simple chemical reaction between two substances, known as a reaction of the first order, proceeding in obedience to the Law of Mass Action. One of the reacting substances was the carbolic acid and the other the bacterial protoplasm. The number of anthrax spores killed in unit time was found to be a constant proportion of the number of survivors, which explained the high rate of mortality at the beginning of the process, and its gradual slowing down as the number of survivors grew less and less. Anthrax spores, after weaklings have been killed by preliminary heating, present a population of almost ideally similar individuals. With other microbes the process was less regular, showing that in an ordinary culture of such organisms there were differences between the individual microbes in their resistance to a germicide which complicated the disinfection process.

When the velocity of the disinfection was measured at different temperatures, the reaction between disinfectant and bacterium was found to be influenced by temperature in a regular manner. The behaviour of the bacteria was in accordance with the well-known formula of Arrhenius for chemical reactions. The increase of the rate of disinfection with rise of temperature was sometimes, however, unusually great, as much as seven- to eight-fold for a rise of 10 °C; a result indicating the great practical advantage in using warm solutions of disinfectant. Similar conclusions about the disinfection process were reached at about the same time, independently, by Madsen and Nyman, working in Helsingfors.

The Chick-Martin test for disinfectants was formulated from these studies. At the time the test in general use had been introduced in 1903 by Dr S. Rideal and Dr J. T. A. Walker. In their method a fixed amount of a suspension of typhoid bacilli in distilled water was subjected to the action of graded concentrations of the germicide to be tested and also of phenol, which was used as a standard of comparison. Equal samples from each set of disinfection tubes were withdrawn after short intervals of time up to fifteen minutes, transferred to tubes of nutrient broth, incubated for three days and examined for evidence of growth or sterility. The ratio of the concentration of disinfectant X to that of phenol which, after an equal interval of time, had sterilized the added bacterial suspension, was called the 'phenol coefficient'. On the value of that figure disinfectants were bought and sold.

There were serious objections to the Rideal-Walker test. It was unrealistic to test disinfectants in distilled water, since in practice they would be used in complicated mixtures containing blood, dust or animal excreta, or as additions to vaccines or therapeutic sera to prevent bacterial contamination. Moreover the studies of Chick and Martin made it clear that the velocity of the disinfection process is different at different stages of the operation and varies with the type of germicide. Hence different 'phenol coefficients' could be obtained for the same disinfectant according to the time taken for the test, which could vary from two and a half to fifteen minutes. When the action continued for only two and a half minutes, the figure supplied would be unreliable for disinfectants which act more slowly than phenol. The Rideal-Walker test is castigated for its unreliability in Topley and Wilson's *Principles of Bacteriology and Immunity* as 'at best a grossly over-simplified answer to a very difficult problem, and at worst little short of bacteriological prostitution'.

The errors in the Rideal-Walker test were avoided by the modifications introduced in the Chick-Martin technique. It was essential to introduce some organic matter into the test mixture. The germicidal value of solutions of pure phenol was much less affected than that of crude coal tar products and certain mineral disinfectants by the presence of materials such as blood serum, animal charcoal dust, albumin or human excreta. Inclusion of three per cent of dried human faeces reduced the efficiency of phenol by about ten per cent, but of commercial cresols by thirty to fifty per cent. The Chick-Martin test, therefore, as finally formulated, was to be carried on for thirty minutes with the addition of three per cent dried human faeces. The test was widely adopted, though the Rideal-Walker test flourished for a long time.

A study of the sterilization of bacteria with hot water exposed another fallacy. It had been supposed that bacteria exposed to heat in water died suddenly when the temperature of the water rose to a critical level, known as the 'thermal death-point', and that lower temperatures left the organisms unaffected. The method of study was much the same as that used for testing disinfectants and, with a variety of infective microbes, it was found that at such relatively low temperatures as 50° and 60°C the population died gradually. In fact bacteria were killed by hot water in much the same way as by disinfectants, that is, according to the law of mass action, but the process was even more sensitive to rise in temperature. For example, the death rate of the typhoid bacillus was increased about 140 times for a rise of 10 °C. The rapid increase in death rate with a small rise in temperature explained why death seemed to take place suddenly at temperatures between 70° and 80°C and how the idea of a 'thermal death-point' had arisen.

The Lister workers suggested that the death of bacteria in hot water was due to heat-coagulation of their proteins, and accordingly studied the effect of heat on pure proteins such as crystalline egg albumin and haemoglobin. When proteins are heated in solution they are coagulated irreversibly. This change of state was supposed to take place at a critical temperature analogous to the supposed 'thermal death-point' of bacteria, and was regarded as a physical constant characteristic of the particular protein. Chick and Martin found, however, that coagulation was a gradual operation, greatly accelerated by heat.

The process of heat coagulation at 60° and 70°C was sufficiently slow for the time relations of the reaction to be studied. The reaction was found to run an orderly course, the amount of protein changed at any time being a constant proportion of the amount remaining unchanged. The analogy with the killing of bacteria by hot water was extremely close and the effect of rise in temperature was even greater. With egg albumin the rate of change was increased about 600 times for a rise of 10 °C, a fact which explains the sudden 'setting' of egg white in cooking.

The results with pure proteins thus offered additional support for the concept of disinfection as a chemical reaction between bacteria and disinfectant. That view, however, aroused sharp opposition.

Some of the early vitalistic beliefs obscuring bacteriology and other biological processes still lingered and there was strong criticism of a mechanistic attitude which likened the behaviour of a biological entity, the living bacterial cell, to that of the non-living substances involved in chemical reactions. The belief prevailed that the gradual death of a population of bacteria in hot water or disinfectant was due to the differing degrees of resistance possessed by the individual microbes. One would expect, however, that such differences would be distributed according to the laws governing biological variation, that is to say the majority would possess the average resistance, and minorities with greater or less resistance would perish, respectively, later or sooner than the majority. This view did not harmonize with the observed course of the disinfection process, where the greatest number are killed at an early stage and the number killed at any stage are roughly predictable by a chemical law.

Chick and Martin then extended their work to the physical state in which the different proteins exist in blood serum, a study of practical as well as of intrinsic interest, for since the time of Sherrington's dramatic use of Ruffer's diphtheria antitoxin the preparation and study of antitoxic sera were an important part of the Institute's work. At first, the serum obtained aseptically from the blood of immunized horses was used without further refinement for injection into patients, who thus received all the proteins present in a 'foreign' blood serum.

The serum proteins can be roughly separated from each other by a process known as 'salting out' with ammonium sulphate or sodium chloride. At a certain concentration of ammonium sulphate a precipitate of protein called 'euglobulin' forms and can be separated by filtration; addition of more ammonium sulphate to the filtrate precipitates a second fraction of protein called 'pseudoglobulin', while the albumin remains in solution. In the years following the discovery of the formation of specific antibodies in the blood of animals which had been injected with an antigen much immunological work had been carried out, and it was established that in antidiphtheritic horse serum most of the antitoxin was present in the pseudoglobulin fraction. The process of 'salting out' was therefore used to concentrate the antitoxin, so that the material used for injection into patients would be highly potent and contain as little 'foreign' protein as possible.

Chick and Martin sought to throw light on the mechanism of

salting out. In solution the different proteins absorb different amounts of water in their molecular aggregates. When much water is absorbed the molecular units are relatively large and the solutions sticky or viscous, owing to the friction of the comparatively large particles slipping over one another. Proteins holding less water will form smaller molecular units and the solutions are less viscous and more limpid. Chick and Martin measured the viscosity of the different proteins in solution and calculated the volume of water held by each. The albumins were found to have absorbed very little water, pseudoglobulins about twice, and euglobulins about three times, as much as the albumin. An interesting light was thus thrown on the sequence in which the serum proteins are precipitated by neutral salts. As water was withdrawn from the molecular aggregate by the action of the salt, euglobulin, needing most water to maintain it in solution, was thrown out first. A higher concentration of salt was needed to throw down the pseudoglobulin and albumin was the last to be precipitated.

The importance of the work done by Chick and Martin was their demonstration that the heat coagulation of protein was an orderly process governed by established chemical laws; it removed the death of bacteria by heat or disinfection from the realms of mysterious vital forces to that of a physico-chemical reaction. The way was thus paved for the development by which proteins became regarded as giant molecules which with suitable techniques could be studied in the laboratory as profitably as simple salts.

To achieve her precise results on the dynamics of disinfection, Harriette Chick used the simplest of glass apparatus. In the work with Martin on proteins, there was greater elaboration. The hydrogen electrode was used to measure the reaction of the solutions and the whole apparatus, though home-made and sometimes cumbersome, embodied the latest scientific principles. Thirty years later, the first Svedberg ultracentrifuge in this country and the Tiselius electro-phoretic apparatus were installed in a new biophysics laboratory at Chelsea, and studies on the proteins of blood serums were renewed with that highly sophisticated equipment.

10. Plague: The Botch of Egypt

Plague has scourged mankind since biblical times. The First Book of Samuel tells how it hampered the military operations of the Philistines against the Israelites in Canaan. As punishment for the sacrilege committed when the ark of the covenant was captured and taken to the city of Gath, 'the hand of the Lord . . . smote the men of the city both small and great, and they had emerods in their secret parts'. According to some authorities by 'emerods' are meant the glandular swellings of plague or plague boils. References in the Bible are probably among the earliest reliable allusions to the bubonic form of plague, which is the commoner form of the disease and the one causing the bulbous swellings or 'buboes' of the lymph glands in the groin, armpits and neck. Unlike the still more lethal pneumonic form of the disease, it is not usually passed on directly from one person to another.

The Israelites spoke of plague as 'the botch of Egypt'. In the ancient Egyptian markets, as in those of Syria and Libya, where the produce of East and West changed hands, the pestilence was an old and dreaded foe. It spread from the market-place along the roads used by camels and caravans, and the sea routes of the corn ships sailing to distant parts, far and wide, to ravage the world.

From the earliest times a relationship has been traced between plague and rodents. When the stricken Philistines decided to pro-pitiate the God of Israel by returning the ark, they included a trespass offering of 'five golden emerods and five golden mice' for 'in the midst of the land . . . mice were brought forth and there was a great and deadly destruction in the city'.

An Indian historian noted that the outbreak of plague in the Punjab, which began in 1615 and lasted eight years, was preceded by the death of mice. He wrote, 'when it (plague) was about to break out a mouse would rush out of its hole as if mad, and, striking its head against the door and walls of the house, would expire. If immediately after this signal, the occupants left the house and went away to the jungle, their lives would be saved.' It was known to many primitive peoples that an outbreak of fatal sickness in rats often heralded the onset of plague. The Chinese used the term 'rat disease' to describe plague and referred to rats as 'messengers of the devil'.

Plague had long existed in endemic form in Arabia, Mesopotamia and Siberia, on the borders of Tibet and elsewhere, but for 200 years had not appeared in Bombay. In 1894, however, there was a severe epidemic in Hong Kong, and the disease spread rapidly along the trade routes and reached India in 1896. Swarms of rats were dying at the docks and in the godowns or warehouses of Bombay, and when the plague bacillus was found in the tissues of sick rats it was inferred that the disease affecting rats and men was the same.

In the autumn of 1896 a sailor just returned from the East was admitted to the Albert Dock Seamen's Hospital in London; though extremely ill, he had little to show for his high temperature beyond enlarged lymph glands in the groin. His physician, Dr Patrick Manson, who was an authority on tropical diseases, was suspicious and excised a piece of the affected lymph gland which was sent to the Institute, then in Bloomsbury, for expert diagnosis. Dr Richard Hewlett made cultures, from which he learned little, and injected some of the material into a guinea-pig. The animal died a week later and from its blood he was able to cultivate a short, thick bacillus with rounded ends; this he recognized as *Bacillus pestis*, the microbe of plague, which had been discovered simultaneously in Hong Kong in 1894 by the Japanese bacteriologist, Kitasato, and the Frenchman, Alexandre Yersin.

Hewlett published his findings, the first British report on the plague bacillus, in the first volume of the Institute's *Transactions*. From that time the bacteriological examination of specimens for diagnosis of plague became a routine service offered by the Institute. At first the work was done in London, and later, when the extent of the risk was more fully realized, in a new isolated laboratory at Elstree.

Meanwhile in the crowded, insanitary warrens of the 'chawls' in Bombay, the disease spread and, when a panic sent half the population fleeing from the city, fresh centres of infection appeared in the villages. It was noted, however, that outbreaks occurred more often in districts to which the rats of Bombay had migrated rather than in

places to which the human population had fled. The authorities did
their best to check the epidemic by a vigorous campaign of inoculation with a vaccine made from killed plague microbes by the government bacteriologist, W. M. Haffkine. But 'Haffkine's fluid' did little
to stem the tide. Treatment with a plague antitoxin, made in horses
by Yersin at the Pasteur Institute in Paris, was also of doubtful
value, and in spite of all efforts plague was widespread in India by
1898.

In 1900 a small epidemic of plague in Glasgow came as a sombre
reminder that Britain was not immune to the Black Death. Two
years later the Secretary of State for Scotland and the President of
the Local Government Board of England asked the Governors of the
Lister Institute if they would build up a reserve of Yersin's anti-
plague serum, the doubtful but only known remedy. As it took six
months to produce this serum, the Government offered to advance
£3,500 to finance the project on condition that repayment would be
made out of the sales of antitoxin. The Institute agreed to make the
serum, using the new isolated laboratory at Elstree, which for many
years was called the Yersin block; special stables were built for the
purpose. By 1903 the Institute was also storing substantial stocks of
Haffkine's fluid, though the clinical value was dubious. The extent
of the plague threat at the time may be inferred from the number of
Colonies to which these materials were sent. The Institute's files
contain the invoices, on the stout buff copying paper that preceded
carbon copies, of the quantities sent to Malta, Hong Kong, Trinidad,
Barbados, the Seychelles, St Helena and Fiji.

During 1903 the plague, which was still spreading in India at an
alarming rate, took over half a million lives, killing four of every
five persons attacked. In the preceding eight years, scientific com-
missions from several countries had sent leading bacteriologists and
pathologists to Bombay to give help. One Indian Plague Commission
in 1898 had included Armand Ruffer, the former director of the
Institute, then President of the Sanitary, Maritime and Quarantine
Council of Egypt. A large amount of experimental and epidemiological information was collected; the air was thick with speculation
but, as late as 1904, the epidemic was unabated and the riddle of how
plague spread remained unsolved.

In the autumn of that year, the India Office sought the Institute's
advice on how to control the pestilence. As Martin saw it, there were
several fundamental problems that had to be solved before the

4

disease could be dealt with radically. It was first essential to discover the habitat and natural history of the plague organism outside the bodies of rats and men. How did the bacillus enter the human body? Was it by infection of chance skin abrasions or from contamination of food with the excreta of plague-infected rats? Or was it introduced by the bite of some blood-sucking insect? These were difficult questions or they would have been answered by some of the numerous investigators who had already tackled them. Martin's views were set out on behalf of the Institute in a letter accepting the challenge.

He suggested that a plan of campaign should be drawn up, administered and supervised by a small advisory committee, consisting of two scientists from the Institute, another two from the Royal Society and a representative from the India Office. This idea was accepted and the Indian Government backed the project with an annual grant of £5,000. The body thus set up was called the Advisory Committee for the Investigation of Plague in India. Surgeon General A. M. Branfoot who had just been made a member of the Institute was nominated by the India Office. Sir Michael Foster and Professor John Rose Bradford, both Governors of the Lister, represented the Royal Society. Colonel David Bruce, F.R.S., the authority on tropical medicine, and Charles Martin represented the Institute, and one of its bacteriologists, A. E. Boycott, was made secretary.

This somewhat unconventionally constituted body met in January 1905, to pick out four promising young research workers, to carry out the plan for field experiments. Two workers came from the Indian Medical Service. One was Captain George Lamb, a talented young Scot from the Indian Pasteur Institute whose researches on snake venom had previously brought him into contact with Martin; the other was Lamb's brother-in-law, Captain Glen Liston, a member of the staff of the Plague Research Laboratory at Parel, Bombay, which was to be the headquarters. Two workers were chosen from Britain, Martin's assistant, Sydney Rowland and George Petrie. Three more doctors and two hospital assistants, seconded from the Indian Medical Service, made up the working Commission.

It was left to Martin to plan the studies, to find out the districts in which they were most likely to be fruitful and to arrange for the organization of the project through the local officials of the Indian Government. No time was wasted. By March 1905 he was on his way to India with the blessing of the Institute, to begin the research adventure whose detailed official reports were to fill three large volumes, issued as supplements to the *Journal of Hygiene*. Rowland and Petrie followed him a couple of months later.

The historic part played by the Lister workers in the great plague investigation in India is largely concealed in the anonymity of the official reports of the Commission. Originally it had been intended to publish each report under the names of the scientists responsible for the research it described, but the work entailed so much mutual co-operation that it was found difficult to allocate the credit. Hence only those studies of plague which were conducted later by the Lister workers in England now carry their names.

The epidemiological approach aimed at collecting all the relevant information about every notified case of plague. District Registrars in Bombay, visiting the houses where cases occurred, filled in the details on case-cards, with mention of any sick or dead rats noticed in the vicinity. When a reward of a quarter of an anna was offered for every dead rat handed in to the laboratory, hundreds were delivered daily. Over 117,000 rats were dissected on long tables and examined for signs of plague. When a rat was found to be infected, its species and the place where it had been found were noted. Street maps were marked to show the houses where cases of human plague had occurred and the spots where rats with plague had been picked up.

Outside Bombay a similar study was conducted among the 6,000 inhabitants of the windowless, mud-walled houses of two small Punjab villages, Kasel and Chand. Rat traps were set in every house where the occupants had no religious objection to destroying animals. The 7,000 rats which were caught were examined for plague. Before they were killed, they were chloroformed in order to examine them for fleas which were already suspected as the possible carriers of plague. The fleas, also anaesthetized, fell from the rats' bodies; they were carefully counted and the species identified. The combined investigations produced for the first time satisfying scientific evidence of a relationship between outbreaks of plague in rats and man. It was noted that the disease generally appeared first in the brown rat (*Mus decumanus*, also known as *Mus norvegicus*). After a couple of weeks the black house rat (*Mus rattus*) became affected. A fortnight later, the plague spread to man. Human epidemics were far commoner in the colder months after the monsoon had broken and the air was more humid.

Experiments were then planned to ascertain how the disease was spread from rat to man. The first experiment aimed at settling finally the much discussed claim that the rat flea was the carrier. Two wire cages were placed close together on trays of sand in a rectangular glass case with a muslin cover. Each cage had a lid through which a rat could be introduced and given water and food. The purpose of the sand was to absorb the animals' urine and provide dry shelter for any fleas which might otherwise die. A plague-infected Bombay rat together with twenty rat fleas was put in one cage. Twenty-four hours after it had died, the body was removed and a rat which had been brought from England and kept in isolation was placed in the second cage. In thirty out of sixty-six experiments of that kind the healthy rat in the second cage got plague. Fleas could jump the intervening space but there was no other communication between the two cages. Infection also occurred when a healthy rat was placed in an isolated flea-proof cage with fleas from a rat that had died of plague; of thirty-eight animals thus treated twenty-one became infected.

Conversely, when contact was close between healthy and infected rats or guinea-pigs *but all fleas were excluded*, the disease did not spread. Large numbers of plague-infected rats were kept together with healthy ones in a confined space but with fleas excluded, and the infection was maintained by the daily addition of other infected animals also freed from fleas. The enclosures were never cleaned out, dead rats were not removed and their carcases were frequently eaten by their healthy fellows. In thirty-one such experiments, each involving from forty to seventy animals, not one of the healthy creatures contracted plague.

Further experiments confirmed that the flea was virtually essential for the spread of plague in animals. Monkeys and guinea-pigs, which readily contracted the disease when they were left for a while in plague houses, escaped infection if they were kept in flea-proof cages. Moreover, the intensity and rate of spread of animal epidemics were shown to depend on the degree of infestation with fleas. People in the poorer quarters of Bombay in close proximity to rats were found by the Commission's workers to be abundantly infested with rat fleas. Further, plague bacilli were often found in the rat fleas caught on the bodies of people visiting plague houses; the ability of these bacilli to produce plague when inoculated into experimental animals clinched the matter. Fleas were found to be less prevalent in the hot weather, a fact which fitted the observation that the human disease was far less common in the summer months. In short, the case against the rat and the flea which fed upon it was established.

The Indian rat flea, *Xenopsylla cheopsis*, proved to be the culprit. Previously, the main argument against the theory of plague transmission by fleas had been that rat fleas do not bite men. That fallacy was soon disproved. *X. cheopsis* was shown to feed gladly on the human subject, especially in the absence of its natural host.

When Martin had seen this monumental investigation well under way, he put Lamb in his place as leader of the Commission in Parel and returned to Chelsea in the late autumn of 1905. Rowland and Petrie remained in India until 1908, when they returned to the Institute.

In the autumn of 1910 there was a new development in this country. Four persons in the East Suffolk village of Freston died from an unusual and rapidly fatal form of pneumonia. It was diagnosed as pneumonic plague by the bacteriologist at the local hospital. Some months earlier a mysterious illness had caused several deaths in the neighbouring village of Trimley. No diagnosis was reached at the time nor was the cause discovered, but from the descriptions available and in view of what happened at Freston, it was judged in retrospect to have been plague. Serious alarm was felt by the health authorities. The Government approached the Institute and commissioned Martin, Rowland and two additional members of the Chelsea staff to visit the scene and investigate the cause of the latest outbreak.

In a survey of the district they caught over 700 wild rats and other rodents, and examined the fleas infesting them. Two rabbits and a small number of rats were found to be harbouring the plague bacillus. It was surmised that plague-infected rats had escaped from ships travelling from the East and had traversed the east coast waterways. The plague rats were found chiefly around the course of the river Orwell which leads to the Ipswich docks. Cats and other domestic animals may also have helped to carry the infection. Fortunately the outbreak did not spread further.

Finding that the wild rats in the Suffolk outbreak were infested with two species of flea, Martin and his colleagues were led to study the feeding preference of the fleas commonly found on the field rat and other wild mammals in England. From personal trials they learned that one English rat flea, *Ceratophyllus argyrtes*, will not feed on man but that the commoner English rat flea *C. fasciatus* will do so. Starving fleas of that species were exposed in a test tube to the temptation of human flesh, and in more than half the tests were seen under a hand lens to 'fall to' greedily. When a woman member of the staff put a bare forearm into a cage containing 100 of the fleas, no less than eighteen insects jumped and struck. The insects' behaviour towards the eight Lister workers who volunteered for the enquiry confirmed the traditional belief that fleas, in picking and choosing their victims, show certain preferences. A more important conclusion was that the English rat flea is just as capable of transmitting the disease as its Indian cousin, although it is a less agile jumper.

An account of Britain's contribution to plague research would be incomplete without mentioning Arthur Bacot. He was one of the most unusual and interesting personalities attached to the Institute, and was its entomologist from 1911 until his untimely death in 1922. After a school life much interrupted by delicate health had ended at the age of sixteen, he became a clerk in a commercial house in the City. He earned his living in that way for twenty-seven years. All his spare time went to his favourite hobby, the life history and ecology of insects, for which he seemed to have a genuine sympathy and affection. He had received no formal scientific education yet he developed a finely trained mind and as an amateur investigator made more than fifty contributions to the *Entomologival Record* during his clerical career.

When by 1909 the Indian Plague Commission had settled the important part played by rat fleas in the spread of bubonic plague, it was clearly of the first importance to get all possible knowledge of the life history and habits of those insects. To his delight Bacot was invited to undertake the necessary studies. At first he retained his clerical post and devoted only his spare time to the work. A whole-time assistant was provided by the Institute to carry out his instructions in an old stable converted into a laboratory, while Bacot was at his desk in the City.

In these primitive conditions Bacot studied intensively the commoner fleas infesting rats and human beings. He investigated their rate of propagation, length of life and reaction to various temperatures and degrees of humidity. The quality and completeness of his work stamped Bacot as a scientific observer of the first rank and in 1911 he was invited to leave his City job and become entomologist to the Institute. For him it was as though a fairy tale had come true; it is said that he wept for joy at the idea that he would actually be paid to do what he so loved doing.

Bacot continued to work on fleas. What was virtually the last word on the life habits of the fleas found on rats, mice, cats, dogs, birds and man, was published in 1914 as a 200-page monograph on 'The Bionomics of Fleas' in one of the plague supplements to the *Journal of Hygiene*. Later work carried out in collaboration with Martin under more precisely controlled conditions showed experimentally how vulnerable the Indian rat flea is to hot and dry atmospheric conditions. It explained the experience of the Plague Commission in India that experimental transmission of plague was always more successful in the cooler winter months, when the spread of the disease among the human population also was greatest. During plague epidemics in northern India a rapid fall in the number of new cases usually occurred with the onset of hot, dry weather. As Martin put it, the ranges of temperature and humidity that occur in India could determine the longevity of wandering fleas so that the climatic conditions encountered before a plague-infected flea could find a new host might decide whether an epidemic of plague would persist or die out. Bacot found experimentally that when fleas remained unfed and conditions were not too unfavourable they could survive for forty-seven days and, when carrying the plague infection, they could still infect a mouse at the end of that time.

The exact mechanism by which the plague-infected flea passed on the disease remained a problem. A Russian investigator D. T. Verjbitski had shown that the infection could be spread from the faeces deposited on the skin by an infected flea either through the wound made by its pricker or by rubbing and scratching. A more certain, and probably the more usual, way in which the infection is transmitted was discovered by Martin and Bacot in a beautiful piece of work. Through a hand lens they could see that some fleas, after they had fed on plague-infected rats, seemed incapable of imbibing any more blood. When placed on a healthy animal the fleas sucked persistently and energetically after the pricker had penetrated the skin, but no revealing pink streak of blood could be seen entering their stomachs. Dissection showed that the entrance to the stomach was blocked by a solid mass of plague bacilli. In attempting to satisfy its hunger the flea went on sucking but, if the suction was relaxed for a moment, there was a recoil, so that both blood and plague bacilli were regurgitated from the insect's gullet and pumped into the punctured wound.

Meanwhile at Elstree, Sidney Rowland, who was still seconded to the Indian Plague Commission, was trying to make a purified plague vaccine as well as an effective antitoxin. The first vaccine made was Haffkine's Prophylactic Fluid. In its preparation, the plague bacillus was grown in beef broth for six weeks and the culture, after being killed by heat, was treated with carbolic acid and bottled in glass ampoules for subcutaneous injection. During the epidemic of pneumonic plague in Manchuria in the winter of 1910–1911, orders for the vaccine could not be met because the method of production was too slow. Charles Martin went over to the Pasteur Institute in Paris and learned there that, by growing the plague bacillus on a solid agar nutrient medium for a few days and washing the culture off the surface of the agar with a saline solution, five weeks of production time could be saved.

Rowland obtained a 'nucleoprotein' from the plague bacillus which was an effective antigen; a horse injected with this fraction produced antibodies in the serum which protected rats and guinea-pigs receiving lethal doses of plague bacilli. He was an expert micro-scopist and spent much time studying the anatomy of the living plague bacillus. With his own special technique, he saw that when the plague bacillus was grown at 36 °C, near to blood heat, about half the microbes became surrounded by a gelatinous capsule; the proportion was much increased if blood serum was added to the culture medium. When the bacteria were grown at a lower tempera-ture, 20 °C, all the bacteria were naked. Moreover the haloed or-ganisms grown at a higher temperature were more lethal. The significance of the capsule was explained years later by Schütze.

The organism of plague, *Bacillus pestia*, used for production of the vaccine, was very dangerous. It was grown in an isolated laboratory and if any worker suspected that he had received a small splash, for instance while inoculating a horse, he immediately had a bath of lysol. But close familiarity with agents of death seems often to breed something close to contempt for danger, and even the best workers may, like rock climbers, have an off day and make a slip in a familiar practice. In 1909, an Australian guest worker, Thomas Carlyle Parkinson, working under Rowland, complained of feeling des-perately ill. He was living at the time in Queensberry Lodge, where several of the bachelor workers were accommodated. It was thought at first that he had influenza and Hartley and Rowland looked after him. When it was realized that his lungs were affected, Martin came out from Chelsea and recognized that Parkinson had pneumonic plague. There was nothing they could do to influence the result; within three days of falling ill, Parkinson died.

Hartley used later to give a dramatic account of this tragedy and his own position as a contact. He was given fifty c.c. of anti-plague serum in the groin, with Martin gloomily saying it was unlikely to do much good. 'I was frightened to death,' said Hartley 'and itching so much from the serum, death seemed almost preferable.' Parkinson's death convinced the authorities that it was not safe for the staff working on plague to be living in Queensberry Lodge, which was used also for other workers, or to be quartered in the neighbouring villages. The Plague Commission, which was still supporting the investigations, therefore erected isolated bungalows on the Elstree estate.

The researches on plague continued to occupy Rowland for some years until, as the *Journal of Hygiene* stated in a footnote to his last paper, 'At this point Dr Rowland's investigations were interrupted by the European War.' Rowland, with the rank of Major, took the first mobile pathological laboratory to France in October 1914. Two years later, while investigating an outbreak of cerebro-spinal fever among the troops, he contracted the disease himself and died at the age of forty-four, in March 1917.

The demand for plague vaccine still continues, for the disease is still endemic in some parts of the world. But the chain of infection — from the rat to the flea, and from the flea to man — had been so clearly worked out by the Plague Commission that the prevention of epidemics today depends to a large extent on the control of rats and fleas in proximity to man.

4*

11. Divers' Palsy: The Bends

Most research workers are embarrassed by the man in the street who asks what their work is worth. They can assert that any addition to knowledge has a price above rubies or proffer an estimate of lives saved or hospital costs reduced, but they cannot often reply firmly in sterling. Captain G. C. C. Damant, R.N., was probably unique in being able to vouch personally for the fact that the research on divers' palsy at the Institute, in which he had taken part, was worth about £5,000,000 on a gold standard.

Shortly after nightfall on January 10, 1917, the *Laurentic* weighed anchor and steamed out of Lough Swilly. The 15,000-ton liner, which had been taken over by the Admiralty and converted into an armed cruiser, had left Liverpool the night before on a voyage to Halifax, and entered the Lough before daybreak to avoid German submarines. The *Laurentic* was barely a mile outside the Lough again, off the coast of Northern Ireland, when she struck a German mine and sank. She had on board 475 people, of whom 334 were lost. She also carried more than 3,000 bars of gold, stowed in the second-class baggage room.

The Admiralty lost no time in attempts to salve the bullion. Captain Damant was in command of the operation, in the *Volunteer*, a small self-propelled mooring lighter with powerful capstans capable of lifting heavy weights. The wreck was located at twenty fathoms (120 feet) depth of water at low tide. The first diver found her lying on her port side at an angle of 60° from the vertical. A water-tight door, half way down the ship's side, gave the easiest access to the strong room. It was blown open with gun cotton. An iron gate barring the way was also blown aside and after two hours spent in shifting further obstructions, diver E. C. Miller reached the steel door of the strong room and opened it with a hammer and chisel. He found himself on top of the gold, which was in small wooden boxes, each weighing 140 lb and worth about £8,000.

Miller brought one box up that night, and three more the next morning. Captain Damant thought that the back of the job was broken; with luck it would be finished in a couple of weeks. In fact, it took seven years, for the wind changed and blew a gale for a week and with the battering it received the wreck collapsed. When the divers got back and blasted their way again to the strong room, they found that the rest of the gold had dropped through a hole in the floor and through decks to end up somewhere far below. It was too risky to follow it, as the five decks above the divers seemed about to break up. It was decided to cut down vertically through the wreck and blow a way to the bullion with explosives. This meant removing the structures plate by plate and beam by beam and hoisting them to the surface for dumping. The exacting task of shifting tons of metal and later, when the divers reached the sea bed, tons of gravel, began at once. Except during 1918, when Captain Damant and his crew of experts were called to the eerie duty of searching for signal codes in sunken German submarines, the salvage continued in the summer months of each year until 1924. The divers had recovered 3,186 bars of gold, all but twenty-five of the number sunk, without one casualty, before the search was abandoned.

Damant described the salvage in 'Notes on the *Laurentic* Salvage Operations and the Prevention of Compressed Air Illness' in the *Journal of Hygiene* in 1926. The success of this dangerous undertaking and others like it can fairly be attributed to the experiments carried out twenty years earlier in the Lister Institute.

Animals are normally called upon to withstand the weight of the air about them, which exerts a pressure of 15 lb on every square inch of the body's surface and inside the lungs as well. Man can, however, support many times the normal atmospheric pressure if the air entering the lungs is at the same pressure as that pressing externally on his body. When a diver, in a helmet and flexible suit, descends in sea water the pressure on his body increases by one atmosphere, that is by 15 lb to the square inch, for every 33 feet of his descent. Unless the air pumped into his helmet is under at least as great a pressure, the external pressure compresses his abdomen and prevents him from breathing and, at greater depths, squeezes his body until blood pours out of his mouth and nostrils. If the air supply to his helmet is under adequate pressure, he can work in comparative comfort at considerable depths.

Breathing compressed air creates the possibility of 'compressed air illness' or, as it is less correctly called, 'caisson disease', since the risk is run by men laying the foundations of bridges and piers as well as by divers. Men may be lowered to a river bed in a bottomless metal chamber known as a diving bell, into which compressed air is pumped. The pressure of the air prevents water from entering the bell, as when an inverted tumbler is thrust into a vessel of water. The open-bottom caisson used for building the piers of bridges is similar to the diving bell except that it is allowed to sink into the mud. It is connected with the surface by a tube wide enough to accommodate a ladder by which the men leave the caisson, passing up through an air-locked compartment known as a 'purgatory'.

Compressed air illness, which appears only after the man reaches the surface, has been known for over a hundred years. In the milder form, the man gets pains in his muscles, joints and trunk, called 'the twist' or 'the bends'; these can be immediately relieved if he is returned to a recompression chamber in which the air pressure is increased until the pains go; the pressure is then decreased slowly. Victims of the more severe forms of the disease vomit, become breathless and develop paralysis, or may become unconscious and die in a few minutes.

In 1878, the French physiologist, Paul Bert, published the results of some experiments on decompression. He placed twenty-four dogs in a metal compression chamber and subjected them to air pressures of about nine atmospheres and then decompressed them in a few minutes. Only one of the animals showed no sign of injury. Twenty-one died. Post-mortem examination showed bubbles of nitrogen in the hearts and arteries, and in the spinal cords of animals which had become paralysed.

Paul Bert recommended that divers who had been exposed to high pressures of air should be brought up slowly and gradually. Since in deep-sea diving the tides and the weather must be taken into account, a slow method of decompression has serious disadvantages. Nevertheless it became the custom for divers to come up at a rate of about 5 feet a minute. The German investigators, Heller, Mager and von Schrötter later declared, after decompression experiments on dogs, that the diver would always be safe if he came up at a uniform rate of twenty minutes for every atmosphere of pressure.

In many countries these precautions were faithfully observed. Nevertheless, in the early years of the present century diving to a total pressure of more than four atmospheres, about 100 feet, was still notoriously dangerous, and fatal accidents were frequent. There was urgent need for a quicker, safe method of decompression, and for rules to guide the diver back safely from different depths and after various periods spent below. In 1905, the Admiralty set up a Committee to 'Consider and Report upon the Conditions of Deep Water Diving'. The scientific member of this Committee was Dr John Scott Haldane, the authority on respiration, who was then Reader in Physiology at the University of Oxford. He was the illustrious father of J. B. S. Haldane, who was perhaps more widely known.

Haldane had been brooding for a long time over the subject of safety in deep-sea diving. The air in the lungs at all times has a pressure equal to that of the air breathed. If this air pressure is increased, the blood and other fluids and tissues of the body will contain more than the normal amount of dissolved air. Then, if the external pressure and consequently that in the lungs is reduced, some of the excess air in the blood will come out of solution; and if the change in pressure is rapid, bubbles may form which may block the blood flow with serious consequences. The bubbles usually consist of nitrogen from the air, since the oxygen, with its greater combining capacity, tends to remain bound in the tissue fluids and a longer time will elapse before it makes its escape, if at all.

Haldane had already noted that there was no record of compressed air illness in divers if the air pressure experienced was not greater than $2\frac{1}{4}$ atmospheres. It was safe to decompress a man from $2\frac{1}{4}$ to 1 atmospheres, irrespective of how long he had been exposed to the higher pressure and of how quickly decompression had been carried out. Haldane considered it probable that if the pressure in the lungs was suddenly reduced by one half the same volume of nitrogen would be liberated from solution in the blood and tissues whatever the original pressure had been. He thought it likely that it would be as safe to reduce the pressure from 4 atmospheres to 2, or even from 6 atmospheres to 3, as from $2\frac{1}{4}$ to 1. If this principle held good, a diver working at 102 feet, equivalent to 4 atmospheres' pressure, might safely ascend to 30 feet depth (2 atmospheres), much more than halfway to the surface. The diver would get rid of surplus nitrogen through the lungs more rapidly than by the traditional practice of uniform, gradual decompression, and shorten his exposure to high pressures.

Dr Ludwig Mond presented the Lister Institute with a large compression chamber to facilitate research on the subject, and Haldane began work there with two colleagues, Lieutenant Damant, R.N., a gunnery officer, and Dr A. E. Boycott, a member of the Institute staff, who was also Secretary of the Advisory Committee on Plague.

Haldane used the chamber, which had been set up in the back yard of the Institute, to find out if his principle was valid within the range of pressures commonly encountered by divers and tunnel workers. The Mond chamber was made from a segment of a $\frac{3}{8}$ inch steel boiler, lying on its side and closed at the ends with curved half inch steel plates. Three stout glass windows were let into the sides and an oval manhole into one end. Wiring for telephone, lights, electric heaters and a motor to drive a fan or a recording drum entered through fibre plugs. A compressor driven by a gas engine was able to vary the pressure within, from 100 lb per square inch above that of the atmosphere to 8 lb per square inch below. The pressure could be regulated from outside or inside by valves in the side. The chamber was $7\frac{1}{2}$ feet long and 7 feet in height and width, roomy enough to hold two or three persons comfortably; it could be used for experiments on animals lasting several hours without the necessity for ventilation.

The workers at the Institute began by using mice, guinea-pigs and rats as experimental animals. These, however, proved to be almost insusceptible to compressed air sickness, because small animals have such a rapid rate of breathing and heart beat that excess gases are swiftly removed from the blood. A mixed collection of ordinary English goats was therefore used. The adult goat, which has about one-third the weight of a man, is curiously insensitive to pain and will even continue to walk on a broken leg; but it was found very suitable for the tests, since it is prone to compressed air sickness, and presents even mild signs in an unmistakable manner. When a goat is experiencing 'the bends' in a leg, it holds the limb off the ground. In milder attacks the animal limps slightly. Some minor gaps in the investigation were caused by the animals' appetite for scientific records. One hiatus appeared 'because the details were eaten by a goat'.

A certain minimum increase of pressure was needed to produce any signs of sickness. As with human subjects, even a long exposure of 4 hours to a pressure of $2\frac{1}{2}$ atmospheres followed by decompression in 2 minutes was almost harmless. Of 45 goats thus treated, 3 showed only slight signs and 42 none at all. With pressures up to 5 or 6 atmospheres the results were more severe even if the time of exposure was shorter and that of decompression longer.

During decompression by stages, however, the relative change in pressure at each stage was more important than the absolute change; this confirmed Haldane's theory. For instance 10 goats were subjected to a pressure of 6 atmospheres for 3 hours and decompressed in $1\frac{1}{2}$ minutes to $2\frac{1}{2}$ atmospheres. Not one of the animals showed any damage when observed through the window of the Mond chamber; nor did they when, after further decompression by stages, they were let out to run about the yard. But when another 10 goats were compressed for 3 hours at $4\frac{1}{2}$ atmospheres and then decompressed in 4 minutes to ordinary atmospheric pressure, only 2 escaped injury; 3 had 'bends', 3 were severely damaged and 2 died. The absolute change in pressure during decompression was the same, $3\frac{1}{2}$ atmospheres in both experiments, but the relative drop was to more than a half in the first experiment and to less than a quarter in the second one.

In another series of experiments, each goat was tested by both methods, first by decompression in stages by Haldane's method and then by decompression at a slow uniform rate according to the conventional practice. In both tests the animals were first exposed to 6 atmospheres' pressure for periods up to 3 hours. After decompression in stages, damage occurred in only 7 out of 96 tests. But after slow gradual decompression, damage occurred in 48 out of 94 tests; in 11 tests the signs were severe and 2 animals died. Pressures above 6 atmospheres could not be tested in the Mond chamber.

The Lister team worked out a set of provisional tables laying down the safe rate of decompression for men working in compressed air and for divers descending to a maximum depth of 204 feet. The total pressure was halved at the first stage. After that, each stage was equivalent to a reduction in depth of 10 feet. In practice the diver would be signalled to stop and wait at every 10 feet of the ascent. The diver's working time was restricted to about 15 minutes at a depth of 204 feet; and to other times according to the depth; for instance 40 minutes at 100 feet or as long as 3 hours at 60 feet depth.

It remained to test the new rules on man. Lieutenant Damant and a Royal Naval gunner, Mr A. Y. Catto, entered the compression chamber and the manhole was sealed. The pumps were started. Damant opened a valve and the air pressure began to rise. When the gauge read a total pressure of $3\frac{1}{2}$ atmospheres the valve was shut and the men settled down to wait an hour. The pressure was then reduced in 7 minutes to $1\frac{1}{2}$ atmospheres and kept at that level for 5 minutes longer. On the telephone Damant told his colleagues watching outside that neither he nor Catto had noticed anything peculiar after the drop in pressure. When they emerged into the open air after being decompressed in two further stages, neither of them had any symptoms to report.

The experiments were repeated on succeeding days at increased pressures. At $6\frac{1}{2}$ atmospheres' pressure the volunteers had the usual experience of finding the pitch of their voices strikingly raised while the mouth and lips felt oily. The pressure was then reduced in 3 minutes to 3 atmospheres. Their only symptom was itching on the exposed parts of the arms. After further decompression lasting 43 minutes, they climbed out into the yard of the Institute and declared themselves unaffected by the ordeal.

The next step was to test the tables of decompression in actual diving. Damant's experience of sea diving was limited to what he had learned in his course as a gunnery officer, and to some experiments made later at Portsmouth for the Admiralty Committee. He had never previously dived below 114 feet. Mr Catto was much more experienced as a diver, but had never been deeper than 138 feet.

Shortly after the human experiments in the chamber at Chelsea, H.M.S. *Spanker*, a torpedo boat equipped for safety with a recompression chamber, arrived at Rothesay on the Isle of Bute with Damant on board. He was met by Dr Haldane, Dr Rees the naval medical officer, and Mr Catto. Next day the pumps were tested up to a pressure of 6 atmospheres, corresponding to a depth of 200 feet, while Haldane estimated to what extent they were leaking at that pressure. He and Dr Rees were compressed in the recompression chamber to check that it was in working order. Diving then started.

Damant and Catto began by diving at 90 feet. Day after day they went deeper. When the *Spanker* was taken to the entrance of Loch Striven, they both went down through darkness to sink into the muddy floor of the loch at a depth of 210 feet. There they took samples of the air from their helmets before and after doing weight-lifting exercises, in order to ascertain the oxygen consumption and carbon dioxide output in such conditions. Every time they followed the new principle and came up quickly more than half way and paused

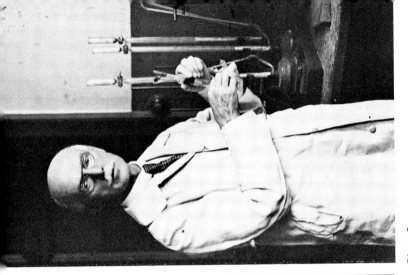

Plate 6:
Lord Lister. First Chairman of the Governing Body. *From the bust by Sir Thomas Brock*

Plate 7:
Sir Henry Roscoe. First Treasurer of the Institute

Plate 8:
Sir Arthur Harden, Nobel Laureate 1929, in his laboratory

Plate 9:
The Lister Institute,
Chelsea
*Photograph by
David Cockcroft*

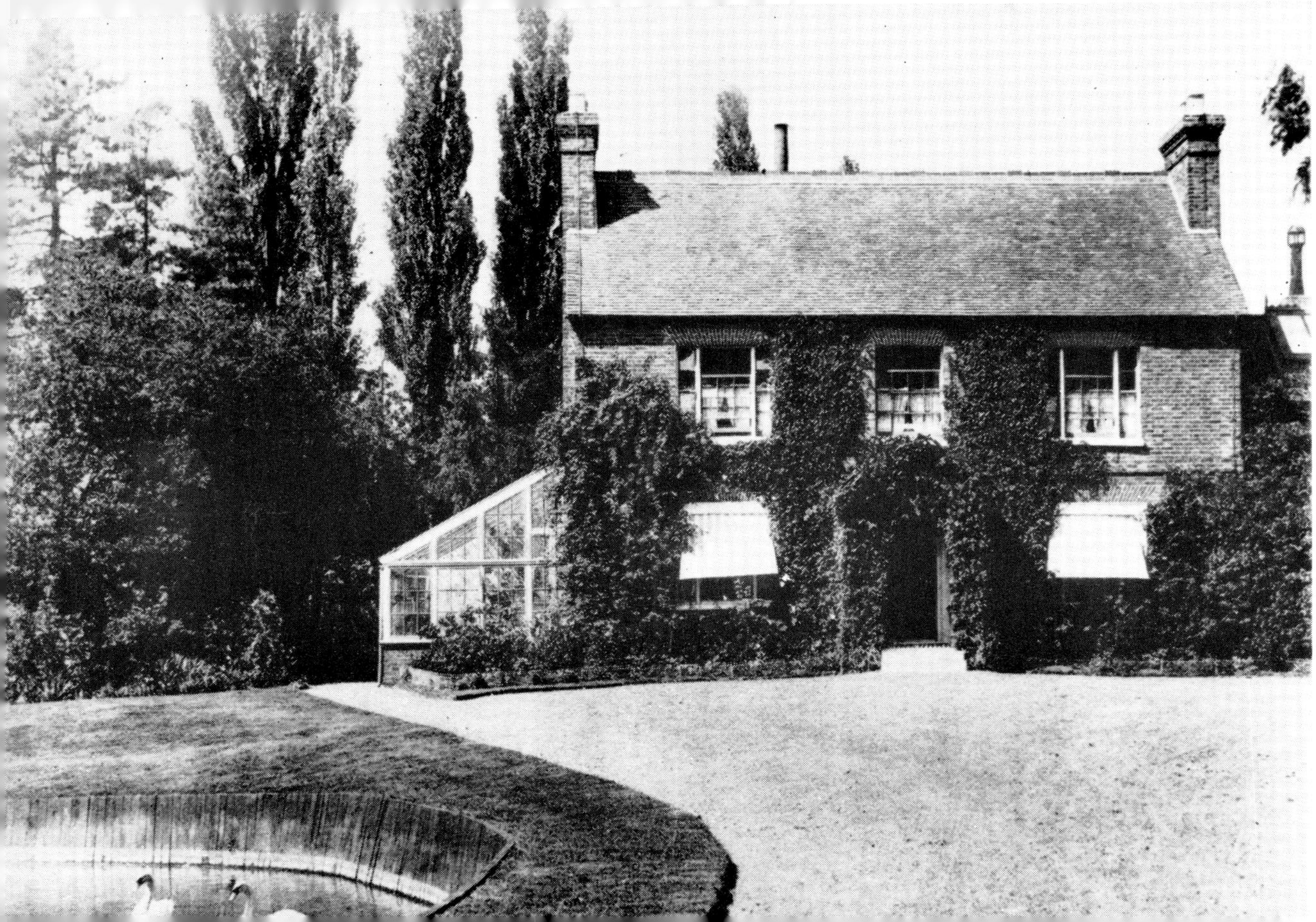

Plate 10:
Queensberry Lodge,
Elstree

Plate 11: The Scientific Staff of the Lister Institute. 1907 *(left to right)*
Top: G. Cooper, E. L. Kennaway, J. Henderson-Smith, G. F. Petrie, H. W. Armit, J. C. G. Ledingham, S. Rowland, H. M. Woodcock, D. J. Reid
Centre: A. White Robertson, F. A. Bainbridge, J. A. Arkwright, G. Dean, C. J. Martin, A. Harden, E. A. Minchin, J. B. Leathes, H. de R. Morgan, W. J. Young
Bottom: Lang Clayton, S. Walpole, P. Hartley, Harriette Chick, W. E. Marshall

at this first stage. Then they made a further slow ascent by stages and came to the surface completely free from symptoms.

With this practical proof that their decompression tables ensured safety for considerable depths, Haldane and Damant returned to the Lister Institute to continue work with Boycott and their goats. They constructed tables of decompression times to cover all depths and durations of dives within the range they had explored. They also drew up a supplementary set of tables to cover emergencies when a man might have to stay down longer than was good for him through vagaries in the weather, a turn of the tide or an accident at work.

During the earlier experiment the workers had got the impression that fat goats were more prone to caisson disease than lean ones. Boycott had left the Institute in 1907 to take a lectureship in pathology at Guy's Hospital, but joined forces with Damant to test the effect of fatness. They subjected goats to degrees of air pressure likely to produce bends or cause death. The total amount of the body fat in each animal was measured post-mortem and compared with the signs that had been observed. Boycott and Damant obtained evidence that fatness does increase the liability to caisson disease. They concluded that really fat men should never be allowed to work in compressed air, that plump men should be excluded from high pressure caissons or from diving to more than sixty feet, and that the time of exposure should be curtailed. This practice is still observed.

In view of their findings, the three investigators condemned as unsafe the Dutch Government's practice of bringing up the diver slowly from the bottom and accelerating the rate of ascent as he neared the surface. As for the more general custom of gradual decompression they said flatly: 'We must emphatically dissent from the conclusion drawn by Heller, Mager and von Schrötter that decompression at the uniform rate of twenty minutes an atmosphere prevents any dangerous retention of gas in the body.'

The rules elaborated in Chelsea were such a sharp break with tradition that it is not surprising that they met with criticism and opposition. The objections came largely from civilian divers who, with considerable personal immunity to the bends, were able to work with less careful decompression. Another opponent was the physiologist, Sir Leonard Hill, who had previously been an advocate of uniform decompression. The Admiralty however incorporated the new rules without delay into the official regulations for diving in deep water. They were contained in the Admiralty's Blue Book on the subject which appeared in 1907 (Command No. GN 1549/1907). Within a year or two all the navies of the world, led by that of the United States, had adopted the new system of decompression, and divers were enabled to reach unprecedented depths and to return in safety.

12. Alcoholic Fermentation

Lord Lister, in the introduction to his classical experiments on the fermentation of milk by *Bacillus lactis*, wrote 'In order that any sure steps may be taken to elucidate the real nature of the various important diseases which may be presumed to be of a fermentative nature, such as the specific fevers of pyaemia, the first essential, as it appears to me, is that we should have clear ideas, based on positive knowledge, with regard to the more simple forms of fermentation, if I may so speak — more simple because they can be conducted and investigated in our laboratories.'

Lister was still Chairman of the Governing Body of the Institute when Arthur Harden was appointed to the staff, and he remained as President until his death in 1912. It may be hoped that he was aware of Harden's pioneer experiments on bacterial metabolism and of the momentous work of Harden and Young on the mechanism of alcoholic fermentation carried out in the first decade of this century. Lister at least would not have thought that alcoholic fermentation was an odd subject for investigation in an institute of preventive medicine, though neither he nor Harden could foresee its full impact on physiology and medicine.

Quantitative studies of fermentation were first made by Lavoisier and later by Gay-Lussac, who recognized that the sugar was broken into two products; one, carbon dioxide, was more oxidized and the other, alcohol, was less oxidized than the original sugar:

$$C_6H_{12}O_6 = 2CO_2 + 2C_2H_6O$$

$$\underset{\substack{hexose \\ sugar}}{C_6H_{12}O_6} = \underset{\substack{carbon \\ dioxide}}{2CO_2} + \underset{\substack{ethyl \\ alcohol}}{2C_2H_6O}$$

The arts of brewing and baking had of course been in existence for centuries but it was only in 1837 that Schwann and Cagniard-Latour independently showed that yeast is a living organism, and that fermentation proceeds from its growth in sugar solution. During the

next fifty years or so, hot arguments raged between those who, like
Pasteur, supported the view that fermentation is a biological process — as in the famous dicta 'No fermentation without life' and
later 'Fermentation is life without air' — and the great chemists,
Liebig, Wöhler and Berzelius, who believed that fermentation was a
kind of slow combustion induced by some lifeless chemical in the
yeast cell. The German chemist, Moritz Traube, suggested that
fermentation might be caused by some soluble agent in the cell,
rather than by the vital activity of the whole cell, and many attempts
were made to extract such an agent. These were unsuccessful until, in
1897, Eduard Buchner ground yeast for a short time with sand and
pressed out the fluid from the ground mass in a hydraulic press. The
juice so obtained fermented sugar with production of alcohol and
carbon dioxide in the total absence of yeast cells. The agent present
in the juice promoted or catalysed the chemical changes of fermentation without itself undergoing a chemical change; it was a ferment or
enzyme, which he called zymase. Buchner had not only solved the
fundamental problem of the Pasteur-Liebig controversy, but had at
the same time provided a most valuable tool for study of the process
of fermentation which, like the oxidation of foods by animals, was
recognized as a main source of energy for growth.

Like most microbiologists at the time, Macfadyen at the Lister
Institute was impressed with Buchner's discovery and wished to
examine it further. He also had the idea of inoculating animals with
yeast juice to find out whether they would produce an anti-zymase in
their serum analogous to an antitoxin. In 1900 Macfadyen, Rowland
and Morris prepared yeast juice and repeated many of Buchner's
experiments. Like others, they found two difficulties; firstly the juice
produced some alcohol and carbon dioxide even before it was mixed
with the sugar and secondly its fermenting power, which was much
less than the corresponding amount of unground yeast, was soon
lost. In the following year, Harden joined forces with Rowland. They
found that the yeast juice contained a complex carbohydrate,
glycogen, expressed from the cells along with the zymase. When the
glycogen had been fermented, no more alcohol was produced until
sugar was added. Later, with Young, Harden showed that yeast
juice contained yet another enzyme which attacked proteins; they
concluded that this proteolytic enzyme decomposed the zymase
itself and so destroyed its fermenting power.

Harden and Young then made two fundamental advances, which

were greatly helped, indeed possibly only achieved, by Harden's introduction of a new technique. Buchner and other workers had measured the amount of carbon dioxide evolved in fermentation by the change in weight of a soda-lime tube in which the gas was absorbed. Harden substituted a volumetric method. A flask containing the fermenting mixture was connected with flexible tubing to a nitrometer, a tall narrow glass cylinder graduated in cubic centimetres by horizontal marks. The nitrometer was filled with mercury, which could escape by a second side tube as the gas passed to the top of the nitrometer. The volume of gas evolved could be determined directly by the height of the mercury, and as frequently as was wanted. The apparatus, described by Harden, Thompson and Young, was simple, cheap and very effective. It consisted of six flasks, each connected to a nitrometer, which were suspended in an enamel bread bin filled with water; this was maintained at a constant temperature with a small gas jet. The change from a gravimetric to a volumetric method, with a consequent emphasis on the *rates* at which things happened, perhaps epitomizes the emergence of a dynamic biochemistry distinct from the orthodox chemistry of the time; although Harden, unlike some later biochemists, was orthodox enough to identify his products as well as measure their volume.

As a necessary preliminary to Macfadyen's experiments on the formation of an anti-zymase in the serum of immunized animals, Harden and Young examined the effect of normal serum on the fermentation of yeast juice. It had a two-fold effect; the action of the proteolytic enzyme was diminished and not only the rate but the total amount of fermentation was increased. They found a similar effect when boiled autolysed yeast was added. Further experiments made it clear that, in addition to zymase and the proteolytic enzyme, yeast juice contained a factor which was not destroyed by boiling and passed through parchment; this factor was destroyed by burning to an ash. They attempted to separate the zymase of fresh juice from this factor by dialysis in a parchment bag, but the process was so slow that in its course zymase was destroyed by the proteolytic enzyme. At Martin's suggestion, they filtered the juice in the gelatin ultrafilter he had used to separate the constituents of snake venom. In a few hours a clear liquid had passed through and the oily protein residue was left on the filter. Neither the redissolved residue nor the filtrate alone would ferment sugar, but when the two were mixed, fermentation occurred at about the rate of the original juice. In a note to the *Journal of Physiology* in 1904, Harden and Young called this filtrate factor the 'co-ferment'; later it was called co-zymase.

Although the co-zymase as well as zymase itself was destroyed by incineration, the ash remaining, which contained the mineral constituents of the juice, considerably improved the fermentation by yeast juice. Knowing that the ash contained phosphate, Harden and Young tried the effect of pure potassium phosphate on yeast juice. The result was startling; in fifteen minutes the rate of production of carbon dioxide was increased seven-fold, as fast as that with fresh yeast, and then fell as rapidly to the original rate. Each time another portion of phosphate was added the rate again rose and fell dramatically.

The added potassium phosphate could no longer be precipitated from the liquid with the conventional reagent, magnesia mixture, but had become fixed in another form. Moreover, the amount of inorganic phosphate disappearing was equivalent, molecule for molecule, with the extra carbon dioxide that had been so rapidly produced. It was found that the missing phosphate had combined with sugar to form a new compound, which was isolated by Young in 1907 and identified as a hexosediphosphate. Young then compared the fermentation by yeast juice of the three commonly occurring hexose sugars, glucose, fructose and mannose. In each case the rate was accelerated by phosphate, and the same hexosediphosphate was formed from the three different sugars.

Harden and Young realized that inorganic phosphate was essential for the fermentation of sugar, and that, once the phosphate added had combined with the sugar, i.e. when the sugar had been 'phosphorylated', the only source of phosphate was the hexosediphosphate which had been formed. They soon discovered that the juice contained an enzyme, a phosphatase, which could decompose the hexosediphosphate. Their observations on the course of fermentation were summed up in the equations

(1) $2C_6H_{12}O_6 + 2K_2HPO_4 =$
     hexose   phosphate
$$C_6H_{10}O_4(PO_4K_2)_2 + 2H_2O + 2CO_2 + 2C_2H_6O$$
    hexosediphosphate   water   carbon   alcohol
                                     dioxide

(2) $C_6H_{10}O_4(PO_4K_2)_2 + 2H_2O = C_6H_{12}O_6 + 2K_2HPO_4$
    hexosediphosphate   water   sugar   phosphate

They supposed that, in some manner not understood, the phosphorylation of one molecule of hexose induced the simultaneous decomposition of a second molecule to carbon dioxide and alcohol; and that the continual slow decomposition of the hexosediphosphate by the phosphatase provided a re-entry of inorganic phosphate into the cycle to maintain the basal rate.

Harden's discovery of co-zymase and the phosphorylation of sugar in yeast juice was immediately recognized as a 'breakthrough' in the field of the intermediary metabolism of carbohydrate, and many laboratories pursued the clues. When Young went to Australia in 1913, Harden himself was joined by Robert Robison, who in his first contact with biochemical problems showed his characteristic enthusiasm and thoroughness. In collaboration with Harden he announced in a note in 1914 the discovery of a hexose-monophosphate in the products of fermentation by yeast juice, in addition to the hexosediphosphate already found.

After his return from service in the sanitary section of the Royal Army Medical Corps in the First World War, Robison resumed work on alcoholic fermentation. By 1922 he had succeeded in isolating the hexosemonophosphate, thought to be a mixture of fructose and glucose phosphates, which was known for many years as the Robison ester. In a series of elegant experiments over the next ten years, with many co-workers amongst whom W. T. J. Morgan and E. J. King were outstanding, Robison isolated the monophosphates of four different sugars — glucose, fructose, mannose and trehalose —from the Robison ester and established their chemical constitution. Robison never concerned himself directly in the enyzmic problems of carbohydrate breakdown. His outstanding contribution was the isolation of glucosemonophosphate, for this turned out to be an intermediate, not only in the anaerobic breakdown of carbohydrate by yeast and muscle, but also in the oxidation of sugar by the respiratory enzymes of cells generally.

Workers elsewhere had begun to explore the reactions by which glycogen, the carbohydrate store of muscle, is broken down to lactic acid during the contraction of muscle. It was soon realized that there were similarities between yeast and muscle, but it was not until 1926 that Meyerhof obtained from muscle an extract which produced lactic acid from glycogen. This extract contained a co-enzyme whch was interchangeable with that from yeast, and sugar phosphates which were formed in the muscle systems were identical with those formed by yeast juice. Later, similar phosphorylation mechanisms were discovered in bacteria, and the brilliant work of Calvin and his associates on photosynthesis established that phosphorylation is also a phenomenon of the vegetable world.

In the twenty years between the discoveries of Harden and Meyerhof, there were enormous advances in chemistry and physics, in theories of organic reactions and oxidation-reduction mechanisms, in enzymology and nutrition and, not least, in microanalytical techniques. The two discoveries were now exploited at a fantastic rate. The co-zymase was isolated almost simultaneously by Otto Warburg in Berlin and Von Euler in Stockholm and identified as a pyridine nucleotide.

In the laboratories of Meyerhof in Heidelberg, of Embden in Leipzig, of Neuberg in Berlin, of Parnas in Cracow and of others too numerous to mention, the enzyme complexes of yeast and muscle were separated into a large number of specific enzymes, each catalysing a single step in the breakdown of glycogen and glucose. The intermediate substances or metabolites were isolated, identified and synthesized chemically; many of them were phosphorylated compounds. A second coenzyme of fundamental importance, adenylic acid, was discovered to be the agent by which phosphate was transferred from one metabolite to another.

A fascinating link with nutritional science appeared when certain of the vitamin B group of accessory food factors were identified as components of glycolytic and respiratory enzymes or coenzymes. Warburg had long been working on the respiratory systems of cells, and in 1933 at last succeeded in getting from animal cells and yeast a soluble yellow enzyme, containing riboflavin, another pyridine nucleotide coenzyme, which oxidized glucose-6-phosphate. Of this important step, Warburg's later comment may be translated: 'The Robison ester has been the substrate for the tests by which the yellow enzyme, both the pyridine nucleotides and the intermediate enzyme were isolated. Probably today none of these substances would have been isolated if the Robison ester had not been available. That we have subsequently also used alcohol as a test substrate does not alter the historic course of events.'

It was a great satisfaction to Robison to know that the ester he had isolated so laboriously was now recognized as a key substance in the aerobic and anaerobic metabolism of carbohydrate in animals and micro-organisms.

During the 1914–18 war, Harden turned to the study of accessory food factors thought to be concerned in the prevention of scurvy and beri-beri. His later work on fermentation, though of interest at the time in the gradual clarification of a problem in which many were now engaged, contributed little of lasting significance.

Harden was not an exuberant man and distrusted the use of his imagination beyond a few paces in advance of the facts. He refrained from speculative theories and from his student days onwards he was an atheist. Perhaps his upbringing in a puritanical atmosphere had stifled his emotions, for he was very equable and indeed said he had never known great elation or great depression. 'A fact for the day' was his motto; he had great precision of observation and a dispassionate capacity to define the significance of his experimental results. His facts on alcoholic fermentation were limited, incontrovertible and seminal; and for them he was justly honoured. He was elected F.R.S. in 1909, received the Davy Medal in 1935, and was knighted in 1936. In 1929 he shared the Nobel Prize for Chemistry with Hans von Euler, who had long been working in the same field. Apart from his scientific contribution, Harden gave great service to the growing discipline of biochemistry. He was an original member of the Biochemical Society, and chief editor of the *Biochemical Journal* for twenty-five years. In this his avowed policy was 'Give a man rope and let him hang himself,' but, as in other affairs, his lucid advice and help were freely given to those who sought them, and many were grateful for his friendship and wise counsel.

Robison was elected F.R.S. in 1930 and soon afterwards, when Harden retired, he became head of the biochemical department of the Institute and Professor of Biochemistry in the University of London. In many ways he was the antithesis of Harden. He was fascinated by the biological problems he encountered, some of which are described later, and threw himself into them with whole-hearted devotion. He habitually over-taxed both his body and his spirit, for he sought perfection and was prone to self-criticism. A man of great charm and fine character, Robison was a stimulating leader and was held in affection by the many who came to work with him. He was sensitive to beauty in many forms and particularly to the solace of music. He was greatly saddened by the agony of war around him from which his sudden death in his sleep in 1941 released him.

Harden and Robison both lived to see the fructification of their work in many aspects of biochemistry and their ultimate fame perhaps is that their work has become largely anonymous and quite axiomatic in textbooks.

13. War and Peace

The researches of Harden and Robison on alcoholic fermentation spanned nearly thirty years. During this time there were changes in other affairs of the Institute, to be recorded. Early in 1913, Sir Henry Roscoe asked to be relieved from the chairmanship of the Governing Body on account of his health, though he remained a member of the board. Sir John Rose Bradford became Chairman in his place. The other members were Lord Iveagh, Mr Pattison, Professor E. H. Starling, Sir William Osler and Sir William Leishman. The last named had been appointed as the representative of the Royal Society during the absence of Colonel Sir David Bruce, who was commanding an expedition to Nyasaland for the study of sleeping sickness.

Two years earlier, the National Insurance Act of 1911 had been passed. One of its provisions directed the Government to set up a National Institute for Medical Research to promote scientific investigations into medical and allied subjects having a bearing on the health of the people. Towards this end a Medical Research Committee (later the Medical Research Council) was created by the Government and began to operate in the summer of 1913 under the chairmanship of Lord Moulton.

It was probably towards the close of 1913 that the Governing Body of the Lister Institute began to consider privately (for the discussion was not minuted at this stage) whether it would not be in the best interests of medical research in this country to offer the Institute to the nation as the nucleus of a National Institute of Medical Research. The proposition might be advantageous to the Medical Research Committee. From the point of view of the Institute the argument which weighed heavily in favour of such action was the economic uncertainty of its future. In the annual accounts for the year 1912, the income from endowments was £8,580; the income at Chelsea from diagnostic and analytical fees and sales of bacterial vaccines was £6,000; put together, the excess over the expenditure at Chelsea was £784. At Elstree, the income from sales of antitoxins and small-pox vaccine was £10,895 against an expenditure of £5,416. The Institute thus was more than solvent, but a large part of the activities of the staff at Chelsea, as well as at Elstree, was taken up with routine work rather than research.

Moreover, most of the earned income came from sales of thera-peutic sera and vaccines. In the early days of the Institute, the preparation of these materials provided a unique service to the public, for there had been little serious competition by pharma-ceutical firms. But by 1912, several firms, and particularly the large firm of Burroughs and Wellcome, were employing in research and production a staff as well qualified as that of the Institute, and the financial success of the Elstree departments was uncertain. In the future it might be difficult to expand the research activities of the Institute or even to maintain them.

A majority of the Governors favoured the idea of offering to present the Institute to the nation. Lord Iveagh, who at the time of his benefaction to the Lister Institute in 1898 had announced it as 'a gift to the nation', was in favour and indeed appears to have been the prime mover in the plan. In February 1914, representatives of the Institute discussed the matter privately with Lord Moulton and it was agreed to negotiate on the conditions of a transfer. During the negotiations, Lord Iveagh offered to build a small hospital on a piece of land adjoining the Institute which he bought for the purpose. The Governing Body was not unanimous about the transfer, the chairman, Rose Bradford, being one of those who opposed it, but by July 1914, the terms of the agreement had been settled with the Medical Research Committee and the Treasury. On July 17 the Governing Body decided, by a majority of five to two, that the transfer should be recommended to the Members of the Institute, the body of people who had signed the Memorandum of Association of the Institute and to whom, as to shareholders in a company, the proposal had to be submitted. Rose Bradford thereupon resigned from the Governing Body and Roscoe resumed the chairmanship.

At this point Sir David Bruce returned from Africa to the Council table. His disapproval was emphatic and expressed with a remarkable assortment of mixed metaphors: 'I was astonished to hear the news, but what astonished me more was to learn that Lord Iveagh favoured the scheme. It seemed to me like a father throwing a favourite child to the wolves. The next thing that struck me as most singular was that the scheme evidently had its birth and emanated from our Director — the Captain of the Ship — I would have thought that he would have been the last to hand over his tight little craft — I won't say to the enemy — but to the melting pot.'

In November 1914, the proposal to amalgamate with the National Committee was submitted to a special General Meeting of the Members of the Institute. A majority of those present was in favour of the proposal, but a poll of the proxies was demanded and, on the final count, thirty-two members voted in favour and thirty-nine against the resolution. The majority of the Governing Body, though greatly regretting the decision, felt that it was inadvisable, in the circumstances of the war, to ask the members to reconsider the proposal at the time. The question was however not reopened, and the Medical Research Committee proceeded with the foundation of the National Institute of Medical Research in the building already acquired at Hampstead.

For better or for worse, the decision of a small majority of the Members forced independence upon the Institute; and although few of those who have worked in the Institute would regret its continued independent existence, the uncertainty of its finances has been a perennial anxiety for the Governing Body and on occasion a cause of frustration for the Director and his staff.

The subsequent relations between the Lister Institute and the Medical Research Council have always been most harmonious. On various occasions, joint committees have been set up for the investigation of urgent problems, and generous financial support for assistance and expenses has been given to individual members of the staff. The Institute at various times has also housed research units wholly financed by the Medical Research Council, whose staff have been welcome colleagues.

In 1915 Sir Henry Roscoe, who had devoted himself to the progress of the Institute for so many years, died at the age of eighty-two. Sir David Bruce then became chairman of the Governing Body. This situation must have been rather unpleasant for Martin, and in that year he joined the Australian Army Medical Corps as a pathologist with the rank of major, a position scarcely commensurate with his status. Bruce's outspoken criticism of Martin was unfair, for though

Martin had been in favour of the transfer of the Institute, he was not a member of the Governing Body and the decision was not his. Nevertheless there is little doubt that for the next few years Bruce indulged in a campaign against the Director.

During Martin's absence, Bruce formed a reconstruction committee bent on suggesting changes in organization which they thought might benefit the Institute. Martin was not consulted on the proposals and when he returned in 1919 protested that the failure to consult him implied a lack of confidence. He proposed to resign and accept the Chair of Preventive Medicine at the University of Cardiff, which had been offered to him. The suggestion excited great alarm amongst the staff, and the heads of all the departments sent a memorandum to the Governors expressing the view that Martin's departure would be a serious loss. Thereupon Martin was assured of the Governors' confidence and agreed to stay.

The proposal made by Bruce's reconstruction committee was that a research hospital like that attached to the Rockefeller Institute in New York should be established in connection with the Institute, in order to bring the scientists into closer contact with the practical problems of disease. It was evidently the intention to create a small hospital for the prevention and treatment of rare, presumably tropical, diseases. The Governors had it in mind to make a public appeal for funds; they also believed that the name of the Institute did not adequately convey to the public the nature of its activities. In fact, by 1919 the Governors had realized that, with increased costs and diminished profits, the Institute would have to curtail its activities unless it got more funds.

At an extraordinary general meeting of members in June, 1919, the proposal to change the name to 'The Lister Institute of Medical Research' was defeated. The proposal to alter the Memorandum of Association to permit the establishment of a hospital, provided that independent funds were raised for this purpose, was carried. It was subsequently found necessary to alter the wording of this resolution to comply with the law; the amended resolution was unanimously accepted by the Members in 1920.

However, no further steps were taken to establish a hospital, or to launch a general appeal for funds. The reason for this is not clear, but it may have been because plans were already afoot, at the instance of Sir Alfred Mond, the Minister of Health, for an institute of state medicine, out of which the London School of Hygiene and Tropical

Medicine arose. According to the *British Medical Journal* in 1922, it was intended that the Lister Institute should be brought into close relation with this scheme, but apparently no action was taken.

Immediately after the outbreak of war in August 1914, the staff of the Institute requested permission to place their services at the disposal of the Army Medical Department in whatever capacity might be deemed suitable; and the Institute itself offered to supply sera and vaccines at cost price to the utmost of its capacity. Within a few months almost all the men amongst the scientific staff, the scholars, and the guest workers, had been accepted for service in the R.A.M.C., and fifteen of the subordinate staff had also volunteered for the Forces. Ledingham, with Penfold and Hartley, took charge of the pathological laboratory of the King George Military Hospital at Waterloo; later he was appointed a member of the Mediterranean Advisory Committee on Tropical Diseases and gave distinguished service in Egypt and Mesopotamia. Rowland and Petrie went to France as pathologists; Arkwright was sent to investigate an outbreak of cerebrospinal fever amongst Canadian troops at Bulford, and later went to Malta. Greenwood, Hartley and Robison served abroad in the Sanitary Section of the R.A.M.C. In 1915, Martin was gazetted to the Australian Medical Corps, and Harden was made deputy-director of the Institute and remained in charge until 1919.

The women workers stopped their own researches and helped in the production work of the Institute. Harriette Chick and Muriel Robertson first went to Elstree to assist in the urgent task of testing and bottling tetanus antitoxin for the Army. The work of the serum department however increased so much that more stables were built and Dr S. S. Zilva, a research student with Harden, and later Dr Annie Homer, were appointed as scientific assistants to MacConkey.

At Chelsea Dr H. L. Schütze was soon the only member of staff left in the bacteriological department; in addition to the diagnostic work, he prepared, with the assistance later of Dr Mary Barrett, large quantities of bacterial vaccines — mainly against typhoid and cholera. The department also made bacteriological culture media for the Army.

Because of the great pressure of work, Harriette Chick took over at Chelsea the preparation of agglutinating sera for the diagnosis of typhoid, paratyphoid and dysentery, diseases prevalent at various times amongst the allied troops in Flanders and the Middle East. The

Institute possessed reliable cultures of the bacteria responsible for those infections, now known as the salmonella group, and for cholera. A rabbit immunized with a culture of a particular organism produces antibodies in its blood serum which specifically agglutinates suspensions of that organism. Thus the rabbit antisera so prepared can be used to identify microbes isolated from the patient, or alternatively the patient's serum can be examined for its capacity to agglutinate suspensions of known bacteria.

Rapid diagnosis was of great value both in the treatment of the patient and in administrative measures to combat epidemics. In this work Harriette Chick was assisted by Dr Elsie Dalyell and Mabel Rhodes, whose real position was that of artist to the Institute, and by other women staff. Not least amongst these was Mrs Soper, whose employment was cleaning and washing up in the laboratories. The doses of living bacteria necessary to immunize the rabbits, particularly those of the Shiga type of dysentery, could easily prove fatal unless the animals were nursed with great care over the critical period. After her day's work Mrs Soper often stayed long into the night, caring for the immunized rabbits and feeding them with milk from a fountain pen filler. Many a tommy may have owed his life to Mrs Soper.

Meanwhile, Muriel Robertson had abandoned protozoology for the time being, to work on an urgent problem of wound infection. In the autumn of 1914, many soldiers in Flanders who sustained severe flesh wounds or fractures were dying of an infection which spread rapidly to healthy tissues. A wounded limb would swell, distended by minute bubbles of gas, from which the name gas gangrene was derived. The source of the infection was found in a group of bacteria known as *Clostridia*, which are prevalent in soil contaminated with human and animal excreta. Two members of this group, one causing tetanus and the other the type of food poisoning known as botulism, were already well defined, and the toxins they produced were known to be responsible for the disease. But the classification of the members of the group causing gas gangrene was in a fantastic state of chaos, largely owing to the technical difficulties of isolating and maintaining them in pure culture. The *Clostridia* are anerobic organisms, that is they grow best in the absence of oxygen and they require special media for the production of their toxins.

The problem was acute, for in the early stages of the war about twelve per cent of all wounded men suffered from anerobic infections and about a quarter of these died. Martin and Arkwright laid the foundations of an investigation into the pathogenic anaerobes before they went overseas. Rowland, Petrie, and other medical colleagues sent back from Flanders specimens of infected muscle from wounded men, and Muriel Robertson carried out the bacteriological examinations. Many difficulties were overcome by improved techniques for cultivation and by patient sub-culturing to make certain that pure cultures were isolated, for much of the confusion of previous workers was due to the fact that they were studying mixed cultures.

As a result, Muriel Robertson, and other English and French bacteriologists with whom she was in contact, succeeded in isolating the three species of anaerobes most commonly causing gas gangrene. They were *Clostridium welchii*, *Cl. oedematiens* and *Cl. septicum*, each of which was eventually shown to produce a soluble toxin. It was a difficult matter to produce these toxins in the amounts necessary for the immunization of horses; it was not until 1918 that antitoxic serum for use in the treatment of gas gangrene was available in limited quantities, and trials of its clinical efficiency were still in progress when the Armistice was signed.

Another investigation at the Institute dealt with an acute problem in nutrition. While Martin was pathologist to the Third Australian General Hospital on the Aegean Island of Lemnos, soldiers evacuated from Gallipoli were being admitted with a malady which baffled the physicians. Martin recognized the disease as beriberi, a deficiency disease which Cooper and Funk had been studying at the Institute just before the war. He found that the men had been living on rations of tinned meat, bread and biscuit made from white flour, and jam. He asked Harriette Chick to organize a continuation of Cooper's work and particularly to look for easily transported foodstuffs with a useful content of the antineuritic factor. Dried eggs and Marmite were found to be most suitable, and supplies were dispatched to Lemnos to treat the men with beriberi. A second nutritional problem was occasioned by outbreaks of scurvy among troops in the Middle East and India; Harriette Chick and her colleague Margaret Hume examined the distribution of the antiscorbutic factor in foodstuffs available for the troops, while Harden and Zilva, in the biochemical department, studied its chemical properties and stability.

In 1919, the members of the staff on active service were gradually demobilized, and most of them returned to their posts at the Institute. It was however some time before research work was again in full swing. The Governing Body decided to restrict the diagnostic work in future to examinations for Public Bodies, because the bacteriological department had always been over-burdened with routine work. With greatly increased costs and diminished profits from the production departments, it was not possible to increase the number of staff, or even to replace some of those, amongst them Greenwood, Hartley and Penfold, who went to other positions.

Moreover, owing to the terrible toll of lives in the war, there was a great shortage of young research workers, and time was needed for training those who wished to come. Before the war many young bacteriologists and chemists had gone to Europe, particularly to Germany and Austria, to study for a doctorate. This practice was necessarily broken by the war, and because of the institution of the Ph.D. degree by the University of London and other universities in this country, and the unsettled conditions in Europe, it was never resumed to the same extent. The Institute had a few scholarships of its own to offer, and a steady stream of research students soon came with scholarships from other countries, notably from Canada and Australia, to fill the ranks of younger workers.

The war had revealed the necessity for research in many fields, and particularly in the chemical and pharmaceutical industries of the country, so that increasing support for research became available from public funds and charitable organizations. At various times the Medical Research Council, the Empire Marketing Board, the Department of Scientific and Industrial Research, and the Ministry of Agriculture provided for specific projects the salaries of senior workers, who usually became honorary members of the staff; funds were also granted for assistance and materials. Help also came from the British Empire Cancer Campaign and the Milbank Fund for infantile paralysis. By these means, the Institute remained as an organic whole and could make full use of its laboratories; in the ensuing years of an uneasy peace, the records of research filled many pages in scientific journals and official reports.

In the first twenty years of the present century, bacteriologists had been largely engaged in systematic investigations of the bacterial causes of disease consolidating the pioneer efforts of Pasteur and Koch. Now more diversified enquiries into the intimate structure of these agents began. The study of the minute rickettsia, as well as of

5

bacteria, and of the sub-microscopic viruses flourished under Ledingham although the department was entitled 'bacteriology' until his retirement.

A particularly fruitful contribution to bacterial physiology was made by Arkwright, with the discovery of variation in the typhoid bacillus whereby the characteristic cell-wall constituent associated with virulence and immunizing power is lost. This and the similar work of Felix paved the way for an attack on the chemical nature of bacterial antigens, to which W. T. J. Morgan, who was appointed as biochemist to the serum department in 1928, made a pioneer contribution.

The rapid development of biochemistry, from the position of hand maiden to human physiology to that of a separate discipline impinging on all aspects of biological research, was a remarkable phenomenon of these years. Work in the department of biochemistry under Robison's guidance was concentrated on two aspects, the chemistry of important biological substances, such as the hexosephosphates, fatty acids, nucleic acids and vitamins, and the biochemical mechanisms underlying normal and pathological processes in the body, such as his own work on ossification.

Under the aegis of the Accessory Food Factors Committee appointed jointly by the Medical Research Council and the Lister Institute, Harriette Chick immediately after the war led a team to Vienna. There they made a classical investigation on the aetiology of rickets among the children of that city. On their return this team, now organized as a Division of Nutrition within the Department of Experimental Pathology, was engaged in research on other aspects of nutrition, particularly on the water-soluble vitamins and their distribution in foodstuffs, research which, continuing into the Second World War, contributed substantially to the increasing general health of the population. Martin himself continued his work on temperature regulation, particularly on the effect of physical work in tropical conditions. In his department also, Vladimir Korenchevsky, who came from Russia in 1920, developed through his endocrinological work on sex hormones his passionate interest in the problems of ageing, and Muriel Robertson returned to the study of protozoa.

During these post-war years, the Institute lost its unique position as a centre of medical research in this country, for the surge of scientific awareness brought many others into being. In London, these included the National Institute of Medical Research at

Hampstead, the London School of Hygiene and Tropical Medicine, the Postgraduate Medical School at Hammersmith and the Chester Beatty Research Institute. In Oxford and Cambridge new institutes for pathology and biochemistry were endowed and in many medical schools the facilities for research in the medical sciences were improved, while institutes of animal and plant pathology offered new outlets for scientists. The scientific societies, which had often evolved from intimate dining clubs, now rapidly increased in membership, so that sadly the Institute could no longer house their meetings in its small but elegant lecture theatre. Yet in the expanding microcosm the Lister Institute retained a unique place and character, and perhaps also acquired a touch of elder statesmanship, for the services of its senior workers were continually in demand on councils and committees and on advisory and editorial boards.

Changes of course were inevitable with time. In terms of bricks and mortar, the view from the river of its façade and turrets, which it had been alleged would be an eyesore to thousands, remained unaltered and unremarked. Internally the rooms, increasingly festooned with pipes, were surprisingly if sometimes quaintly adapted to changing needs; the studio became a monkey house and a tennis court appeared on the site once destined for a hospital. In 1936, an additional building, for the newly established Biophysics Unit, was erected at the rear of the main building, where earlier Haldane's chamber had stood. Here the first Svedberg ultracentrifuge in the country was installed through the generosity of the Rockefeller Foundation, under the supervision of Dr A. S. McFarlane.

The Institute's noble patron, the first Earl of Iveagh, died in 1927, having previously relinquished his interest in the Governing Body to his second son, later Lord Moyne. Professor William Bulloch, earlier a member of staff, became Chairman of the Governing Body on the death of Sir David Bruce in 1931, and Lt.-Col. Addison, the Treasurer since 1915, was succeeded by Sir John Anderson (later Viscount Waverley) in 1938.

Sir Charles Martin, who had been knighted in 1928, retired at the end of 1930 under the age limit, after twenty-eight years as Director of the Institute, though neither his scientific work nor his association with the division of nutrition ceased. Sir Arthur Harden, newly appointed Nobel Laureate and the only survivor in the Institute of the Bloomsbury scientific staff, also retired in 1930. But their successors, Ledingham as Director and Robison as head of the biochemistry department, and many of their colleagues — Harriette Chick, Muriel Robertson, Ida Smedley Maclean, Joseph Arkwright, Harry Schütze, George Petrie and Alan Green had already served many years in the Institute and their presence gave an underlying stability to the corporate life of the Institute amidst the flux of younger workers, a continuity which was shattered in 1939 by the outbreak of the Second World War.

In the next three chapters, which broadly cover the researches during 1919–39, some of the long-continued and outstanding investigations in bacteriology, nutrition and biochemistry are described.

14. Bacteriology

The department of bacteriology in the early days was the largest in the Institute, and its studies ranged widely over microbial infection; not only in terms of the causal agents — protozoa, bacteria and viruses — but of their pathology and epidemiology and of the vaccines and antitoxins for their prevention and cure. In the first two decades of the twentieth century such studies in the Institute, as elsewhere, were largely concerned in extending and consolidating the knowledge of systematic bacteriology and immunology that stemmed from the discoveries of Pasteur and Koch, of Roux and Behring, of Ehrlich and Bordet. In the next two decades the study of more minute agents of disease, the rickettsiae and viruses, began in the Institute, and a new insight into the nature of virulence opened with Arkwright's work on bacterial variation. As the methods of microscopy improved, the morphology and intimate structure of bacteria were increasingly investigated.

Loeffler and Frosch in 1898 had demonstrated that foot-and-mouth disease in cattle was caused by an agent so small that it passed through a bacterial filter and could not be seen under the ordinary microscope. In ensuing years it was established that other diseases, both in animals and plants and even in bacteria, were caused by these invisible agents, which were called viruses; they could not be grown in the usual bacteriological media and their existence was only demonstrable by the capacity of the filtered material from one host to infect another one with the disease. It is difficult already to recall the impassioned controversies that raged forty or fifty years ago upon the nature of viruses. Were they, for instance, simply very small living bodies, multiplying like bacteria by division? Or inanimate poisons, regenerating themselves mysteriously in the tissues of the host? Gradually the techniques were evolved which could answer the questions, and in this Ledingham and his colleagues played a signal part.

John Charles Grant Ledingham, who became bacteriologist-in-chief in 1908, after George Dean had left, was acclaimed as the 'most learned bacteriologist of his time'. Like so many distinguished Scotsmen he was a son of the manse. He had an encyclopaedic memory which was enriched by an unusually long and varied education. When he decided to qualify in medicine, he had already graduated with distinction in classics, mathematics and natural philosophy. His knowledge of the whole subject of pathology was wide and detailed, and in the pre-war years of the century he had done distinguished work on, among other things, the causative agent of the tropical disease Kala-azar, the epidemiology of typhoid fever and the part played by carriers of the infection, and phagocytosis of bacteria by white blood cells in relation to natural immunity.

During the First World War, Ledingham served as a consultant in the Royal Army Medical Corps. One of his studies dealt with trench fever, an illness which was widespread among troops in the trenches of France and Flanders. There was strong circumstantial evidence that the disease was spread by the body louse. It was known also that the excrement of lice which had fed on patients suffering from trench fever contained numerous minute organisms termed rickettsia. When suitably stained they are just visible under the ordinary microscope.

Ledingham obtained a relatively pure preparation of rickettsia from the excreta of lice that had fed on trench-fever patients; but his attempts to transmit the fever by inoculating this material into rabbits and guinea-pigs rarely succeeded. However, the animals had responded actively to the rickettsia in the inoculum, because they produced antibody specific for these organisms; and animals inoculated with excreta from normal lice produced no such antibody. Ledingham's observation supported the view that the rickettsia was the cause of trench fever; but this study soon ended for the disease disappeared with the end of the war.

For the next twenty years the energies of Ledingham and his more immediate colleagues were centred on the group of pock diseases now known to be caused by the larger viruses. They included cowpox (vaccinia), smallpox (variola), fowlpox (variola avium), chickenpox (varicella) and shingles (Herpes Zoster). Most of these viruses give rise to skin eruptions. In 1906, E. Paschen of Hamburg had found enormous numbers of minute bodies in the lesions of smallpox and chickenpox. At that time and as late as 1929, these 'Paschen granules' or 'elementary bodies', as they were called, were not accepted as the causal agent of the disease. It was largely due to the work at the Lister Institute that this causal connection was established.

Ledingham perfected methods of extracting the vaccinia virus from skin lesions; and after ultra-filtration to remove bacteria and cell fragments the extracts were centrifuged at speeds of 15,000 revolutions per minute. He thus obtained relatively pure preparations of the particles, the elementary bodies, and proved them to be the infective virus by inoculation of susceptible animals. With George Eagles he showed that an infective suspension of the granules became non-infective when the granules were removed by high-speed centrifugation, and that the granules so removed were themselves infective. Moreover rabbits or horses inoculated with the granules responded by producing antibodies in their serum that reacted specifically with suspensions of the granules and agglutinated them; this serum would also protect other animals against the virus infection.

The technique of proving the causal role of a microbe in an infective disease by demonstrating that the infected animal makes antibodies which react specifically with the microbe in the test-tube and which, given to other animals, will protect them specifically against that infection, was at that time well established for bacterial disease. The Lister work showed that this technique was possible with virus diseases also, and it was extended to a comparison of the viruses of variola and vaccinia.

During the years after the First World War there was a smouldering but persistent epidemic of a mild type of smallpox with no significant mortality; it was called *variola minor*, or alastrim. Work with monkeys, rabbits and other animals proved that the viruses of variola and vaccinia were closely related to one another, since the serum of animals infected with one type of virus agglutinated the elementary bodies of the other. They, therefore, contained some common antigen. Indeed the immunological similarity of variola and vaccinia was to be expected, in the light of Jenner's original observation that inoculation with material from cowpox lesions could readily protect against the dreaded smallpox.

Another pock disease, chickenpox, was studied by one of Ledingham's colleagues, Russell Amies. Minute round bodies had been found in chickenpox pustules by Aragão in Brazil in 1911 and by Paschen in 1917. Amies' attempts to infect laboratory animals with these elementary bodies from the pustules were unsuccessful. But he succeeded in isolating elementary bodies from pustules in man in the early stages of chickenpox. In the later stage of the disease, antibodies appeared in the patient's serum which clumped elementary bodies in suspension, when the two were mixed. Applied to the contents of pustules in early cases of pock diseases, this 'agglutination' test, by an antibody known to be specific for the chickenpox virus, proved to be a valuable method of differential diagnosis between smallpox and chickenpox.

Amies also demonstrated the existence of an antigen common to the viruses of chickenpox and shingles; for the first time a scientific basis was thus provided for the known clinical connection between the two diseases. Large numbers of elementary bodies were found in the skin vesicles of patients with shingles; suspension of these bodies were agglutinated by the patient's serum and in many instances the serum also agglutinated the elementary bodies of chickenpox. Conversely the serum from patients with chickenpox usually agglutinated the elementary bodies of shingles. There is no doubt that the viruses of these two diseases are closely related, if not identical.

Work on the antigens of vaccinia virus and related problems continued in the department until the outbreak of war in 1939, though after Ledingham became Director of the Institute in 1931 he was himself less actively concerned in experimental work. Though for some time he held the view that viruses were parasitic forms akin to bacteria, he was very open-minded in fostering any lines of investigation which might elucidate the problem. Thus he was largely instrumental in the founding of the biophysics unit in the Institute for the installation of a Svedberg ultracentrifuge, and encouraged younger colleagues to study the physical and chemical properties of viruses.

Ledingham's work on trench fever had been shared by Arthur Bacot, the entomologist, and by Dr Joseph Arkwright, and these two later worked together on typhus fever. Arkwright was the great-great-grandson of Sir Richard Arkwright who, with James Hargreaves, mechanized the cotton industry in the eighteenth century by the inventions of the 'spinning frame' and the 'spinning jenny'. After study at Cambridge, he qualified in medicine from St Bartholomew's Hospital and entered general practice, in which he was successful and happy. Within ten years, however, he was obliged by a hypersensitivity to disinfectants, which resulted in eczema and asthma, to abandon medical practice. As a middle-aged man, he entered the Institute as a bacteriologist in 1906 and proceeded to adorn this calling.

Arkwright's study of the minute rickettsial bodies, found in typhus fever by da Rocha-Lima in 1916, confirmed that they were the cause of typhus fever, with the body louse as the infecting agent from man to man. Bacot's co-operation was essential in tracing the life history of the rickettsia in the louse. He maintained the healthy, uninfected lice he needed by feeding them on himself. He kept them under a body belt in little boxes with muslin covers; in that way he was able to control their blood meals and make a study of their feeding habits.

Typhus is always a serious menace wherever poverty and dirt foster the proliferation of the necessary lice. During and after the First World War it was especially rife in Eastern Europe. In 1920 Bacot was at work in Warsaw during a typhus epidemic in that city. In 1922, when an invitation came from the Egyptian Government to investigate the disease in Cairo, where it was endemic, both Arkwright and Bacot accepted gladly.

The handling of lice infected with typhus is a dangerous business and both workers contracted the disease. Arkwright made a good recovery, after being so ill that his grave had been dug. Bacot died; his fate was the same as that of the pioneer investigators of typhus, H. T. Ricketts and Stanislaus von Prowazek, both of whom died from typhus while investigating it. They are recalled in the name of the organism, *Rickettsia prowazekii*.

For more than twenty years Arkwright was an active member of the committees appointed by the Ministry of Agriculture to study foot-and-mouth disease. Its study presented great problems owing to the risk of spread from experimentally infected cattle unless they were kept in strict isolation. The first investigations were made most inconveniently in an obsolete warship and its attendant lighter moored in the estuary of the Stour at Harwich. Arkwright and his team, which included S. Bedson, H. B. Maitland, M. Burbury (Charles Martin's daughter) and J. T. Edwards, confirmed that the

5*

disease could be transmitted to guinea-pigs; they were also able to infect other small mammals, among them the rat, field mouse, rabbit and hedgehog.

The discovery that hedgehogs infect one another under natural conditions was especially interesting. Hedgehogs can carry the infection even to distant farms. This may explain why eighteenth-century village sextons offered a whole shilling for the body of one hedgehog and only threepence for a dozen sparrows. The farmers believed that hedgehogs sucked the milk of the cows when they were lying down at night, but it is highly probable that hedgehogs gave the cattle foot-and-mouth disease, and so drastically reduced the milk yield.

Further work on foot-and-mouth disease was divided between the London laboratories of the Medical Research Council and the Lister Institute, an arrangement which lasted from 1924 to 1933. During those ten years the Lister workers studied the filter-passing capacity of the virus, its reaction to heat, drying and ultra-violet light, as well as its susceptibility to a variety of disinfectants. They showed that different strains had different antigenic properties, studied the immunity possessed by recovered animals, and attempted to produce a safe vaccine for cattle.

Arkwright's most fundamental contribution to knowledge however was the discovery of biological variation in the typhoid and dysentery group of microbes. The widespread application of the pure-culture technique introduced by Robert Koch had led to the recognition of a large number of distinct bacterial species; and it was largely accepted that the various species were immutable and would continue to propagate themselves indefinitely without change. Bacteria, like all other living creatures, are now recognized as being subject to variation and mutation, which are recognizable by changes, for example, in the way the bacteria grow on artificial media, ferment various sugars, produce disease in susceptible animals, or react with antibody prepared against the parent strain.

Mutations may occur as rarely as one in a million cell divisions and their study in the higher animals and plants is necessarily a slow business. They are however readily studied in bacteria, many of which in favourable conditions have a generation time of less than one hour; so that after a day or two in a culture medium several million divisions have taken place.

Different aspects of bacterial variation had been studied by the

Institute's bacteriologists, Arkwright, Ledingham and Penfold, at intervals during many years. They were impressed by the observation that dysentery bacilli and others of the enteric group, when first isolated from the infected body, produced colonies on solid medium that were smooth-surfaced and circular. In later subcultures, however, another type of colony, irregular in shape and rough-surfaced, began to appear in increasing numbers. By repeated subculture of the two types, Arkwright succeeded in separating the two variants. The rough colony type tended to remain rough but the smooth type occasionally produced rough descendants. The change from smooth to rough was accompanied by loss of virulence in animals and inability to be agglutinated in the test-tube by antibody prepared against the smooth type. Arkwright correctly deduced that the surface of the bacterial cell had changed, the 'rough' bacterial surface having antigenic and physical properties different from those of the 'smooth'.

Motile bacteria were known to possess two different antigens, one in the flagella, the whip-like appendage by which they move, and the other, the somatic antigen, in the body of the organism. Arkwright showed with the motile typhoid bacillus that the rough and smooth varieties contained the same antigen in their flagella, but different somatic antigens.

His most important discovery was the relation of the surface antigen both to the virulence and to the immunizing properties of the bacilli. The rough variants were not virulent and when used as a vaccine had no power to protect animals against infection by virulent smooth forms, whereas a vaccine prepared from a smooth form could protect.

Arkwright's work on bacterial variation attracted the interest of Arthur Felix, who came to the Lister Institute in 1927 as a voluntary worker and later became a member of the staff. He was born in 1887 in Silesia and received his higher education in Vienna. During the First World War he was invited by the Austrian bacteriologist, Edmund Weil, to join him at No 5 Austrian Mobile Epidemiological Laboratory in an investigation of typhus fever which was rife on the Eastern Front. It was here that the curious Weil-Felix reaction was discovered. From the urine of some typhus patients the two bacteriologists isolated a type, type X, of *Proteus vulgaris*, a bacterium commonly found in the gut of man and animals. It clearly was not the cause of typhus; nevertheless, in suspension it was agglutinated by the serum of typhus patients. This Weil-Felix reaction proved of great value in the diagnosis of typhus fever, but its rationale was not evident until many years later, when the organism of typhus was fully established as a rickettsia, and this rickettsia and the type X of *Proteus vulgaris*, though quite unrelated in a systematic sense, were found to have an antigen in common. It was then clear that the typhus patient, in responding to the infecting rickettsia, produced antibodies that would react with the *Proteus*. Felix had spent the six years before he came to London in Palestine working on the antigens of the enteric group of bacteria. At the Institute he investigated the antigenic change in the typhoid bacillus that takes place when, as others had described, it was modified by repeated passage from one mouse to another. After a series of infections, the strain finally isolated was much more virulent to mice than the starting strain, and had greater protective power in mice when used as a vaccine.

With Margaret Pitt, his co-worker at the time, he produced a highly mouse-virulent strain which no longer reacted with antibody specific for the common somatic antigen of the typhoid bacillus. He demonstrated that in his new strain, the bacterial surface was covered by a new antigen, which he called Vi because of its association with virulence. This strain induced animals to form Vi antibody.

The importance of the Vi antibody for protection in mice suggested that the same antibody might be of importance for man, especially since all virulent strains of the typhoid bacillus carried some Vi antigen. In collaboration with Petrie at Elstree, Felix prepared antiserum by immunizing horses with strains of typhoid carrying the Vi antigen, but this antiserum had little effect in the treatment of patients with typhoid fever. Felix's hopes that vaccines made with the Vi antigen would prove to be the best for prophylaxis in man have thus not been fulfilled, for vaccines made with bacilli containing little Vi antigen have in fact proved better. In this instance the argument from mice to men did not justify itself.

Other curious bacterial forms were investigated by Dr Emmy Klieneberger (later Mrs Klieneberger-Nobel), a bacteriologist and refugee from Nazi Germany who in 1933 was given hospitality at the Institute to continue her researches. An ardent microscopist, she had studied aberrant bacterial forms at the Institute of Hygiene of the University of Frankfurt am Main with the aim of discovering how far they could be reconciled with current theories of the origin and nature of the abnormal shapes and sizes of microbes that sometimes occur in both laboratory cultures and diseased tissues.

When she came to Chelsea, Ledingham, who was by then Director, suggested she should put her experience of queer bacterial forms to good use by investigating a group of microbes which includes one that had long been known as the cause of pleuropneumonia in cattle, and another called agalactia which affects milk production in sheep and goats. These organisms are known as the mycoplasmas and differ from ordinary bacteria in being without a rigid cell wall and, as a consequence, assume all kinds of bizarre shapes during their growth.

Klieneberger-Nobel found that other mycoplasmas were harboured by laboratory rats and mice and sometimes produced fatal infections. In rats, the infections take the form of a generalized arthritis or a pneumonia.

A chronic pneumonia is common among elderly rats but rare in young ones. When, however, in a young rat a branch of the bronchus is tied, the disease may appear a few days later in the lobe of the lung supplied by the bronchus, and mycoplasma may be isolated from it. Dr Kleineberger-Nobel therefore suggested that the microbe is naturally harboured by rats, and gives rise to disease only when resistance is lowered; as it appears to be in young rats by experimental interference with lung function and in old rats as part of the ageing process. The recognition in commonly used laboratory animals like the rat and mouse of a prevalent latent infection that can be activated by stress is of obvious importance for those using the animals for the investigation of infectious diseases. Moreover it throws light on the peculiarities of the epidemic spread of mycoplasma diseases among cows and goats. Europe for example is almost free from cattle pleuropneumonia. Its prevalence in places like India, China, Australia and South Africa, where epidemics may occur after the cattle have been driven long distances in hot and humid conditions, may well be due to activation of latent disease by stress.

In man pleuropneumonia-like organisms are found in the mouth and urogenital tract. In the mouth they are almost ubiquitous and are probably harmless. In the male urogenital tract they are frequently isolated from cases of non-specific urethritis where no other bacteria can be found. They are thus suspected of being a possible cause. Unlike gonorrhoea, these infections are resistant to treatment with penicillin.

Dr Klieneberger was at this time also occupied with another microbial form which superficially resembled the mycoplasma. She found small round protoplasmic blobs, 'nodes', associated with a rod-shaped bacterium then called *Streptobacillus moniliformis* (its modern name is *Actinomyces muris*). The bacterium is carried by rats, and is the cause of one form of rat-bite fever in man. Sometimes the nodes were attached to the rods, sometimes free; and by cultivating on special media, apparently pure cultures of node-like forms were obtained. When subcultivated some of them reverted to bacterial forms but others bred true. These Dr Klieneberger named 'L-forms'. The 'L' has no scientific significance; it happens to commemorate the Lister Institute, simply because the first strains she isolated herself at the Institute were designated L1, L2, L3 etc., to distinguish them from strains sent to her by other workers.

Although at first Dr Klieneberger thought the L-form was another microbe living in close symbiosis with the Streptobacillus, she later recognized, with other workers, that they were variants of the bacterial form of the organism; and found L-forms in a number of other bacterial species. The variation consists in loss of the capacity to synthesize a rigid cell wall, and can be demonstrated readily by exposing bacteria to penicillin or other agents that inhibit cell-wall synthesis.

L-forms may be derived from disease-producing bacteria but need not necessarily be pathogenic. Indeed it is uncertain whether the L-forms of pathogenic bacteria play any part in the production of human disease. They resemble the mycoplasmas in being resistant to penicillin and the sulpha group of drugs, but they differ in being rarely found in pathological material and seldom directly from an infected animal.

Most recent work in the Institute and elsewhere confirms the view that L-forms and mycoplasma are different kinds of organism. Examined by electron microscopy, mycoplasmas have proved to be well-defined microbes of great slenderness: they form a class widely distributed in nature of which some are pathogenic, and some not. L-forms are morphologically quite distinct; they appear to be the inner sac-like part of bacteria, known as the protoplast, which contains the nucleus and many enzymes, and are devoid of the usual rigid cell wall.

It is essential in bacteriological work to have authentic strains of different kinds of microbes for reference. The need was realized by Armand Ruffer in the pioneer days in Bloomsbury for in 1894 he reported to the Council the exhibition by the Institute, at the annual meeting of the British Medical Association, of more than 100 pathogenic and non-pathogenic micro-organisms.

Over the years, further additions of tested bacterial cultures were made to the Institute's modest collection; in time, though relatively small, it took its place with similar collections at the Pasteur Institute in Paris, the American Museum of Natural History in New York and the Kral collection in Vienna, and became internationally known to those engaged in the classification of micro-organisms and in medical and bacteriological research. The collection was however largely domestic in scope and organization.

The confusion that had become apparent during the 1914–18 war over the names and identity of the anaerobic bacteria causing gas gangrene made the Lister authorities more than ever aware of the need for a comprehensive collection of bacteria of medical and industrial importance. In 1915 the physiologist, Ernest Starling, who was then a member of the Governing Body, proposed that the Institute should establish a national collection under the care of a trained bacteriologist. A similar conclusion was apparently reached by the Medical Research Council, but it was not until 1920 that the idea took shape. In that year the National Collection of Type Cultures was established under the joint control of the Medical Research Council and the Lister Institute. It was housed in the laboratories at Chelsea under Ledingham's aegis, and financed by the Medical Research Council. Dr Ralph St. John-Brooks was appointed curator, with Mabel Rhodes as his assistant. She had originally joined the Institute staff to make drawings in the department of protozoology.

Two hundred strains of microbes, including Muriel Robertson's anaerobes, formed the nucleus of the collection. Apart from Harden's yeasts, only micro-organisms causing disease were at first included. Year by year, the collection was enriched by gifts from workers in many countries. The microbes were maintained by regular and laborious cultivation on appropriate media. In twenty years the original 200 strains had increased to 5,000. Over the same period the number of cultures distributed to workers at home and abroad had grown from 1,500 to 8,000 a year.

Care of the cultures was not without its hazards, in spite of the precautions taken. A highly infectious organism, the bacterium causing tularaemia — a disease of small mammals first investigated in the U.S.A. — was maintained in culture, with an occasional 'passage' through a guinea-pig to preserve its original properties. During one of these passages, perhaps as a result of the sneezing of the infected animal, both St. John-Brooks and Mabel Rhodes, like so many other workers with the same organism, contracted the disease. Both recovered, but the attack of tularaemia made a very depressing episode in the life of each one.

At the outbreak of the Second World War most of the collection was moved to Elstree for safety. Cultures of fungi causing disease or destruction of timber were transferred to the Forest Products Research Laboratory at Princes Risborough, and most of the viruses went to the National Institute for Medical Research at Mill Hill. Dr St. John-Brooks was succeeded by Dr S. T. Cowan in 1947, who continued as curator of the collection when, in 1950, it was handed over to the Central Public Health Laboratory at Colindale and ceased to be the responsibility of the Institute.

For more than thirty years, Ledingham and Arkwright were the mainstay of the department of bacteriology, working together in amity and rising together in esteem. Both were elected Fellows of the Royal Society, and both were knighted in recognition of their distinguished services to their country. They died within a few months of each other in 1944. The department of bacteriology, which had been disrupted by the secondment of many of its staff to other work during the Second World War, never regained its former size and merged subsequently into a more broadly based department of microbiology.

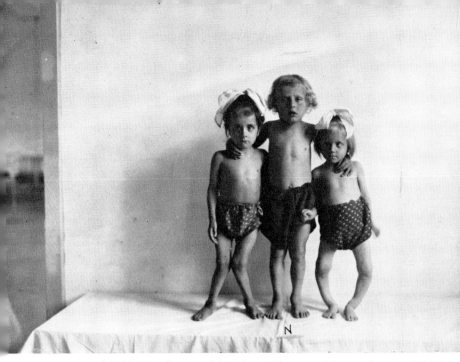

Plate 12: Vienna 1920. Two six-year-old children with severe rickets and a normal child of the same age, at the Amerikanische Kinderheilstätte

Plate 13: Some of the Division of Nutrition in the converted conservatory of Roebuck House, Cambridge, Christmas, 1939. *On the right standing:* Sir Charles Martin, M. El. Sadr, H. G. Hind, Mrs Meeking, T. F. Macrae. *Seated:* Lady Martin, Alice M. Copping, Harriette Chick, Constance Work. *On the left:* E. Margaret Hume, Hannah Henderson Smith, George Flynn

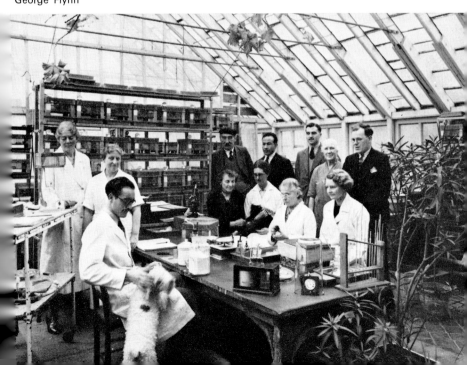

Plate 14:
Sir Joseph Arkwright
Photograph: Walter Stoneman

Plate 15:
Sir John Ledingham, Director, 1931–1942.
From the portrait by Alexander Christie

Plate 16:
Sir Alan Drury, Director, 1943–1952.
From the portrait by Denis Fildes

Plate 17:
Sir Ashley Miles, Director, 1952–

(left to right from top row)
A. E. Pierce, P. Hartley,
A. F. B. Standfast,
D. McClean, E. Margaret
Hume, R. A. Gibbons,
Marjorie G. Macfarlane;
Gillian Harris, Dorothy
M. Parkin, A. P. Mathias,
Margaret Nance, E. M.
Thain, Ruth Sanger,
Jean Walby, Elizabeth
W. Ikin, Margaret E.
Rowatt, Kathleen Cook;
Jean Addy, Y. E. S.
Gabr, B. Cinader,
Winifred M. Watkins,
Mary F. Kelleher,
Margaret Blewett, Joan
Thompson, E. A.
Caspary, J. D. Feinberg,
Jean M. Horton; L. H.
Collier, A. P. MacLennan,
Liza L. Lorenz, A. E.
Mourant, L. Vallet,
C. J. M. Rondle, M. J.
Crumpton, K. Knox, J.
O'Dea, J. G. Buchanan;
F. K. Fox, Margaret E.
Mackay, D. E. Dolby,
W. d'A. Maycock, W. T. J.
Morgan, A. N. Drury,
Muriel Robertson. R. A.
Kekwick, J. Baddiley,
Emmy Nobel. S. A,
White, B. G. F. Weitz

Plate 19:
The Elstree Estate, 1966
*Photograph: Aerofilms
Ltd*

15. Nutrition in Two World Wars.

In 1909–10 the Director was in correspondence with Dr Leonard Braddon on the cause of beriberi, which had reached alarming proportions in Malaya. Braddon was an old friend and school fellow of Martin, and at the time a medical officer of the Federated Malay States. The signs of the malady, including gradual development of nervous disorder, accompanied sometimes by wasting and sometimes by oedema, were suggestive of infection by some slow-acting parasite.

Braddon, however, from epidemiological study over many years had reached the conclusion that beriberi was nutritional in origin and was caused by excessive consumption of the highly milled rice which had displaced rice decorticated in the old primitive manner.

Many years earlier, in the Dutch East Indies where beriberi was prevalent, Christian Eijkman at Batavia had come to the same conclusion, but his investigations were published in the Dutch language in a local journal. Consequently his epidemiological work and successful production of an analogous disease in domestic fowls fed on polished rice were not generally known for some time. Nor was the work of his colleague, G. Grijns, who showed the presence of a protective substance in rice polishings, beans, peas and other foods.

By 1910, however, Braddon had become acquainted with the Dutch work, and he begged that experimental work might be started at the Lister Institute to confirm Eijkman's results and, if possible, isolate and study the preventive nutrient. Braddon's challenge was accepted, and a start made in nutritional research which was to continue successfully for nearly forty years. The group was included in the Director's own department of experimental pathology.

The time was apposite for discovery of unknown nutrients. In the latter part of the nineteenth century N. Lunin and later C. A. Socin, working in Bunge's laboratory at Dorpat failed to rear mice on re-constituted milk, containing its known original constituents, when separated and purified, thus showing that some unknown essential nutrient was missing. These experiments were not immediately followed up, but by 1906 Gowland Hopkins at Cambridge stated that no animal 'can live upon a mixture of pure protein, fat, carbo-hydrate even when the necessary inorganic material is carefully supplied'. This statement was later emphasized in 1912 by the results of his own experiments with rats.

Braddon had observed that while Chinese coolies working in Malaya suffered severely from beriberi, immigrant Tamil Indians escaped the disease as long as the rice they ate was prepared in the Indian manner, that is, parboiled before being milled. This effect of parboiling was finally explained more than twenty years later by W. R. Aykroyd, working at the Lister Institute as a Beit Memorial Fellow. With a small hand-mill for preparing his rice products and young growing rats as his test animals, he found that parboiled rice, even when highly milled and polished, was rich, and its milling offals poor, in the protective substance which by that time had become known as the antineuritic vitamin B_1. When milled in the raw state, on the other hand, the rice was deficient and the polishings relatively rich in antineuritic value. Aykroyd concluded that during par-boiling, the vitamin contained in the germ and outer layers of the rice grain diffuses into even the innermost portions of the endosperm (see page 146).

Experimental work on nutrition was begun at the Institute in 1910–1911, by Evelyn Ashley Cooper, a Beit Memorial Fellow attached to the Director's own department of experimental pathology, and by Casimir Funk, a young chemist from the University of Warsaw, who was working as a guest in the department of biochemistry and later became a Beit Scholar. They repeated the feeding experiments of the Dutch workers and confirmed that rice bran cured polyneuritis in fowls and pigeons fed on a diet of polished rice. The idea sometimes held that beriberi might be caused by an intoxication with infected rice was disproved by producing the classical signs in pigeons with a diet consisting solely of carbohydrate foods other than rice, such as sago and white bread.

Funk set out to identify the protective ingredient in rice polishings.

He induced the characteristic polyneuritis in a large number of pigeons by feeding them on polished rice and used them to test the curative ability of chemical fractions from rice bran and yeast. Eventually, he obtained crystalline substances which he thought constituted the active fraction and for these proposed provisional chemical formulae.

The term 'vitamine' was created at the Lister Institute by Funk. He first used it in 1912, in a paper to the *Journal of State Medicine* where he surveyed the literature on beriberi, scurvy and another disease characterized by diarrhoea, inflammation of the skin and mental disorder, and known as pellagra. In advance of the views held at that time he maintained that all three diseases should be attributed to dietary deficiency. He was even far-seeing enough to think that rickets too was of dietary origin, and suggested that the substances whose absence caused these disorders should be called vitamines, because they were vital and essential to life and because he believed that they contained amine in their chemical make-up. (The correct pronunciation of the first half of the word is therefore vite- and not vitt-amine.) Subsequent research, however, showed that the newly discovered agents were not in fact amines and the terminal 'e' was dropped to make the word still in use today. In the title of his famous paper Frederick Gowland Hopkins in 1912 used the expression 'Accessory Factors in Normal Dietaries' for the unknown essential nutrients which he too was studying. That name, though preferred by scientists, could not stand against the brevity and popularity of 'vitamins'.

The pure antiberiberi vitamin was isolated in 1926 in Jakarta, Batavia, appropriately by Dutch scientists, B. C. P. Jansen and W. F. Donath. Until then it had been called vitamin B_1. They called it aneurin. It was another ten years before it was synthesized and at that point the Lister again came in. In 1937 Franz Bergel and Alexander Todd, later a Nobel Laureate, completed a synthesis almost simultaneously with American workers. The Americans just had priority and chose to call the pure synthetic substance thiamine (from the Greek word for brimstone, theion), because sulphur was present in the molecule. Their word was given precedence over Jansen and Donath's name of aneurin.

It was fortunately not necessary to have isolated the antineuritic agent in pure form before much practical information could be obtained about it. It was known to occur in rice, beans, wheat and yeast, but it was important to know its distribution in other foods. Cooper, doubtless inspired by Martin, devised a roughly quantitative method to determine the smallest amount of a single food which when added to a diet of polished rice prevented the experimental pigeons from developing polyneuritis. With that technique he had shown by 1914 that egg yolk, heart muscle, liver, lentils and certain nuts could prevent the disease. At that point the outbreak of the First World War ended his researches, and Cooper joined the forces.

A year later the research was resumed, once again at the instigation of Charles Martin, and in the dramatic manner described in Chapter 13.

From that time nutrition was a subject of active and productive study for over thirty years. Outbreaks of beriberi and scurvy among our troops operating in the Middle East and India called for an extensive and roughly quantitative study of a large variety of food. Special care was needed for the experimental animals; each had to live in a separate cage, the test material to be given by hand and all uneaten residues conscientiously collected and weighed. More staff was needed and as rough labour would not serve, several young women graduates in science were employed as temporary staff.

The foods examined for antiberiberi value included dried eggs, dried fruits, tinned meat, the yeast extract, Marmite and, on the analogy of the rice grain, different fractions of the wheat grain. Dried eggs and Marmite were found to be the most suitable materials for transport, and a soup cube was devised which contained enough yeast extract to supply the daily requirement to protect an adult. The army was not very ready to adopt the soup cube, but it was finally issued in theatres of war in the Middle East and where it could be issued to the men no further outbreaks of beriberi occurred.

Examination of the different fractions of the wheat grain showed that the germ or embryo was rich in the antiberiberi vitamin, so it and yeast extract lent themselves as suitable material for a study of the effect of heat. When wheat germ was heated for two hours in steam at 100 °C, there was no loss of activity but, when the temperature was raised to 120 °C the vitamin was swiftly destroyed. The effect on bully beef and other foods when they were tinned and sterilized must have been the same.

Guidance from the Lister Institute was sought by the Royal Army Medical Corps after outbreaks of scurvy occurred among troops in the Middle East and in India. As had been done for beriberi, extensive experiments were set up to discover foods in which the antiscurvy or antiscorbutic agent was present in useful amounts and sufficiently stable to be transported. Fortunately a technique of testing with animals was already in existence.

Human experience had long proved that fresh fruit and vegetables had a protective effect against scurvy, but it was only in 1907 that the experimental study of the disease began. A curious condition called ship beriberi had become rife among Norwegian sailors. Their government asked the physiologist, Axel Holst, to investigate the condition. The sailors seemed to be suffering from a mixture of scurvy and of the beriberi found in rice-eating peoples.

Holst repeated the work on beriberi done in Java and confirmed the results. In collaboration with Theodor Frolich he then experimented with mammals and chose the guinea-pig, a lucky choice since, as we now know, very few other animals develop scurvy. The guinea-pigs were fed on a series of whole and milled cereals including polished rice, all of which unexpectedly produced a fatal disease resembling the scurvy of human beings, but no sign of beriberi. A supplement of rice polishings failed to halt the downhill progress of the sick animals, but the addition of fresh vegetables cured them. Fresh cabbage, carrot, dandelion leaves, cranberries and fresh fruit juices all had a protective and curative action when added to a diet of rice, oats or rye. Drying the protective foods or subjecting them to prolonged cooking greatly reduced their efficacy.

The Lister workers again used the principle of finding the minimum protective or curative dose of the food tested. Young guinea-pigs were fed on a diet of grain, and of milk in which the antiscorbutic principle had been destroyed by heat. The animals grew well until the onset of scurvy, when groups of them were given graded amounts of the food under test. In that way it was possible to compare roughly the antiscorbutic potency of one food with another.

Monkeys, though much more difficult to manage than guinea-pigs, were used as test animals also, because in every way they closely resemble man. Curiously, the monkey's antiscorbutic requirement is smaller than the guinea-pig's, so the larger animal proved more sensitive for assessing the efficacy of substances, such as milk, which has only a low content of the antiscorbutic principle. The procedure was extremely tedious, since the validity of the experiments often depended on hand-feeding the sick animals with the selected test dose, which might be large if the antiscorbutic potency was very low.

Repeating and extending the work of Holst, the Lister workers assessed the efficacy of cereals, pulses, meat, eggs, milk, vegetables and fruit juices. The low antiscorbutic value of raw cow's milk is further diminished by heating or drying, a result which lent scientific support for the growing practice of supplementing with orange juice the cow's milk given to infants.

Few guinea-pigs could hold enough raw cow's milk to be protected from scurvy but they could be saved from scurvy if the amount of raw milk taken was sufficiently large. Much smaller supplements of potato, swede, turnip, fruit juice or cabbage sufficed to protect or cure. Weight for weight, raw cabbage leaves were as good as fresh lemon juice, and the juice of raw swedes was nearly as potent. Compared with the antiberiberi vitamin, the antiscorbutic vitamin was much more rapidly destroyed by heat. Its effect was studied by Dr Marion Delf whose observations were of the greatest importance for the kitchen. Raw cabbage leaves lost only about seven per cent of their value when steamed for twenty minutes near boiling point, but about ninety per cent was lost after an hour at a lower temperature.

Holt's colleague Valentin Furst had already discovered that the seeds of cereals and legumes, devoid of antiscorbutic power in the dry state, developed it on germination. The Lister workers confirmed his work and devised practical methods for large-scale germination of peas and lentils. The methods were applied with success to cure scurvy among Serbian soldiers and prisoners in Russian civil prisons around Archangel at the end of the First World War. It is melancholy to reflect how the scurvy which so severely affected the Indian troops in Mesopotania in 1915 might have been avoided if the various pulses, which as 'dhall' formed a substantial part of their diet, had been issued to them in the germinated state. Kut-el-Amara might never have fallen to the Turks if the knowledge had existed there.

Special attention was given to citrus fruit juices because of the persistent reputation of 'lime juice' as a specific remedy against scurvy. Disconcerting reports came from the Middle East of scurvy among British and Indian troops who had been receiving the regular issue of lime juice. Samples of the official preserved lime juice were therefore tested at the Institute; they were found useless. Fresh West Indian limes were very hard to get but a small supply was obtained, sufficient for a test. Trials with guinea-pigs and monkeys showed the fresh juice to have about a quarter of the value of fresh lemon juice which could be preserved in certain ways to retain a large proportion of its original potency.

Such a strange discrepancy prompted an interesting piece of historical research into the Admiralty archives by Mrs Alice Henderson Smith, the wife of a bacteriologist on the staff of the Institute. Her investigation explained why experience with lime juice as a prophylactic had been so conflicting. For instance, the crew of the *Investigator*, which set out in 1850 in an abortive attempt to find and rescue Sir John Franklin, spent two years in Arctic waters with little or no scurvy; a later expedition in 1875, aiming to discover the North Pole, suffered grievously from the disease, in spite of being well supplied with preserved lime juice. In fact Mrs Henderson Smith's scrutiny of the Admiralty's records failed to disclose any instance where scurvy had been prevented or cured by preserved lime juice unless some other antiscorbutic agent had been present in the men's diet. Moreover, it appeared that the terms 'lime' and 'lemon' were often interchangeable so that some of the earlier successes due to lemons had been wrongly attributed to limes. The study revealed also that about 1860 the Admiralty for political reasons substituted West Indian limes for the Mediterranean lemons which had formerly been provided as the antiscorbutic on long voyages.

When, towards the end of the nineteenth century, it was realized that preserved lime juice gave no protection against scurvy, new views about the cause of the disease were advanced. They included theories that bacterial infection or tainted meat was to blame. Tragically, the National Antarctic Expeditions of 1901 and 1910 were provisioned on the basis of the tainted meat theory. As a result Captain Scott and his sledging party developed scurvy so that exhaustion overtook them and they died.

While Harriette Chick and her team were studying the distribution and stability of the antiscorbutic principle, workers in Harden's department were seeking to elucidate its chemical properties and the part it played in nutrition. The finding that the antiscorbutic agent is swiftly destroyed if exposed to alkali was made by Harden and S. S. Zilva, a young chemist from Russian Poland, who devoted most of his subsequent professional life to studying the chemistry of the antiscorbutic vitamin now known as vitamin C, or ascorbic acid. Since even dilute alkali was detrimental, Harden and Zilva gave warning that the practice of adding soda to the water in which vegetables are boiled would soon destroy their antiscorbutic value. They devised also a method for obtaining a concentrated extract from lemons which enabled the London children's doctor, G. F. Still, to give the equivalent of from six to twelve lemons a day to a child with scurvy, and obtain prompt relief in three days. A preparation of concentrated lemon juice made by Zilva was provided for the British Air-Route Expedition to Greenland in 1930–31. One member, Augustine Courtauld, maintained perfect health during a solitary existence for over six months on a diet which otherwise contained no vitamin C. The sample of lemon juice, tested after his return to England, had retained its original potency.

Twenty-five years passed before the substance isolated from rice polishings by Casimir Funk, which he thought was the antidote to beriberi, fitted into place in the jigsaw puzzle of the vitamins. That substance was nicotinic acid and it proved to be the remedy for pellagra, which also Funk had predicted to be a deficiency disease.

Pellagra is a wasting disease characterized by severe dermatitis with diarrhoea, and leading to mental disorder and death. It occurs among peoples living on diets composed chiefly of maize. It is a relatively modern malady which followed the introduction of maize from the New World and has appeared with some suddenness in several European countries since the beginning of the eighteenth century. It was first reported in Spain and later in France and Italy, where it was successfully fought by restrictions on the cultivation and consumption of maize. At the beginning of this century it was a serious menace in the southern United States. More than 170,000 cases were reported there in 1917 and over 7,000 deaths from the disease as recently as 1930.

The connection of pellagra with consumption of maize was well established but its exact cause remained a mystery. About 1933, workers in the Division of Nutrition were attempting to produce the disorder in mice and rats by feeding them on maize diets. Their efforts met with no success because, as is now known, protection is conferred by microbes which inhabit the intestines of those animals and produce nicotinic acid. Since the mouse and rat were useless the pig suggested itself as suitable because it is omnivorous and has an alimentary tract resembling that of man. The keeping of pigs at Chelsea was prohibited by the London County Council's regulations, so an approach was made by Harriette Chick and T. F. Macrae to

Charles Martin who by that time was living in nominal retirement at Roebuck House, Cambridge. Sir Charles, then working as a guest in the Department of Animal Pathology at Cambridge, offered 'to look after a few pigs' and applied himself to the job with all his old enthusiasm.

Pig pellagra which was readily produced on a maize diet could be prevented or cured with yeast or a protein-free yeast extract. Nicotinic acid, which is abundantly present in yeast, had been found by Elvehjem and his colleagues at the University of Wisconsin to cure the condition in dogs called blacktongue, which was the acknowledged counterpart of human pellagra. It proved equally effective with pellagrous pigs. Pig 18, which was described by one of the observers as a miserable, almost moribund 'runt' with severe skin disease and paralysis of the hind limbs, was transformed into a healthy, rosy specimen of the Large White pig by receiving a daily dose of nicotinic acid without any other change in diet. She has become one of the most famous animals in pig literature and her portrait is a feature in many textbooks on nutrition and veterinary science. The researches on pellagra were helped by Dr Philip Ellinger, who was deprived of his Chair of Pharmacology at Düsseldorf under the Nazi régime and received hospitality at the Institute. He made several field studies on the epidemiology and diagnosis of the disease in Yugoslavia and Egypt and also extensive experimental work on the metabolism of nicotinic acid and its derivatives.

Martin was brought into still closer relationship with his old pupils and colleagues by the outbreak of the Second World War. The idea then prevailed that experimental animals housed in London ought to be removed elsewhere or destroyed. At the Institute there was a very valuable stock of piebald Norwegian rats which were essential for nutritional research and also large groups taking part in long-term experiments. No place could be found for them near London, but Martin provided a happy solution by offering the hospitality of Roebuck House. The establishment was made ready for experimental work by converting the conservatory into an animal house and laboratory and adapting an old coachhouse for rough biochemical work such as simple analyses and preparations.

Thus, in the Second World War, as in the First, the nutrition workers were under the guidance of their old chief and found them-

selves as before engaged in the task of assessing the vitamin content
of certain foods, more especially the staple foods, potato and
wheat, and wheaten flours. Vitamin research had progressed so far
that whereas vitamin B, the antiberiberi factor, had been the object
of interest in the First World War, it was by 1939 called vitamin B_1
and had become the senior member of a group, the vitamin B
complex, now known to contain at least six different components,
each with a separate function in metabolism. In the discovery of
three of them Lister workers, particularly Margaret Boas Fixsen,
Honor Roscoe and T. F. Macrae, had been active.

By 1940 the Government was concerned with economizing its
wheat supplies, since much wheat had to be imported in the menace
of German submarines. The problem was put to the Medical
Research Council, which turned to the Accessory Food Factors
Committee, its child of the First World War, still strong and active.

Knowledge was needed as to the type of bread that would be the
most economical and the most nutritious. The wheat grain from
which flour is derived consists of three main fractions; they are the
outer seed coats or bran, the large core of starchy tissue known as the
endosperm, surrounded by a thin envelope of cells called the aleurone
layer rich in protein and B vitamins, and finally the embryo or germ
which, though small in size, contains valuable vitamins and proteins.
In the milling of white flour the 'offals', which include the aleurone
layer and the germ, are discarded. They are much richer in B
vitamins and contain more nutritious protein than the endosperm
from which white flour is chiefly derived. White flour, obtained by
extracting only from seventy to seventy-five per cent of the grain is,
therefore, in the anomalous position of being less nutritious than the
darker wholemeal and of requiring a more costly process to mill it.

The Lister group, which at that time included Harriette Chick,
Margaret Hume and a New Zealand graduate, Alice M. Copping,
turned to the study of wheat and the nutritive value of its several
parts. Like the antiberiberi vitamin B_1, the more recently identified
members of the vitamin B complex proved to be located chiefly in
the germ and outer layers of the grain. The relative nutritive value of
the proteins contained in the different portions was also of practical
and topical importance. For many years the 'biological value' of
different proteins had occupied the attention of Charles Martin and
his Lister colleagues. The worth of proteins as body-building substances was estimated with a technique known as the balance-sheet

method. Adult rats were fed on diets containing known amounts of the protein under study and the amount of nitrogenous matter voided in their excreta was measured day by day. From the results it was possible to compute the relative value of different proteins for incorporation into the animal body for repair of the daily nitrogenous loss.

The relative merits of different proteins can be measured also by studies on the growth rate of young weanling rats fed on diets of fixed protein content, derived solely from each protein under test. Comparison can thus be made between flours of different rates of extraction of the grain, but all coming from the same grist or mixture of wheat. The animals' diets were fully supplied with carbohydrates, vitamins and minerals and the origin of the protein supply was the only variable. The results from both types of experiment emphasized the superiority of the proteins in wholemeal compared with white flour. The gain in weight produced in young rats with proteins of wholemeal flour was about twenty per cent greater than with those of white flour. Further, if the proportion of wholemeal protein in the diet was reduced by twenty per cent, the growth rate induced by the two flours was about the same. When the two flours provided the B vitamins as well as the protein, the difference was more striking, for the weight gain with the wholemeal was twice that with the white flour.

The information available was marshalled for the Medical Research Council by the Accessory Food Factors Committee which recommended that flour for the bread of the people should include the germ of the wheat grain, as much as possible of the aleurone layer, and the finer portions of the bran. A flour of eighty-five per cent extraction of the wheat grain was found to answer the requirements. The corresponding bread was palatable, off-white in colour and a satisfactory compromise in nutritive value between the wholemeal and white flour loaf, being nearer in nutritive value to the former, and in its low content of indigestible fibre, nearer to the latter. There is little doubt that the war-time National Loaf, in addition to reducing the amount of needed shipping space made an important contribution to the satisfactory state of health and nutrition enjoyed by the people of the United Kingdom during the Second World War. With the gradual removal of controls in the years since the war there has been a return to a less nutritious loaf and one made from white flour is now preferred by the majority.

Both before and since Francis Glisson in 1650 published his treatise on rickets in children, the disease has been common in these islands and, since the industrial revolution, particularly in our northern industrial cities. Its cause had remained unknown, but early in the present century attracted much interest and study. Three theories were in vogue. Some clinicians ascribed rickets to a bacterial infection, in accordance with the prevailing fashion. The Glasgow school, including doctors and physiologists, supported the domestication theory which linked the bony deformities with confinement, lack of exercise and bad hygiene. It was pointed out that puppies and the young of wild animals reared in captivity often developed rickets, which was healed if exercise out of doors was allowed.

The third theory, which connected the disease with faulty nutrition, received great support from the experimental work of Edward Mellanby published in 1918. He showed that rickets could be produced or prevented in puppies simply by varying the kind of fat in an otherwise suitable diet. A similar conclusion as to the value of certain fats especially codliver oil, and the uselessness of vegetable oils, for cure of human rickets was stressed by the French clinician Armand Trousseau in 1861, but his work had been forgotten.

Mellanby realized that the distribution of his protective substance in fats was similar to that of the 'fat-soluble A' essential nutrient discovered by McCollum and Davis at Wisconsin in 1913. Unfortunately confusion persisted for years because the original fat-soluble A really represented two factors, one which continued to be called Vitamin A and a second which prevented rickets and was called Vitamin D.

At this period the First World War was raging and ignorance was widespread as to the vital part played by vitamins in our nutrition. The need for spreading the available information on what McCollum has called 'the newer knowledge of nutrition' was keenly appreciated by scientists in England. In 1918, therefore, the Medical Research Committee and the Lister Institute jointly appointed a group of five as 'a special investigation committee upon vitamins and accessory factors in metabolism'. It was known as the Accessory Food Factors Committee and the original members were Drummond, Harden and Mellanby with Gowland Hopkins as chairman and Harriette Chick as secretary. One of their earliest tasks was to publish a series of monographs on vitamins of which the first was entitled *The Present State of Knowledge Concerning Accessory Food Factors* (*Vitamins*).

They appeared from 1919 to 1932 of increasing size to correspond with the rapid increase of knowledge, each one supplanting its predecessor as the current textbook on the subject.

A different sort of enterprise was promoted by the Committee in 1919. In the spring of that year reports began to reach Britain that diseases were rife in Eastern Europe which were there considered to be of nutritional origin and caused by the severe shortage of food. In Vienna, for example, some degree of rickets was said to be almost universal among infants and young children, often leading to grave and permanent deformity. At the same time a clinical condition characterized by softening of the bones, known as hunger osteomalacia, was common among elderly adults of both sexes in the poorer classes. Before the First World War the Viennese medical school had been internationally famous as a post-graduate teaching centre but, during the war, its schools had been cut off from scientific developments in the Western World. Vienna thus offered an opportunity of testing on human subjects the validity of animal experiments on vitamins, and especially of Mellanby's theory that rickets is caused by lack of a fat-soluble vitamin in the diet.

Conditions of acute food shortage have the great advantage for experimental investigation that they inexorably provide what science calls 'negative controls', or a series of individuals left untreated for purposes of comparison. For ethical reasons such a group of human subjects cannot be created artificially to serve a scientific experiment, but can be utilized if they occur naturally. The Accessory Food Factors Committee decided to send a small mission to Vienna to investigate whether the diseases affecting the population were the result of vitamin deficiencies in the diet. In the autumn of 1919, therefore, Harriette Chick and Elsie Dalyell, a medical graduate from Sydney working as a Beit Memorial Fellow at the Institute, set off to Austria on a reconnaissance expedition. They were joined a few months later by Margaret Hume.

They found the state of the public health even worse than had been reported. Scurvy and rickets abounded in infants and young children and could be explained by the shortage of milk and its substitution by cereal gruels. Stunted growth and delayed development were often the result of both diseases. Elderly people among the poorest classes were stricken by hunger osteomalacia. Blindness was met in infants as part of a disorder called keratomalacia due to a serious deficiency of dietary fats.

The new knowledge brought by the ex-enemy visitors was in general met with polite incredulity, but an understanding welcome was given to it by Professor Karl Wenckebach, a well-known heart specialist, Director of the First Medical Clinic of the University, and a person of great importance in the Medical School. He was a Dutchman acquainted with the researches on beriberi of his fellow countryman Eijkman, and consequently prepared to believe in the existence of other vitamins and to hear about them. With his influence arrangements were made for a special meeting of the Vienna Medical Society (Gesellschaft der Aerzte) to hear more about the 'newer knowledge of nutrition' and its clinical implications. The meeting took place in the lecture theatre of Wenckebach's own clinic and was filled with physicians and scientists both old and young. The younger were especially intrigued, for many had been prisoners of war in Russian hands and had suffered from diseases which they now realized were of nutritional origin and due to lack of one or other of the newly discovered vitamins. The foreigners thus gained the sympathetic interest of the Viennese medical profession and opportunities for research were offered on all sides.

The good impression was strengthened after a child had been cured of an ulcer on the eyeball by giving it butter fat and the threat of blindness had been averted. Quick relief of pain in an infant suffering from acute scurvy followed treatment with a preparation made from lemon juice.

Scurvy was common in homes and hospitals for infants and young children, especially in winter and spring. The only recognized treatment was with raw human milk or with raw cow's milk of which there was a great scarcity. It was known as Barlow's disease, pronounced 'Barloff', under the impression that Sir Thomas Barlow, who first described the disease in infants forty years before, was a Russian.

The outstanding problem was, however, to seek evidence on the etiology of rickets in its relation to the newly discovered fat-soluble vitamin. Among those who offered hospitality was Professor Clemens von Pirquet, the well-known children's doctor, Director of the Universitäts Kinderklinik, and world famous for his creative theory of allergy. Pirquet was an Austrian nobleman of cosmopolitan sympathies, who had previously held the chair of paediatrics at the Johns Hopkins University in Baltimore. He was much concerned that rickets usually developed in infants who remained for more than a certain period in his well-run clinic, but he was very sceptical of any specific connection with diet. Nutrition had a high priority in the Kinderklinik and, in spite of shortages elsewhere, rations, ample as regards calories and protein, were provided for his patients. Pirquet believed that rickets was caused by an unknown organism of low virulence which resembled tuberculosis, attacking preferentially susceptible children in poor health through defective general hygiene or insufficient diet.

He was willing and anxious, nevertheless, to give the vitamin theory a fair test and to co-operate in a controlled clinical trial on his own patients. He offered to set aside a ward of twenty cots in the Kinder-klinik and to staff additional wards in a convalescent home under his direction, so that in all from forty to fifty infants could be studied. Equally important would be the resources of his modern X-ray department. The science of radiography had advanced sufficiently to enable the expert to make a precise diagnosis of rickets from X-ray pictures of the growing ends of the long bones. Dr Hans Wimberger was the clinic's radiologist and he would be available to make the assessment. He proved a willing collaborator and was an indis-pensable part of the undertaking.

With assurance of such facilities the Accessory Food Factors Committee planned an elaborate series of trials, to last if necessary for two years. The British staff was augmented by an additional medical colleague, Dr Helen Mackay, who had been working at the Institute with a Beit Memorial Fellowship, and by Hannah Henderson Smith, an experienced hospital nurse who had made a special study of the modern science of nutrition. The cost was to be borne jointly by the Lister Institute and the Medical Research Council.

At the Kinderklinik, Professor von Pirquet had evolved a scienti-fically controlled dietary system whereby each child got the precise amount of food, in calories and protein, required by an individual of its size. Pirquet's system was very important in a country close to starvation because it ensured that no food was wasted since the children got no more than their metabolic needs. The scheme lent itself particularly well to the dietary experiments of the British workers which were planned to assess the value of codliver oil in the prevention and cure of rickets in human infants.

Children are most sensitive to rickets in the first year of life, so healthy infants were selected for the first clinical trial. When X-ray examination of their bones had failed to disclose any rickety changes, they were admitted and received one of two diets. Half were given the diet usual for young infants in the Kinderklinik; it consisted of fresh cow's milk with sugar added to make up from one-half to two-thirds of the total calories. The other half received full-cream dried milk, reconstituted and diluted for the younger babies, with added sugar; all in this group were given codliver oil. Both groups got the juice of raw fruit or vegetables to prevent scurvy and all were nursed under identical conditions of excellent hygiene. One feature of those conditions was the removal in fine weather of all cots to a garden or verandah, where from early in the year the babies were exposed to direct sunshine. It was not then known that such a procedure could have any significance.

The first year's work produced only perplexity. In the early spring the 'Pirquet' babies showed signs of incipient rickets in X-ray, while the 'English' infants showed perfectly normal bones. Later, however, as the season progressed spontaneous healing was noted in the bones of the first group and when summer was advanced all the babies alike had normal healthy bones. The British workers were completely non-plussed. The explanation, however, came to hand in a report of recent observations by K. Huldschinsky in Berlin. He had found that the bony changes of rickets could be healed by exposure to the ultra-violet rays from a mercury vapour quartz lamp, an observation which he had verified by X-ray examination.

Accordingly, when in the second year the experiment was repeated, exposure to the direct light of the sun which includes ultra-violet rays was taken into account. It was found that, in the absence of direct light from the sun or from any artificial source of ultra-violet rays, the slight degree of rickets allowed to develop by the 'Pirquet' babies very early in the year showed no healing as long as they remained indoors. The wards were bright and sunny but the vital ultra-violet rays, which do not pass through ordinary window glass, could not reach them. The 'English' babies who received codliver oil showed not the faintest sign of rickets.

A further test, which was purely therapeutic, was made on older children admitted with severe rickets, all of whom received the Pirquet diet. Those who were exposed to direct sunshine or to the rays from a mercury vapour lamp showed swift calcification of the growing ends of the long bones; the same thing happened to those who remained in the wards but were dosed with codliver oil. All three methods proved equally effective, whereas with rachitic children left untreated no improvement could be detected radiographically, even after long periods in hospital. When even one limb of an affected child was exposed to the rays of the lamp, rickets was healed in the other limbs which were covered, proving that the reaction was general and not local.

The discovery that light or codliver oil could prevent or heal rickets did much to reconcile the environmental and dietary theories about its origin, but did not provide a complete explanation. That came some years later when it was discovered that irradiation of an inert fatty substance, ergosterol, and other related materials produced the anti-rachitic vitamin, similar to that in codliver oil. Such a compound is present in the skin of animals.

Dietary experiments like those made on rickets were made on the sufferers from hunger osteomalacia. A notable feature of that painful and crippling disease as it occurred in Vienna was its seasonal appearance. Like rickets it developed in winter and early spring with remission in summer and autumn, except in housebound people. Many sufferers were found among elderly persons of the poorest class applying for relief at the offices of a large sick benefit organization. Treatment had previously been made with a vegetable oil containing phosphorus in the belief that the latter had a curative value. The results, however, had been disappointing. A controlled trial on 177 patients was carried out by Margaret Hume with the collaboration of an Austrian colleague, Dr Edmund Nirenstein. The tests had to be made in spring but, when dosage with the 'Phosphoroel' was compared with that of codliver oil, even large doses of the former gave results inferior to small doses of the fish oil.

Hunger osteomalacia was unusually severe in the enclosed convents of the city. Both the younger and older nuns were affected and no improvement occurred in summer, especially if there was no garden or opportunity for outdoor exercise. In those communities food deprivation had been specially acute, partly because of their isolation and partly because of the antagonism existing at that time between the secular authorities and Catholic institutions. With the active co-operation of the Mother Superior, tests were made in an Ursuline convent on the effect of supplementing the diet with different groups of foods, which were provided by the generosity of the relief mission of the Society of Friends. Extra calories in the form of sugar, jam, olive oil or rice had little effect but animal fats,

6

especially codliver oil, worked a swift cure. The result was confirmed in a series of severe bedridden cases in hospital; to some of them the effect of codliver oil was so rapid as to seem miraculous.

Perhaps the greatest contribution of the Lister team's work on rickets was to the public health. Many others contributed to the complete picture of scientific fact, particularly Edward Mellanby in England and scientists and paediatricians in the United States. The Vienna experiments were unique in providing a dramatic and easily comprehensible demonstration that rickets can be prevented or cured equally by codliver oil or by ultra-violet light. It was no longer necessary for stunted and bowlegged men and women to be seen every day in the streets. Those responsible for child health in Britain quickly learned the lesson and acted upon it.

The age-old mystery of the so-called 'English disease' (*Englische Krankheit*) was a mystery no longer, but the rays which had penetrated the darkness were the X-rays. It was their discoverer, the German scientist Wilhelm Röntgen, who made it possible to look inside the growing bones within the living body and so settle the crucial question of what was really happening at any given moment of time in relation to the method of treatment given.

16. Biochemistry

The department of biochemistry, created in the Institute in 1907, was the second of its kind in the country, the first, founded in 1902, being at the University of Liverpool under Benjamin Moore. Like the department of bacteriology, it undertook at first certain routine examinations of water samples and other specimens, but these duties were not so onerous and soon petered out, so that for many years the department has been almost wholly engaged in research. The practice of the Institute in making appointments *ad hominem*, rather than to a predetermined scheme, is nowhere more apparent than in this department, for over the years a succession of likely young chemists were appointed to the staff, some to stay, others to depart to senior posts elsewhere, but all free to develop their own ideas. To the Institute, this practice gave recurring contact with topical aspects of chemistry and new techniques; to the men themselves it gave a period free from teaching and administrative duties in which they could concentrate on their research, whose course was often influenced, sensibly or insensibly, by their sojourn in the Institute.

Thus R. L. M. Synge, who was a member of the staff from 1943 to 1948 writes: 'These were the most connected and single-minded five years of my research so far, and were spent nearly completely on studies of the chemistry of antibiotic polypeptides of the gramicidin-tyrocidine group. I got a much more spacious room with more bench space than I have ever had before or since, and a technical assistant. My main impression is of a spacious place in which highly interesting individual workers were getting on with their own work in their own highly effective ways and you could talk with them as much or as little as you liked. I learnt a great deal from such discussions. I have specially clear memories of discussion of Almroth Wright's now too-neglected ideas, with H. Schütze while he was giving me a course of

autogenous staphylococcal vaccine for the recurrent boils from which
I suffered. I also remember discussing with Muriel Robertson about
1947 whether proteins could diffuse in gels, and how she was cate-
gorical that anti-Trichomonas antibodies *could* diffuse through agar
gel. The inventions of Oudin, Ouchterlony and Grabar came later. That
certainly stimulated my own interest in molecular-sieve effects in gels.'

Broadly speaking the activities of the department fall within two
aspects of the expanding fields of biochemistry — the isolation,
structure and synthesis of complex biological substances on the one
hand and the elucidation of the biochemical mechanisms underlying
physiological or pathological processes on the other. This latter
aspect was not confined to the biochemistry department proper, for
similar activities were soon scattered in other laboratories and some
can be conveniently mentioned in this chapter.

Robert Robison, who was head of the department from 1931 till
1941 had an interest in both aspects and the groups formed round him
were the mainstay of the department from 1922 until his death. His
part in the unravelling of the process of phosphorylation in yeast and
the structure of the hexose phosphates has been told in Chapter 12.
His other absorbing interest was the process of calcification in bone.
It may seem a far cry from alcoholic fermentation to the biological
process by which bone is formed, but the one investigation led quite
logically to the other once his mind had turned on the problem. His
work, with its brilliant combination of histological and chemical
techniques, opened a field in biochemistry which was almost un-
touched.

Chatting one day with a medical colleague about the bone disorder
of rickets, Robison was surprised to hear that the mechanism by
which calcium salts are laid down during conversion of cartilage into
bone was still a chemical mystery. At the time he was testing the
ability of various enzymes to break down hexose phosphates into
simple phosphate, and for the purpose was using the barium and
calcium salts of hexosemonophosphate which dissolved easily in
water. While testing the action of a crude enzyme called 'emulsin'
on these salts, he was struck by the fact that the insoluble barium or
calcium phosphate liberated by the enzyme was sticking to the sides
of the vessel. The presence of the deposit on the walls of the vessel set
Robison wondering if that might not be the way in which calcium
phosphate is laid down in the cartilage destined to become bone. His
first experiment was simplicity itself. He placed portions of bone from

a young rabbit in a solution of barium hexosemonophosphate. In a few hours, there was a marked deposit of insoluble barium phosphate in the bone structure.

To test the possibility that bone contained an enzyme, he made a watery extract of bone from a young rabbit immediately after it had been killed. A solution of barium hexosemonophosphate was added and the mixture was incubated; after eighteen hours barium phosphate was deposited in the dish. The same thing happened when bone from normal or rachitic rats was used: Robison often used the bones of rachitic rats for his experiments because in rickets the cartilage at the ends of the bones goes on growing but does not calcify; the area of cartilage available for the study of calcification is thus much larger than in normally growing bone. Robison concluded that bone-forming cartilage, normal bone and rickety bone, as well as other tissues, all contain an enzyme capable of breaking down the hexose phosphate and setting free inorganic phosphate. The enzyme is known as bone phosphatase.

With other colleagues he showed that the activity of phosphatase is at its greatest in the ossifying cartilage of the developing bones and teeth of young animals and declines as the animal grows older. There is little or no phosphatase in the cartilage of the *very* young, before it reaches the stage at which it begins to change into bone, nor is there any phosphatase present in the kind of cartilage that never normally ossifies. Such is the gristle which occurs in the windpipe or joins the ribs to the breastbone. The overgrown hypertrophic cartilage of rachitic bone, on the other hand, is rich in phosphatase, but has the peculiarity that it does not ossify as long as the rachitic process persists.

With Honor Fell, then a Beit Memorial research fellow at the Strangeways Research Laboratory, Cambridge, of which she was later director, Robison proceeded to investigate the process of ossification in embryonic bone. Honor Fell is a specialist in tissue culture, the growth of living tissues apart from the animal body. The tiny thigh bones from chick embryos of six days' incubation were cultivated in blood plasma and embryo extract. Portions were examined microscopically at various stages of culture, and the amount of the enzyme phosphatase was measured. At first, before cartilage began to change into bone, no phosphatase was detected, confirming the results obtained with bone taken from very young rats or rabbits. As cell differentiation in the tissues increased, with the formation of hypertrophic cartilage and periosteal bone, the amount of phosphatase increased in proportion. Support was thus given to the idea that normal cartilage cells produce the enzyme only at the appropriate phase in their development.

At an early stage of his studies Robison propounded a simple theory to explain the chemistry of ossification. Blood, he thought, is normally saturated with calcium phosphate, which means that it contains as much of the compound as it can hold in solution. Phosphatase elaborated by the bone-forming cartilage cells breaks down the calcium hexose phosphate circulating in the blood and liberates calcium phosphate. The blood, therefore, becomes super-saturated with calcium phosphate, so that the slightest disturbance can throw the dissolved salt out of solution and deposit it in the groundwork of the cartilage cells.

That, however, was not the whole story as he was quick to realize, for no such deposition takes place in tissues like kidney, lung and liver, where phosphatase is present but calcification never normally occurs.

In a search for a further unknown agent Robison, with his colleagues, Adèle Rosenheim and Morna Macleod, studied the conditions favouring or inhibiting calcification in the test-tube of slices of cartilage from the bones of rachitic rats. Workers at the Johns Hopkins Hospital in Baltimore had noted that, if growing bone was first soaked for several hours in chloroform or strong acetone, no calcification took place, whatever the strength of the nutrient solution. The Lister workers were able to show that the phosphatase mechanism was not impaired by such harsh treatment, but that some other process was seriously damaged. That process appeared to be the trigger action favouring the deposition of bone salts from the supersaturated solution. The absence of that second mechanism from other tissues, which contain phosphatase but do not ossify, may explain why they do not become calcified under normal living conditions.

Robison was prevented by the Second World War from pursuing the problem further. Much work has since been done on the process of bone calcification but a complete scheme has not as yet been worked out.

Another stalwart in the department with interests both in pure chemistry and in biological processes was Ida Smedley-Maclean.

She was a Girton student and came to the Institute in 1910 with a Beit Memorial Fellowship from Manchester, where she had worked with H. E. Armstrong. Here she developed her life-long interest in the metabolism and chemistry of fats. In 1913 she married Hugh Maclean, a fellow worker in the biochemical department, who at that time was also working on fats; later she became a member of the Institute's staff. She was a fine chemist and her work made a valuable contribution to the subject, and particularly to our knowledge of the methods of oxidation of fatty acids *in vitro* and to the processes by which fat is synthesized from carbohydrate in living organisms.

Her researches on the biological side of fat metabolism were extended in 1938 when she followed up the classic work at Berkeley University of G. O. and M. M. Burr, who had described a state of deficiency in young rats totally deprived of fat, which was thought to be due to deficiency of certain highly unsaturated fatty acids. In this work she collaborated with Margaret Hume in the Division of Nutrition. They confirmed the results of the Burrs, and reproduced the condition in rats in which there is a characteristic failure of growth and a dry scaly state of the skin. This condition could be cured by either of the two 'unsaturated' fatty acids — linoleic and linolenic acid. Mrs Smedley-Maclean also prepared very pure specimens of another highly unsaturated fatty acid, arachidonic acid, which had first been isolated many years before in the Institute by Percival Hartley; she then worked out its structure on very small quantities of material. This acid was as active biologically as linoleic acid.

The three acids, linoleic, linolenic and arachidonic, came to be known as 'essential fatty acids' because without one or other of them in the diet the characteristic signs of deficiency appeared in rats. It has not yet been established that the same is true of man, but these 'essential' fatty acids have a special interest because of a theory that an insufficiency may play some part in arterial degeneration leading to increased blood pressure and thrombosis. This degeneration is often associated with a high concentration of cholesterol in the blood, which can be lowered by replacing animal fats in the diet with certain vegetable and fish oils which are rich in the essential fatty acids. However, the causal connection between a high cholesterol level and arterial disease has not yet been established.

Amidst all this work, and her devotion to her family, Ida Smedley-Maclean found time for other activities. She was largely instrumental in founding the British Federation of University Women, which owes much to the service and the breadth of vision she brought to its work, and later did equal service for the International Federation at Crosby Hall. She was indeed one of those who earned the enfranchisement of women in this country, not by militancy but by evoking sheer respect of their capacities.

Chemists working on the nature of biological substances have three main problems: the first is to isolate the substances that interest them from all the other constituents of the tissue or cells, which may be a mammoth task when the substance is only a very small part of the whole, as with many vitamins and coenzymes. The second is to find out the probable structure by analysis and degradation to recognizable bits; and the third, the crown of the work, is to synthesize the substance in the laboratory and show that it has indeed the biological activity sought. It is no fault of the chemist that the subtlety and elegance of their work is in general lost on those who are not chemists, but thought expressed in symbols and diagrams is not readily transposed into plain English; like Greek and Gaelic, it should be savoured in the original.

Among such chemists in the biochemical department was James Masson Gulland, who from 1931 until 1935 when he accepted the Chair of Chemistry at the University of Nottingham, worked in the Institute on the nucleotides that make up the all-important nucleic acids of cells. Another was Alexander Todd (later Lord Todd and Nobel Laureate) who, with Franz Bergel, completed the synthesis of vitamin B_1 begun in Edinburgh and went on to synthesize vitamin E in his brief years at Chelsea, whence he went to Manchester in 1938. R. L. M. Synge, already famed for his work with A. J. P. Martin at the Wool Industries Research laboratories at Leeds on chromatographic methods, for which they shared the Nobel Prize for chemistry in 1952, spent much of his sojourn from 1943 to 1948 on studies of the antibiotic polypeptide gramicidin, which he thought might provide a key to the normal processes of protein biosynthesis.

After Synge left to go to the Rowett Institute at Aberdeen, James Baddiley, who had been a student of Todd's at Manchester and later at Cambridge, established a lively group who were mainly concerned in establishing the structure and achieving the partial or complete synthesis of various substances active as coenzymes. These included Coenzyme A, which contains the vitamin pantothenic acid and plays a part in the building up of acetate into fatty acids and other substances in the body, and also the coenzyme pyridoxal phosphate, which is another vitamin derivative and is concerned in transamination, the transfer of amino groups from one compound to another. Baddiley and Mathias also began a project on the biosynthesis of coenzyme A which led to their discovery of two entirely new types of coenzyme in bacteria. When at the end of 1954, Baddiley moved to the Chair of Chemistry at the University of Newcastle-upon-Tyne this work developed into the study and isolation of new types of antigens from bacterial cell walls.

Such a catalogue does scant justice to many important activities which were in a sense fragmentary in the history of the Institute. Yet in them lies the fruition of the earlier work of Harden on the mere existence of a mysterious coenzyme, and of the laborious work of the Nutrition Division in the elucidation of a variety of vitamin-deficiency diseases. It can be appreciated how extensively the concepts of biological activity, in which the cell, the tissue or the animal are units, have been underpinned by knowledge of the specific nature and interactions of the molecules concerned.

The recognition of the specificity of an immunological reaction, that is the reaction between an antigen and the antibody it has induced in immunized animals, followed almost immediately on the discovery of the phenomenon of immunization at the end of the nineteenth century. It was soon accepted that this specificity must reside in the chemical structure of both antigen and antibody, but the concept had to be expressed in pictorial terms, like Ehrlich's, of jigsaw-like complementary structures for antigen and antibody, and Fischer's 'lock and key' simile to express the specificity of enzymic reactions. Bacteriologists had long been interested to discover what makes each species of bacterium distinguishable by the antibody it induces in blood, and to know the precise chemical nature of the constituent which gives the microbe its power to act as an antigen.

In this field of immuno-chemistry the work done by Walter Morgan in the serum department at Elstree on the antigenic complex of the Shiga dysentery bacillus was a landmark. It was already known that soluble substances were extractable from several different kinds of bacteria — typhoid bacilli, pneumococci, streptococci, staphylococci and others — which in the test-tube react with the specific antiserum to form a precipitate. These substances were found to be complex carbohydrates, called polysaccharides. Usually, the polysaccharide

6*

isolated from a particular species was incapable by itself of exciting the production of an antibody after its injection into an animal. It came to be accepted that the antigen in many bacteria owes its specificity to the polysaccharide portion of its make-up, but that the power to evoke an antibody in an animal requires combination of the polysaccharide with some other substances present in the antigenic complex.

Morgan went from Chelsea as biochemist to the serum department in 1928, at a time when Arkwright's work on bacterial variation, described in Chapter 14, had indicated that the virulence and the immunizing power of certain bacteria were associated with the presence of a particular antigen on the cell surface. At that time, one of the products of the serum department was an antiserum for use in the treatment of the severe toxic form of Shiga dysentery, whose clinical efficiency was open to question. For those engaged in devising prophylactic vaccines against bacterial infections the dysentery bacillus first described by the Japanese bacteriologist, Kiyoshi Shiga, presents special difficulties. Even when killed, the Shiga organism is highly toxic and dangerous to use as a vaccine. Morgan conceived the idea of isolating the antigenic complex in pure form from the virulent strain of the Shiga bacillus, so that it could be used for active immunization against the disease.

To avoid the risk run by his predecessors of altering the antigenic complex by exposing it to acid, alkali or raised temperature during the process of isolation, Morgan introduced a new way of extracting the antigenic material. He treated the bacillus with diethyleneglycol, an extracting agent which is neither acid nor alkaline and which mixes readily with water and can be used at ordinary temperature. Morgan first isolated the polysaccharide on which the specificity of the antigen was known to depend. He found that it consisted of three simple sugars, D-galactose, L-rhamnose and N-acetylhexosamine.

It took Morgan and his colleagues several years to elucidate completely the composition of the Shiga antigen, and to prepare purified material which, on injection into animals, induced the same antibody response as the intact microbe. The purified antigen proved to be a large, macromolecular complex containing a protein component, the specific polysaccharide and a phospholipid. Morgan broke down the complex step by step, and determined the part played by each of the components. For instance, when the phospholipid portion was removed from the macromolecule, what remained was still able to excite the production of antibody when injected into rabbits. The residual polysaccharide-protein complex was treated with a protein-digesting enzyme, trypsin, and, for the first time, a pure specific polysaccharide was obtained. Injection into rabbits made it clear that the polysaccharide fraction alone could not induce the production of antibodies.

Next to be investigated was the protein constituent. The Lister team showed it to be a 'conjugated protein', that is, a protein intimately attached to another chemical substance not a protein. Like the other components, the conjugated protein by itself failed to induce specific antibodies against the Shiga bacillus. If however a small amount of the conjugated protein remained joined to the polysaccharide, the two together constituted a unit which could evoke the formation of antibody. The idea of trying to make the complex artificially, by joining together separate pure specimens of the polysaccharide and of the conjugated protein, was attractive and exciting. The attempt was crowned with success and the resulting artificial complex proved to be an antigen with a potency equal to that of the whole natural antigenic complex.

It was thus clear that the essential constituents of this kind of bacterial antigenic complex are a polysaccharide which is specific for the organism and responsible for its characteristic reaction with the antibody, and a conjugated protein which endows the polysaccharide with antigenic properties. The main phospholipid constituent appeared not to be essential but the small, non-protein component of the conjugated protein is now known to be a phospholipid also, but a different one. More recently the work of Otto Westphal and his colleagues, at the University of Freiburg im Breisgau, has shown that the phospholipid conjugated with the protein is an important constituent of the antigenic complex and is responsible for certain of the other biological reactions, such as fever, induced by the whole microbe.

Specific polysaccharides obtained from certain organisms of the typhoid and dysentery group were found by Morgan and his colleagues to become full antigens when combined with conjugated protein from the antigens of other bacterial species within the group. Antibodies formed in response to the artificial antigen thus derived were specific for the organism which provided the polysaccharide component. Even more remarkable was the discovery that artificial antigens could be made from vegetable polysaccharides, such as gum acacia, plum gum, cherry gum and the agar-agar used in culture media. All these substances are of themselves totally without any antigenic property but, when combined with the conjugated protein isolated from the Shiga antigen, become complete antigens which can evoke antibodies against their respective vegetable polysaccharides.

A specimen of the purified Shiga antigen was tested by injection into twelve volunteers from the Institute's staff early in the Second World War. After inoculation the amount of Shiga antibody in the blood increased sharply. When the blood serum of the subjects was injected into mice infected with a particularly lethal variety of Shiga dysentery, it proved to be strongly protective. The volunteers experienced no ill effect.

The use of a purified antigen for routine immunization against Shiga dysentery was ironically obviated by another important advance in medical science. The sulphanamide family of drugs had been introduced for combating bacterial infections and provided the means for curing Shiga dysentery in a matter of days. Instead of trying to immunize men before exposure to the risk of infection, it was simpler to let them contract the disease and dispose of it promptly by treatment with sulpha drugs. Since then, as happened with the early antiseptics and later with the antibiotics, particularly penicillin, strains of bacteria resistant to the sulpha drugs have risen in numbers through natural selection. It is possible that necessity may re-awaken interest in vaccination with the Shiga antigen. Be that as it may, Morgan's work has been fruitfully developed by other workers with other antigens.

Morgan's studies were essentially on the chemical nature of antigen contained in a bacterial cell. In contrast to this, two other biochemical studies were focused on the mechanisms by which the toxins and other soluble antigenic factors liberated by bacteria produced a pathological effect. Between the two world wars extensive studies of bacterial toxins had shown them to be proteins, but nobody under-stood how they could kill in amounts far more minute than the lethal doses of such poisons as cyanide or strychnine.

At the outbreak of war in 1939, Marjorie Macfarlane in the bio-chemical department at Chelsea began to collaborate with B. C. J. G. Knight, at that time biochemist to the serum department.

She had graduated in physiology in the University of St Andrews, and came to work under Harden in 1926 with a Carnegie Research

Scholarship. She was later made a member of the staff in the bio-chemical department and was engaged on studies of enzymic activi-ties in vaccinia virus and of phosphorylation processes in yeast. Knight had been trained as a chemist at University College in London, and had worked later under the distinguished bacteriologist Sir Paul Fildes; he was an expert on various aspects of bacterial metabolism. Their immediate interest was in methods of standardization and purification of the antitoxin against the gas-gangrene organism *Clostridium welchii*, but a common background of biochemical con-cepts soon led them to consider the nature of the toxin itself; they thought it might be an enzyme which attacked some constituent of the animal cell. A clue came from Australia, where Dr F. P. O. Nagler in Sydney had found that when *Cl. welchii* was grown in human serum, small globules of fat rose to the surface of the culture medium, but only when toxin had been formed. Similarly, bacterio-logists at the Wellcome Laboratories found that when *Cl. welchii* was grown in an emulsion of egg yolk and salt solution the emulsion broke down and a layer of fat rose to the surface, but again, only when toxin had been formed.

It occurred to Macfarlane and Knight that the toxin might act by decomposing lecithin. This is a fatty substance, a phospholipid in which fatty acids, glycerol and phosphorylcholine are linked together. It has the property not possessed by normal fats of becoming emulsified in water and of holding other fats as well as proteins in the emulsion; for this purpose it is used in various food industries. Pure lecithin was prepared from egg yolk, which contains a lot of it, and emulsified in water; when the toxin of *Cl. welchii* was added, the emulsion broke up and the fat floated to the surface.

Further tests soon showed that the toxin contained an enzyme, a lecithinase, which split lecithin into two parts, a fatty part containing the fatty acids still linked to glycerol and a water-soluble part con-taininig phosphorylcholine. The activity of this enzyme corres-ponded exactly with the killing power of the toxin. Moreover, the power of the antitoxin to neutralize the lethal effect of the toxin ran exactly parallel with its power to prevent the toxin from destroying lecithin in a test-tube.

The question remained; why is lecithin so important in the animal economy that its destruction may prove fatal? Lecithin is present in the walls or membranes of many cells including red blood corpuscles and cells of muscle fibres. In most cells there are tiny bodies called mitochondria which, besides containing lecithin, house many of the enzymes concerned with vital processes of oxidation. Marjorie Macfarlane found that the activity of the mitochondria, the chemical laboratories of cells, was impaired when the lecithin they contained was destroyed by the lecithinase of the toxin. If sufficiently widespread in the body, such an effect might prove fatal.

She went on to explore the behaviour of lecithinases excreted by other species of *Clostridia*, which were distinct immunologically from that of *Cl. welchii*. Some of these appeared not to be toxic to animals although the enzymic activity in the test-tube was the same. This seeming paradox was confirmed, and it was shown that a particular toxin may be a lecithinase, but a particular lecithinase is not necessarily a toxin. This power of a bacterial enzyme to discriminate between the kinds of cells it will attack is doubtless one of the factors which determine what kinds of animals or plants a particular kind of bacteria will attack. The importance of the function of the phospholipids in maintaining the normal activity of cells led Macfarlane into further studies on these substances in collaboration with G. M. Gray.

Another enzyme study followed directly on some investigations made by Ledingham and Douglas McClean into the significance of the skin lesions produced by ordinary smallpox vaccination. Francesco Duran-Reynals at the Rockefeller Institute in New York noticed in 1928 that if an extract from rabbits' testicle was injected into the skin at the same time as the vaccinia virus, the resulting lesion was much more severe.

McClean, then working at Elstree, confirmed that observation and in doing so made an important discovery. When testis extract was added, the vaccinia diffused rapidly into the skin so that, instead of the usual sharply outlined bleb, there was a relatively large lesion with blurred edges. The difference was striking, like the difference in the behaviour of a drop of water placed on glazed paper or on blotting paper. The substance responsible for the spreading action was exceedingly active, for the testicular extract could be diluted 100,000 times and still be effective.

Water extracts of some bacteria, notably of those in the gas gangrene group, also possessed a substance which helped other microbes to invade the body. At the same time the diffusing substance passed into the blood stream causing a general increase in the permeability of the tissues. It was noticed that in skin tests with toxins made on horses prior to routine immunizations, diphtheria toxin remained circumscribed at the site of injection. But with gas gangrene toxins the local bleb disappeared immediately and the lesion extended downwards for several inches.

Such diffusing substances are widespread in nature. Significant amounts have been found in extracts of certain tumours, in snake and spider venoms and in leeches. The agent responsible for this phenomenon is not the enzyme lecithinase which renders *Cl. welchii* so deadly but is something quite different.

In 1939, Karl Meyer and his colleagues, in New York, discovered an enzyme in the pneumococcus which could break down a sticky substance, a mucopolysaccharide, which acts as a cementing material in the skin, muscle and other tissues. An enzyme which behaved in the same way was found in cultures of *Cl. welchii*. Meyer called the polysaccharide hyaluronic acid, and the enzyme which broke it down hyaluronidase. Then in 1940 Ernst Chain and K. S. Duthie at Oxford showed that the diffusing factor in animal tissues was also a hyaluronidase. McClean had already produced immune sera that could neutralize the spreading factors present in bacterial filtrates and testicular extracts. The immune sera also inhibited the hyaluronidase activity of the preparations, which was additional evidence that the two activities were due to the same factor.

Within the gas gangrene group of microbes McClean found a striking difference in the appearance of wound infections caused by strains producing hyaluronidase and those without it. With the former a thin watery fluid spread through the body as the infection proceeded; with the latter the fluid was relatively localized and very sticky. The viscosity of the fluid was due to hyaluronic acid, and it could be broken down by hyaluronidase from any source. McClean and his colleagues made many other experiments to determine the effect of hyaluronidase in wound infections. It is highly probable that this enzyme influences the spread of microbes in infected tissues, but their complete role in the mechanism of infection has not been cleared up.

The spreading factor was first discovered in testicle extract. It is also present in spermatozoa, and is probably of importance in fertilization. Work by I. W. Rowlands at the National Institute for Medical Research, in collaboration with McClean, suggests that hyaluronidase is intimately concerned with enabling the spermatozoon to penetrate the ovum. When unfertilized eggs collected from a rat's uterus are placed in a clear fluid, a cloudy mass of cells and jelly is seen surrounding each ovum. If sperm is added the cells melt away and the eggs, denuded of their surrounding jelly, fall freely to the bottom of the vessel. Spermatozoa are not alone in this capacity to liberate the ovum; it can be done also by hyaluronidase from other sources such as bacteria and snake venom; the rate at which the ovum is denuded is proportional to the concentration of the enzyme.

McClean suggested that during fertilization, at least in some species of animal, the hyaluronidase elaborated by the sperm dissolves the jelly surrounding the egg and thus facilitates penetration. A large number of spermatozoa may be needed in the neighbourhood of one egg to produce a sufficiently high concentration of hyaluronidase to liquefy the jelly and permit entry of the single effective spermatozoon.

The world's most pressing social problem is over-population and the trouble is most acute in countries where ordinary methods of contraception are rejected. The mind, therefore, at once leaps to the idea that a substance which could inhibit the effect of hyaluronidase might serve as a contraceptive and be especially valuable if it could be taken orally.

It may well be asked of the various researches carried out in the Lister Institute whether there was anything in this work that is characteristic of the Institute? Would it have been done at all, or would it have proceeded along other lines, if the Institute had not backed it? No doubt it would have been done some time, perhaps by other workers in other places. But some things were done when and how they were done because there was in the Institute a near association of different disciplines, which not only sparked off an idea but laid the combined tools for its exploration ready to hand. This chapter illustrates how chemical thought impinged upon biological problems encountered in a sense by chance, but a chance that was heavily biased by the existence and the nature of the Institute with its varied staff. To a greater or lesser extent, these researches were milestones in the permeation of chemistry into the elucidation of mysterious vital processes.

17. The Second World War and its Aftermath

The threat of a second world war had of course caused the Government to make emergency arrangements. Amongst the plans which particularly affected the Lister Institute were those for the supply of bacterial vaccines, smallpox vaccines, and antitoxins, and the establishment of an Emergency Public Health Laboratory Service. There was also the reservation from military service of persons in certain categories of skills who could be directed to war work, and the dispersal of people from areas likely to be heavily bombed. At the outbreak of war in September 1939, most of the bacteriologists of the Institute were attending the Third International Congress of Microbiology in New York, to which the Director, Sir John Ledingham, was the chief Government delegate. Professor Robison was in charge of the Institute at Chelsea. Surprisingly enough, as the Treasurer of the Institute was at the time also the Secretary of State for Home Affairs, no decision on a general policy of dispersal had been made earlier, although, as pre-arranged, the National Collection of Type Cultures was transferred immediately to Elstree. With the immediate threat of bombing, it was decided to evacuate from Central London the units using infectious materials and experimental animals.

In the poignant sunshine, while London lay waiting, the scientific and technical staff at Chelsea stripped fittings and furniture, books and apparatus from the building and packed them in hastily mobilized lorries and cars. At Elstree, where the production laboratories were already geared up, Dr Amies, successor as bacteriologist-in-chief to Dr Petrie, found accommodation for the bacteriology department and for the assistant secretary, S. A. White, with the records of the Institute. With the energetic help of Mr F. K. Fox, the Elstree secretary, disused rooms and bungalows were brought into service and the library of some 10,000 volumes was arranged in a large room lent by the nearby Aldenham School. With the exception of Dr Zilva and his staff, who went to the East Malling Research Institute in Kent, the nutrition division was evacuated to Sir Charles Martin's house at Cambridge, Muriel Robertson to the Institute of Animal Pathology in Cambridge and Dr Korenschevsky to the Department of Zoology and Comparative Anatomy at Oxford.

By the end of September, the Institute at Chelsea housed only the biochemical department, the biophysics unit, Dr Ellinger of the nutrition division, the Secretary of the Institute, Mr A. L. White, and some of the maintenance staff. Most of the dispersed staff had resumed their ordinary work in new quarters. Dr Felix and Mrs Barratt, however, were seconded to the War Emergency Public Health Laboratory Service. In 1940 Dr Henderson was seconded to the Ministry of Supply at the Experimental Station at Porton, and Dr T. F. Macrae was lent to the Royal Air Force for special nutritional work. In that year also, Dr Amies was released at his request for service with the Royal Army Medical Corps, in which later Dr G. H. Eagles also served, while Dr Petrie resumed his former post as head of the serum department for the duration of the war.

In contrast to the First World War therefore, in spite of dispersal and awkward conditions, there was for the most part little disturbance of the rhythm of scientific life, though the work was often focused on problems accentuated or presented by the war. The important contribution of the nutrition division to the problems of rationing has been described in Chapter 15. Much of the bacteriological work on the nature of bacterial antigens and virulence was continued and harnessed to practical problems of immunization and epidemiological control, particularly of typhoid, dysentery and plague by Felix and Schütze; the latter, as in World War I, was in charge of the bacterial vaccine laboratory, which was housed at Elstree. The work of the other production laboratories, the smallpox vaccine department under Dr D. McClean and the serum department under Dr Amies and Dr Petrie, was greatly increased by demands from the Services and was continued at full capacity throughout the war. The staff, although coping in cramped conditions with many technical problems, also continued the researches embodied in other chapters. It is convenient to describe here work on two subjects whose significance is peculiarly associated with war injuries. These are the anaerobic infection of wounds, and the provision of blood or plasma for the treatment of surgical shock.

In the First World War the incidence of tetanus and gas gangrene amongst men wounded in Flanders had led to much work on infections with various species of *Clostridia*, the anaerobic bacteria often present in manured soil, as has been described in Chapter 13. In the intervening years, tetanus toxoid had been established as a prophylactic agent, and was used to immunize the British forces. In consequence the incidence of tetanus in the Second World War was almost negligible.

Antitoxins for use in gas gangrene infections had not been available until near the end of the First World War in 1918, and there was little knowledge of their efficiency or proper dosage. These antitoxins were being made at Elstree, where Dr Henderson had evolved satisfactory methods for the production of the toxins used to immunize the horses. At the outbreak of war, Professor Robison offered the services of the biochemical department at Chelsea to the serum department as might be required, and subsequently Marjorie Macfarlane collaborated with B. C. J. G. Knight in various studies on gas gangrene antitoxins. Out of this work arose their discovery, described earlier, that the lethal toxin of *Clostridium welchii* was in fact an enzyme, whose activity was inhibited by the antitoxin.

In 1941, the War Wounds Committee of the Medical Research Council, perturbed by the reports of the ineffectual treatment of casualties suffering from gas gangrene, appointed an Anaerobes Sub-Committee, which included Sir John Ledingham, Muriel Robertson, who had resumed work on anaerobic infections, and Marjorie Macfarlane as secretary. One problem of this committee was to find out whether antitoxin would decrease the high death rate of gas gangrene, for even academic opinion was divided on this point. 'People are so damn ready to cure things,' Martin had said over the confused bacteriology of the First World War, 'I wish they tried to investigate them first.' It is difficult enough to get clinical trial of a new measure in civil practice. For harassed medical officers in the wake of battle it is virtually impossible both physically and ethically to make a controlled investigation on gravely wounded men. It was in a sense fortunate that in the early stages of the war the practice of surgeons with antitoxin was so diverse that it was possible to compare the fate of those given antitoxin with that of those receiving none.

A statistical analysis of these results by Marjorie Macfarlane showed that the death rate was much lower amongst the patients who were promptly given proper doses of the antitoxins. Thereafter antitoxin was commonly used in treatment. The incidence of gas gangrene was, however, very low in the campaigns fought by the British Army in 1944–5, because the excellent arrangements of forward surgical units ensured prompt treatment of the wounded, which to a large extent removed the risk of the infection. Nevertheless, gas gangrene remains peculiarly a war risk, for its prevention is closely linked to the success of military operations which can ensure the early treatment of casualties.

Another investigation begun in the Institute during the war has since grown into a major enterprise of the National Health Service. In 1940 Dr A. S. McFarlane, in the biophysics laboratory, began a study of the conditions governing the drying of human serum for transfusion, and designed a plant for drying serum from the frozen state. He found that a solution of the powder so obtained had all the physical properties of the native serum except for a milky appearance due to fat particles, and devised a method by which the fatty constituents were removed from the serum before drying by extraction with ether at a low temperature. The technical facilities for freeze-drying on the required scale were at this time very limited. Accordingly, in conjunction with Dr R. A. Kekwick and in association with the Medical Research Council Emergency Blood Transfusion Service, the technique of ether extraction was applied to the processing of blood plasma and serum; the products were issued for use in liquid form and kept well. The biophysics unit moved for a time to the London County Council Serum Institute at Carshalton, where room was available for the extension of the work, in association with the London Blood Supply depots. In 1943, the unit, which had been joined by Dr Margaret Mackay, returned to Chelsea, where the Medical Research Council, which was administering the London Blood Supply depots on behalf of the Ministry of Health, set up a blood products unit. Here Dr Kekwick and Miss Mackay devised the techniques for the fractionation of plasma and for the freeze-drying of the products in a research of great interest and practical benefit; it is described more fully in Chapter 19.

Sir John Ledingham retired in March 1943, after thirty-eight years on the staff of the Institute and thirteen years as Director. His wide knowledge of pathology and bacteriology and his personal distinction as an investigator had rendered services of great distinction to the Institute and the nation. He was succeeded as Director by Dr Alan N. Drury, F.R.S., a member of the Scientific Staff of the Medical Research Council, and Huddersfield Lecturer in Special Pathology in the University of Cambridge.

Dr Drury had been associated at University College Hospital with Sir Thomas Lewis, one of the early workers on the problem of surgical shock; and his own investigations were particularly concerned with heart block. At the beginning of the war in 1939 he came to the headquarters of the Medical Research Council and had been actively engaged, as Chairman of the Blood Transfusion Committee and on allied committees, in the organization and development of the Blood Transfusion Services.

Dr Drury resumed occupation of the Director's flat at Chelsea. Dr Zilva and his unit had already returned there from Kent, and the small staff of the biochemical department was reinforced by the appointment of Dr R. L. M. Synge. With the reoccupation of the laboratories for experimental pathology and the establishment of the Medical Research Council unit for the filtration of plasma, the Institute stirred with new activities; the return of the Library from Aldenham early in 1945 was a welcome augury of peace.

But the austerities of peace were scarcely less than those of war and the Director faced a bleaker period of office than either of his predecessors. The finances of the Institute were uncertain, and expenses rocketed. Repairs to old and bomb-damaged buildings, provision of new production laboratories and equipment were all urgently needed, yet subject to restrictions, quotas and seemingly interminable delays. In these frustrating conditions the Institute, depleted of many of its pre-war staff, had to adapt itself to the needs of a changing world and to a new era of scientific work.

The Governing Body itself did not escape the democratic wind of change. In 1949 the Institute, as a School of the University, received a statutory visit of inspection from the Principal; the inspectors made some recommendations on the constitution of the Governing Body, which were accepted. The Memorandum of Association was accordingly changed so that the Director of the Institute became *ex officio* a member of the Governing Body, and a representative was elected to it by the scientific staff. During the war there had been several changes in the Governing Body. Sir Henry Dale became chairman in 1942 after the death of Professor Bulloch, and following the tragic assassination of Lord Moyne in Cairo in 1944, the second

Earl of Iveagh, who had inherited the rights of nomination to the Governing Body, himself joined the governors and continued the generous interest and support of the Guinness family.

The organization of the Institute, which had been substantially the same for more than thirty years, now changed considerably. The department of bacteriology had suffered grievous losses by the deaths of the Emeritus Professors Ledingham and Arkwright in 1944 and of Dr H. L. Schütze in 1947; and after the retirement or resignation of other members of the staff it never returned to its former state. Dr Felix took a permanent position with the Emergency Public Health Laboratory Service, which later was the basis of the Public Health Laboratory Service. The National Collection of Type Cultures remained housed at Elstree under Dr Cowan until in 1950 he moved with it to the Central Public Health Laboratory at Colindale, where it came under the control of the Medical Research Council and the Ministry of Health. Dr Henderson remained with the Ministry of Supply to become Director of the newly-established Microbiological Research Station at Porton, where in the years to come his former colleagues often received generous hospitality and facilities.

The diagnostic work of the Institute at Chelsea, much of which had been concerned with diphtheria, vanished almost overnight in 1939 with the evacuation of school children from London. Subsequently, owing to the virtual disappearance of clinical diphtheria as a result of mass immunization and also the establishment of the Public Health Laboratory Service, it was no longer necessary for the Institute to provide a diagnostic service. The other routine activity of the bacteriology department, the preparation of bacterial vaccines, remained at Elstree.

In the place literally of the former bacteriology department, a new activity was established which still fulfilled one of the original aims of the Institute: 'to prepare and supply to those requiring them such special protective and curative materials as have already been found or shall in future be found of value in the prevention and treatment of disease'. The Medical Research Council's Unit for filtration of plasma, in association with the biophysics unit, extended its work to the preparation from blood of such valuable products as fibrino-gen, gamma-globulin and anti-haemophilic factors for clinical use. It was later to be transformed into the Blood Products Laboratory at Elstree. Alongside of this unit, the Blood Group Reference Laboratory of the Medical Research Council, under Dr A. E.

Mourant, was established in 1946 for the production of sera for blood-grouping tests, and for the investigation of clinical blood transfusion problems. The Blood Group Research Unit of the Medical Research Council, under Dr R. R. Race, began their brilliant studies on the inheritance of blood groups and their application to problems of human genetics. The tale of these advances in our knowledge of blood, which includes Morgan's work in the biochemistry department on the chemistry of blood group antigens, is recounted in Chapter 19.

Harriette Chick retired officially in 1945, but continued in control of the nutritional work for some time, and both she and Margaret Hume, as honorary members of the staff, remained in close contact with the Institute in literary activities after the division of nutrition had disbanded. Like the department of bacteriology, the activities of the division had in many ways fulfilled the aims for which it had been established, the discovery and function of unknown factors in nutrition.

Dr Muriel Robertson returned from Cambridge to continue the work on trichomoniasis in cattle which she had begun during the war. She was elected F.R.S. in 1947. Although officially retired in 1948 she remained at work with undiminished zeal for many years, and taught her skills to younger colleagues. During these years work on trypanosomiasis, which when she joined the Institute in 1906 was a main object of the protozoology department, was resumed in the Institute by G. F. B. Weitz and his colleagues, with the support of the Colonial Medical Research Committee; the tale of these later studies on the vectors of this disease, carried out like the earlier ones both in the laboratory and in the field, is told in Chapter 20.

Meanwhile there was a new venture in microbiology. In 1952 the Governing Body announced that they had accepted a charitable endowment from Messrs Arthur Guinness & Co Ltd for the establishment in the Institute of a Guinness-Lister Research Unit, to deal with fundamental problems in general microbiology. Here was formal recognition of the need for a wider basis of enquiry into the problems of infective disease than strictly medical bacteriology, and in 1953 the pioneer attitude of the Institute was apparent in the establishment for the first time in this country of a unit for research in bacterial genetics, under B. A. D. Stocker.

The financing of research carried out in other departments was an increasing problem. Heretofore the needs of an individual worker engaged in a problem of his own choice, as distinct from one who worked on some special project by arrangement with an outside body, had in general been met by the Institute. After the war there was not merely a rise in the cost of living, but a new scale of expenditure for research. The increasing complexity of techniques demanded a far heavier budget for the provision and maintenance of facilities such as cold rooms and workshops and specialized apparatus. Moreover the variety of methods available and the intensity of international competition tended to lead to the extinction of the solitary worker, and to the formation of groups able to attack a problem simultaneously from several angles. The Institute itself could not afford all-round expansion, but the Nuffield Foundation in particular, with generous grants over five-year periods, and other bodies, came to the rescue of several members of the staff, who were thus enabled to pursue their chosen problems.

For some years after the war, the Institute had to spend much of its limited resources on the buildings at Elstree, which in places were literally falling down, for little had been spent on their maintenance since their establishment forty years earlier. A start was made with new laboratories for the production of smallpox vaccine, which were opened in 1947; by 1952 new animal houses had also been completed. Bigger plans on foot for the increasing demand by clinicians for blood products, which the unit at Chelsea was unable to satisfy, led to the establishment of the Blood Products Laboratory on the Elstree estate. In the planning of such a building much thought was needed for the engineering problems involved in low temperature work under sterile conditions. Although the laboratory was not in operation until 1954, Sir Alan Drury, who had done so much for its inception, had the satisfaction before his resignation in 1952 of seeing the start of the building.

Drury was succeeded as Director by Dr Ashley Miles, who had been deputy-director at the National Institute of Medical Research at Mill Hill and had previously held the Chair of Bacteriology at University College Hospital. Under his guidance the department of experimental pathology received fresh impetus. With the laboratories at Elstree and Chelsea rebuilt or rejuvenated, the Institute passed from the doldrums of post-war austerity into more favourable winds.

18. A New Look at Elstree

One of the main functions of the Lister Institute since its foundation has been the production of vaccines and sera to combat specific diseases, and the sale of these products has been a major source of income for its research activities. At the time the Institute was conceived the foundations of bacteriology and immunology were being laid in Europe and in the United States. Much of these new sciences had grown from the need to apply the new knowledge to the prevention and cure of infectious diseases. The technology demanded by this need was not a consequence of the new sciences; it had to grow with them. The rural façade of Queensberry Lodge has changed little since the day the serum department moved there in 1903, but behind it lie new buildings and streamlined production lines that reflect the development both of the medical sciences and of a competitive pharmaceutical industry. There is a sign also of a new era in social medicine, the Blood Products Laboratory, established in 1953 on behalf of the Ministry of Health to supply human blood products for the National Health Service.

The three laboratories producing immunological substances are all now housed on the Elstree estate. The smallpox vaccine department returned from Cornwall in 1935 to the care of Dr Douglas McClean and the bacterial vaccine laboratory, transferred from Chelsea in 1939 as an emergency measure, had remained there in the charge of A. F. B. Standfast. In 1948, Dr W. d'A. Maycock was appointed superintendent of the Elstree laboratories, and head of the serum department, which throughout has been based at Queensberry Lodge. Maycock later became head of the Blood Products Laboratory, and Bernard Weitz succeeded him as head of the serum department.

The work of these three laboratories has changed little in essence since their inception, but in those days the products, though bacterio-logically safe and clinically efficacious, were comparatively crude. As knowledge of the nature of antigens and antibodies grew, so also the methods used for production were altered to meet the demand for highly refined and stable preparations.

Fluctuations in the sale of the Institute's products have often reflected major advances in medical science, and sometimes even political crises, as in the cessation of the sales of antiscorpion serum to Egypt in 1956. Since antisera are more often used in treatment than in prevention of disease the serum department has usually been the more seriously affected; the new methods of prophylaxis, as for instance active immunization against diphtheria, may radically alter the demand for its products.

The first dramatic result from mass inoculation of children with attenuated toxin (toxoid) of diphtheria was announced from the town of Hamilton in Ontario, Canada. Injection of the toxoid pro-duced a state of active immunity and by 1930, there were no more deaths from diphtheria in Hamilton; after 1933, when inoculation had been in use for eight years, there were no more cases. It was not, however, until 1940 that the British Ministry of Health found it possible to contemplate the mass inoculation of all children with diphtheria toxoid and, in the circumstances of the Second World War, the scheme did not get under way until 1942. Between the years 1935 and 1942 there was in England and Wales an annual average of more than 55,000 cases of diphtheria, of which more than 2,700 were fatal. In 1959, although there were 102 cases, none was fatal. Such great success in preventing the disease has, therefore, lessened the need for curative serum in Britain, but there is still a demand from Eastern Europe and the less developed countries.

The fate of some other Elstree products was decided by the notable discovery of the sulphonamide drugs, of penicillin and of other anti-biotics which had revolutionized medical treatment. As a result of those new trends in medicine, the Institute no longer makes many of the antisera on which doctors used to rely — such as those against dysentery, pneumonia and meningitis, and those against infections caused by staphylococci and streptococci. With the continued dis-covery of new chemotherapeutic agents and antibiotics, the need for antitoxins in the treatment of those diseases has dwindled. Up to 1942 the main product of the serum department continued to be diph-theria antitoxin. Nowadays, tetanus antitoxin comes first on the list, gas gangrene antitoxin second, and the diphtheria antitoxin last.

The method of concentrating the antitoxin in horse serum simply by 'salting out' the active globulin fraction with ammonium sulphate has been superseded by a process of digestion with the proteolytic enzyme pepsin, which destroys a large part of the serum proteins but leaves the antitoxic property of the remainder virtually unimpaired. A great advantage of this process is that the product is less likely to cause serum sickness in the recipient, as much of the 'foreignness' of the horse protein which causes the allergic reactions is destroyed in the digestion.

In 1959 new extensions to the serum laboratory were built, and the older part reorganized. The new arrangements permit a modern, labour-saving flow line for the processing of the horse serum from the time it is drawn in the stables to the automatic filling of ampoules with the concentrated antitoxin in sterile rooms.

Smallpox vaccine has been made by the Institute for more than sixty years; its earlier history is recorded in Chapter 8. The Ministry of Health had inherited responsibility for making smallpox vaccine from the Local Government Board, but in 1946 by arrangement the Lister Institute took over production for the National Public Health Services and for H.M. Forces. About two million doses of vaccine are issued on behalf of the Ministry every year. It is also a responsibility of the laboratory to hold sufficient reserve of vaccine to replace any stocks suddenly depleted at the threat of an epidemic, and the department is admirably geared to meet such a demand. Thus in 1962, when an outbreak of smallpox occurred, more than two million doses were issued within a week.

Thanks to the vigilance of the health authorities in watching airfields and ports, smallpox only rarely gets a serious footing in Britain. Elsewhere, however, the menace is by no means ended. Throughout the world, every year, it takes a toll of many thousands of lives. In India and Pakistan alone in 1959, there were nearly 53,000 cases with 14,500 deaths.

In those tropical countries where the disease is still a day-to-day hazard, efficient vaccination has been difficult because ordinary vaccine quickly loses its potency unless it is stored at temperatures below freezing point. The vaccinators seldom have rapid transport or efficient refrigeration at their disposal. Villagers often refuse to go to the large towns where the vaccine is stored and if, as often happens, it takes the vaccinators several days to reach the villages, the vaccine may have deteriorated on the way. It may also be difficult to keep sufficiently large reserves of the vaccine at local depots for immediate use during an epidemic. Interest has, therefore, centred on the possibility of making a vaccine that would remain stable and still usable after long periods in the tropics where refrigeration might not be available.

Early in the nineteenth century it was known that if a pointed quill or bit of ivory was repeatedly dipped in lymph of a calf with cowpox and allowed to dry, the material which accumulated on the point could still effect successful vaccination even after several months. The numerous attempts since made to preserve the virus of vaccinia alive have included several techniques of drying.

In 1951, Leslie Collier, then assistant bacteriologist in McClean's department at Elstree, produced a new smallpox vaccine whose preparation depended on a process of freeze-drying by which the fluid containing the virus is exposed in the frozen state to a vacuum which removes the moisture leaving a dry spongy mass. In 1952 the World Health Organization arranged a trial of the keeping properties of freeze-dried smallpox vaccine from four countries. In laboratory studies conducted at Elstree, Copenhagen and Paris, the preparations under test were stored at various temperatures for different periods and then used to vaccinate rabbits or produce 'pocks' in chick embryos. The samples of dried vaccine from the different laboratories varied greatly in their keeping properties but all proved to be more resistant to heat than the corresponding wet vaccine. In a second combined laboratory and field trial, the best of the four vaccines and one produced at the Lister Institute were compared. The Lister vaccine was found to be the most stable of all.

In further laboratory and field studies, involving Royal Air Force personnel, the Lister product produced 100 per cent of successful vaccinations after storage at 45 °C (113 °F) for two years. After long exposure in hot climates the dried vaccine could, therefore, be relied on to be effective in the maximum number of cases. In fact the Institute's new vaccine has proved its value in the Middle East and Africa, and vaccines of this type have made possible the recent worldwide campaign for the eradication of smallpox initiated by the World Health Organization. The vaccine is also used with uniform success by the armed forces; and a large stock is kept in reserve in the event of an epidemic in Britain.

An even purer vaccine was prepared at Elstree by Dr Colin Kaplan by growing the virus in the tissues of macerated chick embryo. The technique of tissue culture has been greatly improved by the use of antibiotics which prevent the contamination and destruction of the cultures by bacteria. An important advantage of this vaccine is its bacteriological sterility and freedom from the products of inflamed animal tissues. Since neither sheep nor calves are used, its production is also cheaper.

Although vaccination against smallpox has saved hundreds of thousands of lives in countries where the disease is endemic, in countries like Britain that are today free of smallpox the risks of vaccination must be weighed against the desirability of protection. From 1955 onwards the department has worked towards an effective killed vaccine, because killed vaccine virus, unlike the live virus in the conventional vaccine, does not multiply in the tissues of the subject and is therefore unlikely to provoke the rare, but often serious, complications of conventional vaccination. The killed vaccine that was finally devised proved to be safe, and to be capable of stimulating the body's defences against smallpox. It is likely to be particularly useful for persons in whom vaccination with live vaccine is contraindicated, for example, children and adults with eczema; or for giving as a *first* vaccination, to protect against the hazards of a subsequent vaccination with live vaccine.

An extension of the work of the department to viruses other than vaccinia had been contemplated for some time, and to this end, a new research and production laboratory was completed in 1963. The first product to be made there, however, was not strictly a virus vaccine, but a trachoma vaccine for trial by the Trachoma Research Unit.

Douglas McClean retired in 1961, after thirty-two years in the Institute and twenty-six years in charge of the smallpox vaccine laboratory. In his way, he was as much a 'character' as MacConkey had been. Tall and spare, with a beard acquired as a surgeon-probationer in the Navy during the First World War, he had something of an Elizabethan charm and indeed could sometimes rival Drake in calm. On one occasion, when a smallpox scare put sudden demands on his department, he said 'I detect a certain coolness in the powers above because I went to a committee meeting at the Wine Society yesterday; but I had pressed the button for the emergency arrangements I had already made and there was no point in hanging

around to give everybody the jitters.' He combined a patrician taste
for the good things of life with a passionate belief in democracy and
was well known for his fearless tilting at sacred cows. He died in 1967
after several years of ill-health. Dr Kaplan, who joined the department as assistant bacteriologist in 1954, became its head in 1961.

Earlier in this chapter, it was said that the work of the production
laboratories had changed little in essence since their inception. This
is true of the Bacterial Vaccine Laboratory in the sense that its object
then, as now, was the production of vaccines which would protect
against diseases caused by bacteria, such as plague and typhoid. But
its methods changed much more as a result of subsequent discoveries
in bacteriology and immunology than those of the other departments.
Arkwright's classic discovery in the 1920's, described in Chapter 15,
that changes in the nature of a bacillus could profoundly affect its
virulence and antigenic quality was a landmark in the development
of vaccines and was soon exploited.

For instance, Dr Schütze, then in charge of bacterial vaccine production, soon showed the significance of Sidney Rowland's observations on the envelope of the plague bacillus made eighteen years
earlier. Schütze showed that *Bacillus pestis* possesses two antigens,
one in the body of the bacillus, the so-called somatic antigen, and
another in the gelatinous envelope. Vaccines were prepared from
strains of plague bacilli grown at 26 °C and at 37 °C, and their
protective action compared on rats injected with a lethal dose of the
organism. The vaccine from bacilli grown at 37 °C possessed considerably greater prophylactic power. Since growth at the higher
temperature, as had been noted by Rowland, favoured the development of the envelope, and increased the virulence of the bacteria,
Schütze concluded that it is the envelope antigen which is pro-
phylactically important. Cultures grown at 37 °C were therefore used
for the preparation of plague vaccines, for which there has been a
continued demand.

Another landmark in the development of bacterial vaccines was
Morgan's isolation of the antigenic complex of the virulent Shiga
dysentery bacillus described in Chapter 16, and the elucidation of its
chemical composition and immunizing power. Similar investigations
of antigens belonging to other pathogenic organisms have yielded
valuable new knowledge. For instance, work at the Microbiological
Research Establishment at Porton, in Wiltshire, under the direction

of Dr D. W. Henderson, a former colleague of Morgan in the serum department at Elstree, led to the production of highly purified vaccines against woolsorter's disease and other forms of anthrax infection.

There are, however, often manifold difficulties to be overcome before a vaccine of known efficiency can be issued. These can be exemplified by the studies on whooping cough vaccine made at Elstree by Dr A. F. B. Standfast and his colleagues. The microbe causing whooping cough, the *Haemophilus pertussis* of Bordet and Gengou (lately renamed *Bordetella pertussis*), can readily be grown in the laboratory, and the possibility of preventing the disease by means of a bacterial vaccine has been abundantly demonstrated. The success of vaccination was shown in recent field trials made under the direction of the Medical Research Council, in which the Lister Institute collaborated both in preparing and testing some of the vaccines used. The trials involved over 35,000 children who were followed up for from two to three years in Leeds, Manchester, Oxford and several places in the London area.

Unfortunately all vaccines used in the past have not been equally potent, some even being useless. One difficulty was the lack of a convenient laboratory method for measuring the protective power of pertussis vaccines and another was an almost total ignorance of the part played by the various antigens of *B. pertussis* in producing immunity in man.

For these reasons A. F. B. Standfast and his colleagues at Elstree studied both the mouse protection test and the antigens of *B. pertussis* and their corresponding antibodies. The laboratory protection tests for potency were examined, in conjunction with extensive field trials in man, of a number of vaccines made under the direction of the Medical Research Council, so that the behaviour of a series of vaccines in laboratory animals and in children could be compared. In the past, vaccinated mice had been challenged in one of two ways; by the intranasal route, in which the living *B. pertussis* was instilled into the nose of the mouse; and by the intracerebral route, in which it was injected into the mouse's brain. Surprisingly, for the intranasal challenge might be expected to resemble more closely than the intracerebral the natural genesis of the disease in children, it was the assays with intracerebral challenge that corresponded closely to tests of the vaccines in children.

As Standfast and J. O. Irwin of the M.R.C. Statistical Research

Unit found in a statistical analysis, the errors of this test were large and, although the method was reliable, the number of mice required for a single accurate assay was very large. Nevertheless, with this reliable test of vaccine efficiency as a guide, it was possible to study the antigens of *B. pertussis* and the part they play in inducing immunity to whooping cough. Of the many distinct antigens that were known in this bacillus — the agglutinogens, the haemagglutinin, the toxin, the histamine-sensitizing factor and two mouse-protective antigens — all but one was rejected as the antigen effective in man. The remaining antigen protected mice against intracerebral challenge; and was eventually isolated in a non-toxic form, for use, it is hoped, as an immunizing antigen in human beings.

The highly artificial intracerebral route of infection was further analysed. In the brain of an unprotected mouse the injected *B. pertussis* increased steadily in numbers for six or seven days, when a critical concentration was reached that killed the mouse. In mice protected by antiserum or by vaccination the number of bacteria increased steadily for about four days and then began to decline quite dramatically until the brains were free from bacteria. Even when the circulating blood contained potent antibody from the start of the infection, the numbers did not decline until the fourth day. It appeared that at first antibody could not pass from the blood to the infected brain tissues, but that by the fourth day the infection was sufficient to damage the cerebral blood vessels so that antibody passed through the vessel walls into the tissues.

The fourth production department at Elstree is the Blood Products Laboratory. In contrast to the other departments, its work is not primarily directed to the prevention or treatment of infectious diseases, nor are its products sold to augment the income of the Institute. It was erected in 1953 at a cost of £175,000 with funds supplied by the Government, and is entirely supported by the Medical Research Council. Its function is to receive the surplus out-dated blood collected from voluntary donors at the eighteen regional centres of the National Blood Transfusion Service, and to recover from this blood the constituents which are of use in clinical medicine. These products are sent to the regional centres for the use of hospitals and clinics under the National Health Service.

The Blood Products Laboratory is the culmination of much research carried out in the biophysics department of the Institute and the Blood Products Research Unit of the Medical Research Council set up in the Institute under Sir Alan Drury during the war. The new building at Elstree soon became too small for its expanding work and an extension was built in 1964. Since its inception the laboratory has been under the direction of Dr W. d'A. Maycock. The history of the development of the Blood Products Laboratory is bound up with that of the biophysics department and together with an account of other researches on blood is recorded in Chapter 19.

With the extension of the original production departments and the creation of the Blood Products Laboratory, the establishment at Elstree, which includes many skilled technicians, has increased about tenfold since MacConkey's day. It enjoys the facilities of a canteen, a library, a well-equipped machine shop and transport to near-by places. The scientific staff are appointed primarily as research workers, who are free if they wish to tackle problems with no direct relation to the production for which they are responsible, a condition which has the same beneficial effect as the opportunity for active research provided in a teaching establishment. Examples of some of the research closely related to the technology of production have been outlined in this chapter; the contributions of workers at Elstree to other problems are told in other pages.

19. Blood and Blood Products

'For the blood is the life'

Every year in Britain over three-quarters of a million people visit the regional centres of the National Blood Transfusion Service and give freely a part of their blood for unknown recipients. The blood is drawn from a vein in the forearm into a glass bottle containing sodium citrate which prevents the blood from clotting. Bottles are labelled according to the blood group of the donor and stored at the centres in 'blood banks' kept in refrigerated rooms, until they are distributed to hospitals and other centres according to their need. Such blood will keep only for three weeks; after that time the red cells begin to disintegrate and the blood becomes unsafe for transfusion. Surplus outdated blood is however, not wasted. The bottles are returned to the regional centres and there the blood plasma is separated from the red cells, and sent from all parts of England and Wales to the Blood Products Laboratory at Elstree. There, various protein constituents of the plasma are extracted by an elaborate process, and the invaluable products made available for clinical use.

For more than twenty-five years, blood has been a major theme of work at the Lister Institute, particularly in the departments of biochemistry and biophysics. The various aspects studied range from the immunochemistry and molecular structure of plasma proteins and blood-group glycoproteins, through blood-group serology and genetics to the isolation of therapeutic blood substances. For the most part these studies, however academic they may seem, arose from problems encountered in transfusing the blood of one individual into another.

It was a Cornishman, Richard Lower, who in 1665 was the first man to make a blood transfusion from one animal to another, but later attempts to transfer blood from an animal into man, as a means of resuscitation after haemorrhage, were unsuccessful. In 1875 the German physiologist Leonard Landois noticed that when the red blood cells of one animal were mixed with serum from an animal of another species, agglutination usually took place. The red cells behaved like bacteria, which agglutinate when mixed with serum from an animal previously immunized against them. In fact, red blood cell agglutination was soon recognized as an immunological phenomenon.

At the beginning of the century the Austrian immunologist, Karl Landsteiner, made a striking observation on the blood of six of his colleagues at the Pathological Institute of Vienna University. Having separated the red cells from the serum, he tried the effect of mixing each sample of red cells with each of the other specimens of serum. He found that in some of the mixtures the cells agglutinated or clumped together. Extending his researches, Landsteiner came to the conclusion that the red cells of an individual possess one of two chemical factors which for convenience were later termed factors A and B. In the serum of certain other individuals there are antibodies (anti-A or anti-B) which, when mixed with the corresponding cells, cause them to clump together. Those antibodies occur naturally and must obviously be so distributed that an individual's serum does not agglutinate his own red cells. Landsteiner observed also that while the red cells of some people have either factor A or factor B, the cells of others may possess both factors, or neither. On that basis human beings can be divided into four sharply distinct groups according to whether the individual's red cells possess one (A) or the other (B) factor, or both (AB) or neither (O). Landsteiner's classification has remained valid to this days and is known as the ABO blood group system.

The particular blood group of any person is of critical importance when a blood transfusion is needed. When an individual belonging to one blood group is transfused with blood of another group so that the donor's cells are agglutinated in the recipient's blood stream, the result may be grave and even fatal. Blood transfusion is used nowadays not only for the replacement of lost blood but in the treatment of some diseases. In the pathology department of a modern hospital certain members of the staff are responsible for 'typing' the blood of patients as they are admitted. The National Blood Transfusion Service, for its part, is responsible for sending out blood labelled correctly with its type.

The ABO system forms the simplest basis of classification, but many other factors are known now, including one called the Lewis factor which is linked with the ABO system, and the *rhesus* factor. The whole subject of blood groups has become in its own right a profoundly complicated branch of genetics. Students of genetics who have investigated the distribution of blood groups among the members of the same family have concluded that the property of belonging to any particular blood group is inherited, transmitted from the parents to the child in the genes of the germ cells. Since 1946, the Lister Institute has housed two units of the Medical Research Council which have done outstanding work in this field; the Blood Group Research Unit directed by Dr R. R. Race and the Blood Group Reference Laboratory established under the direction of Dr A. E. Mourant.

A fundamental investigation on the chemical basis of blood group specificity undertaken by Walter Morgan was however underway in the Institute before 1946. Morgan returned from the serum department at Elstree to the biochemical department at Chelsea in 1939, and became head of the department after Robison's death in 1941. His work on the isolation of the antigenic complex of the dysentery bacillus is described in Chapter 16. For his distinguished work in immunochemistry, Morgan was elected F.R.S. in 1949, and delivered the Croonian Lecture in 1959.

The specific substances which cause certain red blood cells to agglutinate in the presence of an appropriate antibody are known as 'blood group substances'. Each of the chemical structures responsible for any one of the blood group substances seems to be controlled by a single one of the thousands of genes present in a single human chromosome. To know the structure of the individual substance should help to explain in biochemical terms the way in which one gene may influence another, and should be of value also in understanding the phenomenon of immunity, for these substances are antigenic.

The blood group substances are components of the surface of the red cells of the blood, but they are not confined to the blood cells. In water-soluble forms the blood group substances may be secreted into body fluids such as the saliva, the gastric and intestinal fluids and the urine. There are considerable difficulties in obtaining the substances from red cells, and the amounts in saliva and gastric juice are meagre. Morgan and his team found that the substances often exist in considerable amounts in the mucinous fluids present, sometimes to the extent of several gallons, in human ovarian cysts. Cystic fluid obtained from the operating theatres of hospitals was thenceforth used as the source of blood group substances.

The material from each patient was freeze-dried and then treated with ninety-five per cent liquid carbolic acid (phenol); the extraneous proteins were thereby dissolved and the residue which was insoluble in phenol possessed most of the specific blood group activity of the original fluid. The group substance thus concentrated was subjected to further purification, and its purity assessed by exacting physical, chemical and serological tests. Material obtained from patients of blood group A is called the A-substance, that from the B group, B-substance and so on. Morgan, however, called the substance from the donors of blood group O, the H-substance; it was found that this substance is present in all the other groups as well.

Chemical studies showed that the blood group substances belong to a class of compounds called mucopolysaccharides or glyco-proteins. In the state in which they occur naturally, they consist of giant molecules or macromolecules containing 80–90 per cent of carbohydrate and about 10–20 per cent of amino acids firmly bound together in a protein-like structure.

The next phase of the work established that the four sugars, L-fucose, D-galactose, D-glucosamine and D-galactosamine, and a minimum number of eleven amino acids were present in each substance. The first clue that any one of the four sugars present in each group substance is more closely involved in its characteristic serological behaviour than the other three, came to light from some experiments made by Morgan and his colleague, Dr Winifred Watkins. In that work they used reagents obtained from the blood serum of the eel and from the seeds of certain plants. Eel serum contains a protein that reacts as an antibody to the H-substance, which although present in all the blood groups represents the only specific substance secreted by individuals of the O group.

If eel serum is added to human red cells belonging to group O, agglutination takes place. The Lister team utilized a principle which had been expounded earlier by Landsteiner and tried the effect of adding fucose and other sugars separately to the eel serum before mixing it with the red cells of group O. The process of agglutination was prevented by fucose, but not by the other sugars. It seemed that the fucose had blocked the power of the antibody, the H-agglutinin, in the eel's serum and prevented it from reacting with the red cells.

Since fucose was the only sugar that could prevent clumping of red cells bearing the H-substance, the implication seemed clear that fucose was, in some way, the most important or dominant structure in H-substance. Further support for that conclusion was obtained from experiments made with the seeds of a plant (*Lotus tetragono-lobus*) belonging to the pea family, which like eel serum contain an anti-H substance. The ability of the material from this seed to agglutinate red cells of the human O group was strongly inhibited by fucose.

By a similar approach other blood group specificities were found to depend on the presence of one or other of the four sugars in the blood group substances. Thus a substance which agglutinates the red cells of the human A-group is found in the seeds of the common blue vetch (*Vicia cracca*). Morgan and Watkins found that a sugar called *N*-acetylgalactosamine inhibited the A-agglutinin.

Another approach to the problem was to examine what happens when the blood group substances are decomposed step-by-step by enzymes known to be capable of rendering them serologically inactive. Such enyzmes have been isolated from the liver of snails and from certain micro-organisms.

The protozoon, *Trichomonas foetus*, which causes sterility in cattle, was under study at the Institute by Muriel Robertson. Winifred Watkins found that it would yield extracts which destroyed or changed the serological activity of A, B, H and Lewis blood group substances. One purified enzyme from *Trichomonas* destroyed the specific activity of B-substance and liberated galactose almost exclusively and in large amounts. The mucopolysaccharide remaining then possessed H-activity. In the same way the appropriate enzyme was found which destroyed the activity of A-substance and left a substance which was H-active. It was, therefore, clearly possible to change the specificity of a blood group substance by removing a simple sugar component. Thus a probable scheme could be formulated for the biosynthesis of the blood group specific substances which was in agreement with genetic, serological and chemical findings.

Morgan and his colleagues then tried the effect on the blood group substances of two enzymes, ficin and papain, which decompose proteins. These proteolytic enzymes caused minor changes in the amino acid-containing moiety of the specific substance and gave rise to smaller units than the original macromolecule, but did not attack the carbohydrate part. It was surprising therefore to find that much of the original blood group activity had been lost, showing that the structure of the specific substance had been profoundly disturbed by the treatment. A similar result followed exposure of the blood group substances to ultrasonic vibration and thus confirmed the conclusion that the *shape* of the macromolecule as well as its chemical constitution plays an important part in its immunological specificity.

One might perhaps envisage the macromolecule as a building where the polysaccharide component forms a scaffolding which supports an interior structure of amino acids. In the process of attacking the amino acids with proteolytic enzymes, the configuration of the polysaccharide scaffolding also is upset and the original serological specificity is damaged.

The results strongly suggest that the carbohydrate portion of each blood group substance is associated with its specificity, that only a small portion of each carbohydrate moiety is directly involved and that the macromolecular structure of the blood group specific substance, as it occurs naturally, is also an important factor in the immunological reactions of the mucopolysaccharide macromolecule.

Later, Morgan and his colleague Terence Painter made another step forward by the use of a polystyrene resin as a hydrolytic agent instead of acid or alkali or enzymes. By this method, the specific blood group substances were broken down into a number of small chains of sugar molecules, which were still linked in the order in which they occurred in the whole substance. The separation and identification of these products, by a variety of means which involved much ancillary work on methods, was a stiff problem with much intricate chemistry. As a result, in 1965 Professor Morgan and his team were able to offer an explanation, in terms of chemical structure, on the nature of the inherited differences in the blood group specific glycoproteins. Winifred Watkins is now attempting to characterize the enzymes formed under the influence of the blood group genes and to elucidate the steps by which these specific substances are synthesized in the body.

The history of the Blood Products Laboratory at the Lister Institute is bound up with the development of the biophysics department, which has for the most part concerned itself with a study of the different proteins present in blood and plasma. In 1935 Dr A. S. McFarlane came to work at Chelsea as a Beit Memorial Fellow. He had already spent a year in the Laboratories of Professor Thé Svedberg at the University of Uppsala, studying the physical properties of proteins. Proteins are giant molecules, many thousand times heavier than the molecule of hydrogen. Each different protein is made up of a different chain of amino acids, which coils upon itself to form a complicated structure much as a strand of wool may be wound into balls or skeins of different shape. If a suspension of particles, such as sand, is whirled round in a centrifuge the sedimentation of the particles is greatly accelerated. When a protein is dissolved, the giant molecules dispersed in the liquid are minute in comparison with sand, yet if the solution is centrifuged at an enormous speed they are large enough to settle to the bottom of the container. The rate at which the molecules settle is decided, among other things, by their shape, size and weight, and from the precise measurement of the rate of sedimentation much knowledge of the properties of the protein can be gained. The ultracentrifuge devised by Svedberg to subject giant molecules to a centrifugal force about 250,000 times that of gravity was a great step forward.

Soon after McFarlane's arrival at the Lister Institute, the Director, Ledingham, suggested to the Governing Body that the Rockefeller Foundation might be asked to give the Institute an ultracentrifuge. The Rockefeller Trustees readily agreed to provide £3,400 for the machine, which was to be made in Svedberg's workshops. A new isolated building was essential to house the apparatus and its auxiliary equipment, and this was built at the rear of the main building in Chelsea. The steel rotor, which is the very core of the machine, is only about eight inches in diameter, but it took a powerful electric pump driving an oil turbine attached to the rotor to achieve the required centrifugal force. Concrete piles were driven deep into the Thames mud to provide a foundation free from vibration for the forty-ton concrete plinth on which the rotor and its casing were mounted. The casing, of massive steel, served to protect the operator and his surroundings from the danger of the rotor flying to pieces under the strain of the intense centrifugal forces which are developed.

The purpose of this complex piece of engineering is to spin rather less fluid than would fill a thimble. The solution of the protein under study is placed in a small cylindrical metal cell with quartz ends and centrifuged at 60,000 revolutions a minute. A beam of light which is passed through the cell strikes the boundary formed by the sedimenting protein molecules, creating a characteristic image which can be recorded on a photographic plate. Exposures are made at intervals during the centrifugation which may last several hours, and the pictures are interpreted by complex mathematical means.

It took two years to erect the new building and install the new machine, which was the first of its kind to be used in Britain. By the time the ultracentrifuge was installed at Chelsea, Dr Arne Tiselius, also of Uppsala, had perfected another extremely useful instrument for identifying proteins in solution. It was based on the principle that when electrodes are dipped into a protein solution and a current passed through, the protein molecules migrate towards one or other of the electrodes, a phenomenon known as 'electrophoresis'.

Just as the sedimentation rate in the ultracentrifuge can be used to identify a protein, the rate of movement in an electric field is also a characteristic which helps in its identification. In the Tiselius apparatus for electrophoretic analysis the speed of the protein molecule is measured under controlled conditions. The optical system for viewing and recording is similar to that used with the ultracentrifuge. It is possible to distinguish between several proteins present in the same solution which have about the same size but different electrophoretic properties, and to measure the amount of each. Thus it was found that the globulin fraction of blood plasma consists of three main components which are named alpha, beta and gamma globulin. In 1937 the Institute added a Tiselius apparatus to the Svedberg equipment.

In the same year McFarlane was joined by R. A. Kekwick, a graduate in chemistry from University College, London, who also had worked in Professor Svedberg's laboratory in Uppsala, with a grant from the Medical Research Council. They applied the new apparatus to studies on viruses and on the proteins, especially the immunoglobulins, of blood plasma. Three years later, after the outbreak of war, the department of biophysics was of necessity moved from London, and McFarlane and Kekwick were evacuated to the London County Council's Serum Institute at Carshalton in Surrey. At that point they began to be involved in the practical problems raised by blood transfusion and the products that could be prepared from blood.

As soon as war started, mobile units travelled up and down the

7*

country collecting blood from volunteers. Of the four main groups, the blood of group O, formerly known as the universal donor, is suitable for most patients. This type of blood was therefore generally used for transfusion during the early war years but, as a matter of policy, no donor's blood was refused by the collecting teams. There was, therefore, a surplus of all types of blood other than group O, so it became a matter of urgency to find ways of salvaging the plasma from out-of-date blood.

The technique of freeze-drying offered one solution but, at that stage in the war, facilities for freeze-drying were limited, and other methods had to be sought for producing a liquid plasma derivative which would keep. All existing products of the kind had the disadvantage that a precipitate gradually appeared making the liquid look as if it had been contaminated by bacteria. In fact, the cloudiness was harmless and consisted of insoluble fatty (lipid) material. In the biophysics department McFarlane had the idea of extracting the lipids with ether, but that made the plasma froth. In seeking to control the frothing he froze the ether-treated plasma at $-20\,^{\circ}C$ and then removed the ether with an air spray. In that way he obtained a solution of undamaged plasma protein which remained clear, and was used for transfusion. His work showed also that, among the lipoproteins (compounds of protein and fat) present in human plasma, there were differing categories distinguishable by their varied stability.

As long ago as 1908 at Oxford the physiologist John Mellanby showed that, if ordinary alcohol (ethanol) was added to the blood of a horse previously immunized against diphtheria, the antitoxin with other proteins was thrown out of solution. The principle of precipitating proteins with alcohol was applied by Dr E. J. Cohn and his colleagues in the United States to the preparation of purified albumin from human plasma. The albumin could be concentrated for use in transfusion and could be stored for long periods even in the tropics.

By fractionating blood with alcohol, the American workers obtained several other useful fractions, including gamma globulin and the proteins thrombin and fibrinogen, which react with one another to make fibrin, the insoluble substance formed when blood is clotted. Small amounts of those fractions were sent from the United States to Britain for clinical trial and the surgeons and physicians who used them reported favourably. The Medical

Research Council's Blood Transfusion Committee decided therefore that the substances should be made generally available for British medicine. That decision was supported strongly by the Committee's chairman, Dr Alan Drury, a member of the Medical Research Council's external scientific staff at Cambridge, who had been largely responsible for developing the Blood Transfusion Services in Britain and was in close touch with researches on blood products carried out at Cambridge.

When Sir John Ledingham retired in 1942, Dr Drury was appointed director of the Lister Institute. In the following year he arranged the establishment of a Blood Products Unit at Chelsea, sponsored jointly by the Institute and the Medical Research Council. The purpose of the Unit was to obtain protein fractions from blood and also to prepare large amounts of plasma for freeze-drying at the Medical Research Council's unit at Cambridge. When that unit was closed down at the end of the war the Chelsea laboratories took over the preparation of all the freeze-dried plasma needed for Britain.

The biophysics department returned to Chelsea in the autumn of 1943; McFarlane had gone to the National Institute for Medical Research and Ralph Kekwick was in charge. He was joined by Dr Margaret Mackay, an Australian graduate of Adelaide University who had been working with the Medical Research Council Serum Drying Unit at Cambridge.

When Kekwick, Record and Miss Mackay were asked by Drury to fractionate human plasma, much of the equipment needed for the Cohn alcohol method was not to be had in Britain and ether was more easily obtainable than alcohol. The Lister workers, therefore, set out to find an alternative method that would be simple and yet give a high yield of proteins pure enough for clinical use. While using McFarlane's procedure for ridding the plasma of unwanted fats by extracting with ether, they found that the ether also threw fibrinogen out of solution. That gave them the idea that, by varying the dilution, temperature and acidity of the plasma, they might be able to use ether to separate and purify other proteins as well. In fact, the ether technique lived up to their expectations.

Over a period of ten years Kekwick and Margaret Mackay collaborated to produce a new and complete system for isolating and purifying the chief proteins in human plasma; these fractions were produced on a pilot-plant scale for clinical use.

The demand for human blood products ultimately became so great that the Blood Products Research Unit from Chelsea had to move to new buildings at Elstree. This was done in 1954, when the Unit, with greatly expanded facilities, was renamed the Blood Products Laboratory and put in charge of Dr W. d'A. Maycock with Mr Leon Vallet responsible for the technological developments.

The useful fractions were separated from the blood plasma by the ether method of Kekwick and Mackay, adapted to large-scale production in a cold laboratory at 4 °C. The fractions are precipitated successively from the plasma by varying the concentrations of ether, plasma proteins and salts, at different temperatures and different degrees of acidity. The high volatility and inflammability of ether, however, is a disadvantage in large-scale work, and in 1963, in preparation for further expansion of the laboratories, a move was begun to replace ether by the less volatile and inflammable ethyl alcohol. The crude fractions so produced are purified and the products, which include thrombin, fibrinogen, immunoglobulin ('gamma globulin') and anti-haemophilic globulin, are sent to hospitals and public health laboratories all over the country.

Thrombin turns soluble fibrinogen into an insoluble fibrin clot. A mixture of fibrinogen and thrombin has proved to be a useful adhesive for holding the nerve ends together during nerve repairs and on grafts for keeping skin grafts in position. When it is used instead of a 'pressure dressing', new blood vessels form readily in the clot, the graft 'takes' in two days instead of a month and the cosmetic result is much better. Transfusions of fibrinogen are also used to correct a tendency to bleed in patients whose blood fibrinogen has been depleted.

Normal immunoglobulin from adults is the protein fraction which contains antibodies against the viruses and bacteria to which adults have been exposed during their life time. Among these are the viruses of measles and German measles and of hepatitis. A single injection of immunoglobulin will for several months protect susceptible individuals exposed to infectious hepatitis and is particularly useful for controlling outbreaks of hepatitis in institutions. It also prevents or attenuates measles in weakly or sick children who have been in contact with measles, and prevents German measles in pregnant women, thus obviating the risk that their babies will be born blind or with other congenital defects. Because of the wide variety of anti-bodies present, normal immunoglobulin is given for a rare condition, hypogammaglobulinaemia, in which the ability to make antibodies is deficient or lacking. Sufferers from the disease are liable to chronic infections of varying severity; when treated regularly with immuno-globulin, many of them are able to enjoy better health and to live more normal lives. Donors of blood may be specifically immunized, for example against tetanus, before they are bled, and so provide a potent, deliberately stimulated, immunoglobulin for the treatment of that disease. Anti-D immunoglobulin is of special interest. It was first made in the Laboratory in 1963, from the blood of Rh-negative people who had acquired a high content of antibody to the Rh antigen D; and has been used by the Department of Medicine of Liverpool University in a pioneer attempt to prevent the sensitization of Rh-negative mothers by the D antigen, and thus prevent haemolytic disease in any Rh-negative children they might have.

The albumin in blood, which constitutes about fifty per cent of the plasma proteins, is largely responsible for maintaining blood volume; it exerts nearly all the osmotic pressure in the plasma which in its turn controls the total amount of fluid. Concentrated solutions of albumin are very stable and are used conveniently to increase total blood volume when it has been diminished by haemorrhage. They are also a valuable means of giving protein to people with an excess of fluid in the body tissues, often promoting a decrease of the excess. Albumin is also available in the 'plasma protein fraction', whose production as a more easily made substitute for purified albumin was begun in 1964. This fraction also has advantages over whole plasma because, unlike plasma, it can be safely heated to destroy the virus of serum hepatitis that is a not uncommon contaminant of transfusion blood.

The preparation of the antihaemophilic factor from blood plasma is of special interest. The mechanism which brings about the clotting of blood after injury is very complex; twelve distinct components have been recognized as taking part and there may be more. One of the components, the antihaemophilic factor or Factor VIII, is missing from the blood plasma of those males born with haemophilia, a disease rare in females though they transmit the defect. Factor VIII disappears quickly from normal blood or plasma even if stored at low temperatures. Until 1954, the only effective way of checking bleeding in the haemophiliac was to transfuse him with fresh whole blood, fresh plasma or reconstituted quick-frozen plasma which had been stored at $-20\,°C$ or below. Because there is relatively so little

Factor VIII in blood, and because it is rapidly destroyed after transfusion, large volumes of blood or plasma were needed to raise the Factor VIII to a level when clotting could occur; there was thus a danger of overloading the circulation.

An important advance was made in 1953, when a group of workers, led by Dr R. G. Macfarlane at Oxford, devised a quantitative laboratory test for Factor VIII. The Oxford workers also succeeded in preparing a Factor VIII fraction from bovine blood, which their new test showed to be especially rich in the factor. The bovine factor was effective in controlling haemorrhage in haemophiliacs but, since the protein was not of human origin, it sensitized them to future injections of the same material.

Another laboratory test for estimating the Factor VIII potency of fractions from human plasma was devised in the biophysics department. With the new test as a guide, the first concentrated preparation of Factor VIII was obtained from fresh human plasma. It was used successfully on over seventy haemophiliacs, including some under dental treatment or suffering from wounds and broken bones after traffic accidents, as well as in others undergoing major operations. A distressing condition frequent in young haemophiliacs is caused by haemorrhages into the joints. One dramatic incident involved a seven-year-old boy who, from that cause, had been unable to walk for eighteen months. He could not receive physical treatment for fear of causing further bleeding. After a course of human Factor VIII, however, the condition of his blood was so much improved that physiotherapy became possible and he was on his feet again in six weeks. Such a course of treatment, involving regular and repeated injections, is only possible with material of human origin. The Factor VIII concentrate has the advantage over the whole blood in that its antihaemophilic potency is known to the clinician; in the freeze-dried state it is stable at ordinary refrigerator temperature for at least six months and can be safely transported at normal temperatures.

This account has traced the beginnings in the biophysics department of an enterprise, the Blood Products Laboratory, of outstanding value in clinical medicine. For his distinguished work on proteins, Kekwick was elected F.R.S. in 1966. The biophysical work at Chelsea still centres on biologically important macromolecules. It is a commentary on the rapidity of progress in this field that the Svedberg ultracentrifuge, which in 1936 was the centrepiece of the new department, has in thirty years become literally a museum piece, which will have an honoured place in the Science Museum. It has been replaced by an even more sophisticated apparatus, the Spinco analytical ultracentrifuge, in charge of Dr J. M. Creeth, who joined the biophysics department in 1961.

20. Trypanosomiasis and Trachoma

By the end of the first half of this century, the picture of infectious diseases in Great Britain had changed radically from that confronting the founders of the Institute. With the virtual elimination of the rapid mass killers — typhoid and tuberculosis, diphtheria and scarlet fever, smallpox, plague and typhus — much medical research today centres on other diseases such as cancer and rheumatism, arterial degeneration and mental illness, congenital diseases and allergies. The study of infectious diseases, however, is still one of the functions of the Institute and embraces in a comprehensive way the nature of the protozoa, bacteria and viruses which cause them. Two of these studies, worthy successors to those on plague and sleeping sickness described in earlier chapters, have taken members of the Institute staff into field work abroad on problems which are world wide and involve international collaboration. One of these concerns the vectors of trypanosomiasis, malaria and yellow fever, and the other the cause and prevention of the crippling eye disease, trachoma.

Sleeping sickness caused by trypanosomes is, in Africa, no longer a grave menace to human beings; modern drug therapy, wise sanitary measures and a considerable degree of fly control have changed the picture in recent years. Trypanosomiasis in cattle however is still a cause of serious economic loss, and by limiting severely the supply of milk and meat it also impoverishes the people's diet. It was realized that more information was needed about the habitat and feeding preferences of the blood-sucking insects which carry the trypanosomes, and about the ecology of the wild beasts on which the insect prefers to feed and from which it infects domestic animals. It might be feasible to exterminate the creatures most seriously incriminated, and thus clear the scourge of cattle disease from large tracts of land.

In 1947, at the instigation of the late Professor P. A. Buxton, the Colonial Medical Research Committee of the Colonial Office mapped out an ambitious programme of field and laboratory research to ascertain the feeding habits and preferences of the tsetse fly and other insects. A suggestion by Buxton that the Lister Institute might undertake the laboratory side of the investigation was at once accepted by Sir Alan Drury. Bernard Weitz, a veterinary scientist who a year before had joined the serum department at Elstree from the Ministry of Agriculture's laboratories at Weybridge, took charge of the project. His part was to identify the animal on which the insect had fed by immunological tests on the blood found in the insect's gut.

Samples of blood from a wide variety of tropical animals on which the flies might have fed were needed as standards in the tests. So in 1949 Weitz set off on a preliminary safari in East Africa to see how they could be expeditiously collected and brought back to England. He was greatly helped by members of the East African Tsetse and Trypanosomiasis Research and Reclamation Organization (EATTRRO) at Shinyanga in Tanganyika, and notably by the late Dr D. H. N. Jackson, whose technical staff played an important part in the field work.

Another valuable ally was William Hilton, who was seconded by EATTRRO for the collection of blood samples. Though William Hilton is described as 'field assistant', he is perhaps better known as a crack shot big-game hunter. His presence in the camp was indispensable because, in order to obtain blood, the wild animals had to be shot without damaging the heart. Ideally the beast was stunned with a bullet in the brain or across the vertebrae of the neck. Once the quarry was immobilized the arteries in the neck were cut and the blood collected. Usable sera from the blood of twenty-five species of wild animals were brought back to Elstree.

Weitz then designed a mobile laboratory for the collection of sera in the field from a further twenty-five species, including birds, reptiles, and mammals, ranging from the elephant to the porcupine.

The next step was to prepare for each species of blood serum an antiserum to be used in what is called the precipitin test. That test is based on the fact that an animal of one species, after receiving an injection of the blood proteins of another species, will produce antibodies to the foreign proteins. Such antibodies, conveniently raised in the rabbit, react with a specimen of the original foreign protein, but not with unrelated proteins, to form a precipitate. Thus, antibody to pig serum proteins precipitates the serum proteins of the pig, but not of the zebra or elephant. Given a whole battery of such antisera, each of them specific for the blood proteins of a particular species of animal, the blood found in the gut of a blood-sucking insect can be identified. The same technique is commonly applied in medico-legal practice where antisera specific for the blood proteins of man and domestic animals are used to decide whether suspect blood stains are of human or animal origin.

The precipitin test had already been applied to insect blood meals but the results were unreliable through lack of the right antisera. But even with the correct antisera the test did not always distinguish sharply between the blood proteins of closely allied animals such as the warthog and the bush-pig.

Weitz accordingly devised a version of the so-called inhibition test whereby the unknown proteins are identified by their power to inhibit the precipitin reactions between known blood proteins and their corresponding antibodies. It proved to be extremely sensitive and reliable as a means of identifying the species of origin of a blood meal.

When the gorged tsetse fly had been captured, it was placed on a piece of fine filter paper and dissected so that the abdominal contents were squeezed out on to the paper and allowed to dry. At Elstree the dried blood meal was extracted by soaking the paper in saline solution. Since each sample had to be tested against a wide range of antisera, Weitz saved time and labour by devising an apparatus with which a single technician, in the course of a morning's work, can test from 100 to 200 blood meals against half a dozen antisera.

The precipitin test seeks first to decide from which of five likely families of mammals the blood may have come. They are the Primates, including man, baboon and monkey; the *Suidae* or pig family, including the warthog, giant forest-hog, Red River hog, bush-pig or domestic pig; the *Equidae*, including the horse, donkey, mule and zebra; the *Bovidae*, including the buffalo, eland, reedbuck, hartebeest and many others, and the *Canidae*, including the dog and fox. Any unidentified specimens are then tested with antisera to the blood of birds, reptiles and mammals such as the elephant, rhinoceros, hyaena and porcupine. The individual species within the group is then determined by the inhibition test.

With the help of Dr Jackson, a field trial was made to check the validity of the results in the Daga-Iloi district of Tanganyika. Wild tsetse flies of the species *Glossina swynnertoni* were captured and caused to feed on man or on the ox, donkey, domestic pig or Thomson's gazelle. They were then marked with coloured paint according to the host bitten, released and recaptured after about a day at large. All of twenty-eight smears of stomach contents were assigned to their correct families by the precipitin test; and twenty-two out of twenty-five meals to their correct species by the inhibition test.

Accurate knowledge of the tsetse fly's natural hosts was now possible, and a wide study was made by Weitz in collaboration with J. P. Glasgow of the Central Tsetse Research Laboratory at Shinyanga in Tanganyika. The origin was determined of 1,433 blood meals from seven species of *Glossina* captured in the Sudan, Uganda, Kenya, Tanganyika, Zanzibar and Southern Rhodesia, from seventeen areas representing the habitat of the tsetse fly in Africa.

The survey showed that each species of *Glossina* preferred one particular host. *Glossina morsitans*, the fly responsible for transmission of sleeping sickness to cattle, as well as the related species *G. swynnertoni*, fed most readily on the warthog, whose blood was detected in about one-half of the blood meals examined. Only a relatively small proportion of feeds was derived from other wild game animals; the hartebeest and zebra were apparently never bitten.

G. palpalis, the fly responsible for the transmission of human sleeping sickness, was known to depend for its food on large reptiles such as the crocodile and monitor lizard. That fact was confirmed by the inhibition tests but, in areas where the crocodile had been hunted and eliminated, the fly maintained itself by biting other animals or human beings coming down to the water's edge. Other species of *Glossina* preferred the rhinoceros, elephant or porcupine. Thus the particular fly was usually found in those situations favoured by its preferred host.

The results of the blood meal analyses are leading to a new approach in the control of trypanosomiasis, for it should be possible to eliminate the fly from a given area by removing the species of animal on which it prefers to feed. Studies are now being planned to show whether in fact such discriminative hunting would be effective.

Malaria is also spread by the bite of a blood-sucking insect. The cause of human malaria is a protozoon of the genus *Plasmodium*, carried from man to man by mosquitoes of the genus *Anopheles*, and its life cycle runs partly in the mosquito and partly in man.

Malaria is accepted as the greatest single destroyer of human life, not excluding war or cancer. More than 1,100 million people, nearly half the world's population, live in malarial regions, and as recently as 1955 there were records of 200 million sufferers and two million deaths from the disease. Eradication of the disease means eradication of the mosquito, an aim placed in the forefront of its activities by the World Health Organization at the Assembly in 1955. For that purpose it is necessary to know the breeding and feeding habits of different species of *Anopheles* in different parts of the world.

As part of the world-wide campaign to eradicate malaria the Lister Institute unit at Elstree offered a centralized service to determine the origin of the blood meals ingested by anopheline mosquitoes. Between 1955 and 1959, with the same technique as for tsetse flies, Dr Weitz and his team tested more than 56,000 blood meals from about fifty species of mosquito captured in thirty different countries.

Several species of *Anopheles* prefer human blood, for more than seventy-five per cent of the blood meals proved to be human; other species prefer the blood of horses or cattle. Changes in feeding habits can, however, be caused by alterations in the environment, such as are brought about by spraying the habitat with insecticides. Treatment of villages with DDT (dichlor-diphenyl-trichlorethane) was found, for example, to reduce the proportion of blood meals that were of human origin. With one species it was reduced from 93 to 76 per cent and with another from 97 to 14 per cent — clear evidence of what is known as 'avoidance behaviour' on the part of the mosquito.

Weitz and his team later studied the immune reactions of animals infected with *T. brucei.* In these infections the number of trypanosomes in the blood — that is the degree of parasitaemia — rises to a maximum and then declines sharply, only to rise and fall every few days until the animal dies or recovers. They discovered that during the first rise the trypanosomes released into the blood an antigen, against which the animal formed the appropriate antibody. The first decline in numbers coincided with an abundance in the blood of this antibody, which presumably acted as a protective antibody. From the trypanosomes in the next bout of parasitaemia a new antigen was released, against which a correspondingly distinct protective antibody was formed; and similarly with each successive bout. It was clear that after each decline, there was among the trypanosomes remaining in the animal an antigenic mutant which was not susceptible to any antibodies already present, and which consequently proliferated, until it in turn stimulated an antibody active against it. Up to five antigenic changes in the parasitaemic population of trypanosomes were observed; and others have since extended the number to over twenty. This versatility of the infecting protozoon emphasizes the difficulty of immunizing against this variety of trypanosomiasis, unless the full range of possible antigenic variants was known, and their number small enough for all of them to be included in a single vaccine.

The antigens were discovered as soluble material present in small quantities in the blood of the infected animals. If the nature of the antigens is to be effectively analysed, large numbers of trypanosomes are required. Large-scale cultivation of trypanosomes in artificial media is not only difficult but, even when successful, grossly modifies the character of the organisms, including their antigens and their infectivity. The difficulty was ingeniously solved by the team under Dr D. G. Godfrey, who took charge of the trypanosomiasis research when Dr Weitz became Director of the National Institute for Research in Dairying at Reading. Godfrey's colleague, Sheila Lanham, taking advantage of the differences of the electrical charge on the surface of blood cells and of trypanosomes, passed infected blood through columns of a special absorbent cellulose that held back the blood cells, and so obtained for study pure suspensions of living trypanosomes in abundance.

This technique has also made it feasible to examine samples of blood from animals in infected areas of West Africa, to uncover infections hitherto unrecognized because of the very small number of trypanosomes in the blood.

Trachoma is the most widespread of all eye diseases and the greatest cause of blindness in the world. According to the World Health Organization, it affects about 500 million people, a sixth of the human race. It is prevalent in China, Japan, India, Russia, Africa, the Eastern Mediterranean, Australasia and, nearer home, in the poorer regions of Spain and Portugal. Egypt and North Africa are gravely affected and many of the 25,000 blind beggars that chant their way through the narrow streets of Moroccan towns have lost their sight through trachoma. During the Napoleonic wars 'military ophthalmia' was spread with appalling results throughout Europe by the allied armies engaged on the Continent and, from the Egyptian Campaign of 1798–99, many blinded British soldiers returned home carrying an infection generally thought to have been trachoma. The first introduction of pensions by the Government was to compensate soldiers incapacitated in that way. A contemporary wrote that 'in England, Egyptian Ophthalmia now became familiar to every medical practitioner'.

Throughout the nineteenth century, trachoma was common among children in the schools maintained by the Poor Law authorities in and around London. Examination of 9,000 such children in 1875 revealed that only one-fifth had eyes free from infection. Two special ophthalmic hospital schools were opened in 1903–4 for the segregation and treatment of children suffering from trachoma and this measure led to a speedy decline in its incidence. Nowadays the disease is uncommon in the indigenous population of this country; and the general improvement in living standards minimizes the risk of its importation and spread by immigrants or visitors.

Trachoma is a chronic and contagious inflammation of the conjunctiva, the delicate transparent membrane covering the eyeballs and the inner surface of the eyelids. If the inflammatory process extends to the cornea which forms the window in front of the pupil, opacities may be formed and cause partial or total blindness. The infection often begins in the first six months of life and secondary contamination with bacteria adds to the seriousness of the original infection. The primary cause of the disease was generally accepted to be a virus which, however, for many years resisted all attempts to grow it in the laboratory. Although trachoma is susceptible to treatment by modern drugs, isolation of the causal organism is of prime importance to any campaign aiming at its eradication.

In 1956, the Lister Institute established a new department of virology at its Chelsea Laboratories, equipped with all the necessary modern facilities for cultivating viruses in different kinds of tissue. Leslie Collier, who had previously worked at Elstree on vaccinia, took charge and decided that his main objective would be isolation of the trachoma organism. He soon made contact with a group from the Institute of Ophthalmology which, under the leadership of Sir Stewart Duke-Elder and supported by the Medical Research Council, had set up a research unit in the new Ophthalmic Hospital of the Order of St John of Jerusalem, situated on the Jordan side of that city. There is an appallingly high incidence of trachoma among the million Arab refugees from Israel, living mainly in camps in Jordan. Eye swabs taken from patients on the spot were sent to Chelsea, but when material from them was inoculated into cultures of kidney and other cells, there was no growth of the virus. However, this work had not been long in progress before the Suez crisis dictated the return of Sir Stewart's team to England.

The Medical Research Council had for some years been maintaining laboratories for studying the indigenous diseases of the Gambia, and members of Sir Stewart Duke-Elder's team then investigated the suitability of that country for trachoma research. They reported favourably, but soon afterwards were disbanded, and Collier became Honorary Director of a re-formed Medical Research Council Trachoma Research Unit based partly at the Lister Institute and partly in the Gambia.

Meanwhile, a claim was made from Peking that the virus of trachoma had been isolated. It came from a group of workers led by Dr T'ang Fei-Fan at the National Vaccine and Serum Institute and the Municipal T'ung Jen Hospital. They reported that after sixty-eight experiments on ninety-three specimens obtained from the eyes of trachoma patients, they had obtained three strains of a virus-like organism. In the *Chinese Medical Journal* for 1957, the Peking team described how, after treating eye swabs with antibiotics to destroy contaminating organisms, they had inoculated the material into fertilized hens' eggs after they had been incubated for from six to eight days. The inoculum was injected into the yolk sac of the developing chick embryo. The eggs were then incubated for ten to fourteen days at 35°C, the temperature of the human conjunctiva. In most of the tests no change could be detected in the cells of the yolk sac membrane either with the naked eye or microscopically. Material from the yolk sacs of eggs thus inoculated was injected into a second series of eggs, and so on for up to five 'passages'. Eventually, it was observed that injection of material originally derived from three patients caused death of the embryo after two or three passages. Microscopic examination of the yolk sacs from the dead embryos revealed numerous 'elementary bodies' similar in size to those of trench fever or vaccinia. T'ang was able to show that this infective agent was highly resistant to streptomycin, but that penicillin was deleterious, which probably explains why other investigators had failed to isolate it. The Chinese workers inoculated two of their three strains into the eyes of seven monkeys, and induced in them a conjunctivitis with some of the clinical features of trachoma. On that and other laboratory evidence they felt justified in claiming that they had isolated the causal virus.

When Collier read the exciting report of the Chinese work he at once wrote to Dr T'ang to ask if he could have freeze-dried samples for study. At the moment when the letter reached Peking, Professor Spooner of the London School of Tropical Medicine and Hygiene happened to be visiting Dr T'ang and he was given an ampoule of the precious yellow powder to take back to Britain. Collier repeated Dr T'ang's technique on the samples brought from China and had no difficulty in recovering the micro-organism.

Collier then went himself to the Gambia to see if a virus could be isolated from trachoma patients on the spot by the Chinese method. On November 28, 1957, material from the eye of an eight-year-old Mandingo girl was inoculated into chick embryos. On December 6, the bacteriologist in charge there, Josef Sowa, examined portions of the yolk sac under the microscope and saw unmistakable elementary bodies. Freeze-dried samples of infected yolk sac were sent to Chelsea and from them Collier propagated the virus in the London laboratory. The claims of the Chinese workers were so far confirmed.

To fulfil the requirements laid down by the World Health Organization Expert Committee on Trachoma it still remained to be proved that the virus could cause the disease in human beings. To do that involved a crucial experiment on man. The Expert Committee had set up the following essential requirement for assessing claims to have isolated the trachoma virus: 'In all cases the final proof should be the production of typical trachoma in human volunteers after sufficient passages in culture to eliminate the dilution factor. Although the committee deplores the necessity for human inoculation (not at present a dangerous procedure in view of effective chemotherapy) it insists that this criterion be fulfilled, as at the present time experimental trachoma cannot be diagnosed with certainty in hosts other than man.'

The course of events had been followed closely and with great interest by Sir Stewart Duke-Elder. He offered Collier two male volunteers, both of whom were hopelessly blind from other causes. It had been explained to them that results from the trial might provide an important link in the chain of evidence that was being forged by scientists of the East and West in their attempt to wipe out the terrible scourge of trachoma. The two men were assured that their general health would not suffer and that any infection that might develop could be promptly cured. With their consent, therefore, on March 11, 1958, the conjunctiva was stroked with a suspension of the virus. In one man the result was doubtful but in the other, signs of trachoma appeared within seven days and progressed to the characteristic picture of the disease. The patient was observed and treated for several months, during which typical elementary or inclusion bodies were repeatedly demonstrated in conjunctival scrapings, from which the virus was cultivated on eight occasions.

Thus Collier proved that he had produced, with a cultured virus, the first case of experimental trachoma in a human subject. The virus of trachoma is now being grown at Chelsea and in the Gambia. It has been successfully cultivated in the developing chick embryo and in tissue culture; in both, the microscope shows the cells to be crowded with elementary bodies. The preparation of a vaccine has thus become a possibility.

Trachoma can be cured by certain antibiotic or sulphonamide drugs; but in some countries where the disease is endemic the sheer numbers of those afflicted, coupled with difficulties of access to large sections of the population, make general and sustained treatment extremely difficult. An effective vaccine would greatly simplify the prevention of trachoma, and much energy in Collier's unit is therefore devoted to this end. Laboratory tests and preliminary field trials in the Gambia and in Iran have given some hope for such a vaccine. At the Institute, this work is supported by research on the immunopathology of trachoma, and on the properties of the causal micro-organism. Because the trachoma agent cannot be grown on artificial culture media, it has been referred to as a virus; but as recent researches show, it is much more like a bacterium, albeit one that is unable to multiply outside living animal cells.

Both newborn infants and adults in Western communities occasionally suffer from another form of infective conjunctivitis, known as inclusion conjunctivitis or inclusion blennorrhea. The infection is carried in the adult genital tract and is mainly transmitted by sexual contact; but the eyes of babies may be infected at birth and the eyes of older people by contact with infectious discharges, for example in swimming pools. Inclusion conjunctivitis in some ways resembles trachoma, but it clears up without treatment and without permanently damaging the eye. There were good grounds for supposing that the causal organism is very similar to that of trachoma, and in 1959

Collier, with Professor Barrie Jones of the Institute of Ophthalmology, undertook to prove this.

Jones, who had been closely associated with the earlier volunteer
experiments on trachoma, provided material from the uterus of a
woman whose baby contracted inclusion conjunctivitis soon after
birth. From it, both Collier and Dr C. H. Smith, who was formerly
microbiologist in Sir Stewart Duke-Elder's unit in Jordan, isolated
an agent virtually identical with that of trachoma; and Jones and
Collier succeeded in infecting the eye of a human volunteer with it.
Similar microbes were found in the eyes of babies and adults with
inclusion conjunctivitis and, as with the isolation of the trachoma
agent itself, these observations have now been confirmed in many
other laboratories. Some of the inclusion conjunctivitis agents have
properties that make them particularly useful for laboratory study,
and research on them has thrown much new light on the behaviour of
the trachoma group in general.

21. The Seventh Decade

Ashley Miles became the fourth director of the Lister Institute in 1952, just on half a century after Martin took up the post. From the time of Martin's coming to the present day, the Institute has grown from six departments, with twenty graduate scientists, to twelve departments, with usually about sixty graduate workers, and has maintained its flexibility in creating new departments and discontinuing old ones as needs arose or interests shifted. Today, the Chelsea departments are biochemistry, biophysics, electronmicroscopy, experimental pathology, microbiology and virology, and the heads of five of them are professors of the University of London. The Medical Research Council's Trachoma Research Unit is attached to the virology department, and two other of the Council's units, dealing with the genetical and immunological aspects of blood groups, are housed at Chelsea. The accommodation has been increased by the transformation of the director's flat and various basement rooms into laboratories, and by new premises, built on the site of the tennis court, provided by the Ministry of Health for the Blood Group Reference Laboratory of the Medical Research Council. At Elstree, there are four research and production departments, three concerned with vaccines and antisera and one with blood products.

The climate of opinion in Great Britain in recent years is very different from that which greeted the founders of the Institute. The indifference and even hostility of public opinion towards medical research has largely disappeared and governments are no longer cautious about associating themselves with it. The Institute, which then stood alone, is now physically dwarfed by many of the research institutes and the laboratories of medical schools and pharmaceutical companies engaged in similar fields of research. Its comparative smallness still carries the virtues of ready collaboration and exchange of ideas between individuals and departments.

Nowadays, however, it is difficult for those in different disciplines to understand each other's work. The difficulty is not simply a matter of highly specialized techniques and instrumentation. It is the growth of a specialized language within disciplines which makes communication difficult. Thus the geneticist who designates a particular blood group as 'O; MNSs; R_1r; $K+k+$, $K_p(a-b+O)$' conveys as much wealth of precise information and as much potted history of research as the chemist who writes $K_2HP^{32}O_4$ on a radioactive phosphate; but like W. S. Gilbert's castaways, they cannot chat together, they have not been introduced. What is difficult for the specialist is even more so for the layman; so that recent researches in the Institute, besides those described in Chapters 19 and 20, will be dealt with only briefly — mainly to indicate the new frontiers of knowledge and the kind of approaches made in the Institute for their exploration.

The Director, Ashley Miles, together with Don Wilhelm — who later became Professor of Pathology in the University of New South Wales — re-established the department of experimental pathology as his own department. Miles had specialized in bacteriology and immunology after qualifying in medicine and in 1935 had been apointed to the Chair of Bacteriology at University Hospital Medical School. During the Second World War he was engaged also on research on wound infections. In 1944 he joined the staff of the National Institute for Medical Research at Mill Hill as deputy-director. There his interest shifted from the study of bacteria to the study of the tissue changes they induce in the body, especially those reputed to have a defensive value.

All animals, including man, live in an environment of microbes, some innocuous and others potentially infective, and are continually subject to the risk of the entry of microbes, by skin, respiratory or alimentary tracts. One of the important defences against infection is the reaction to the infecting microbe when it first lodges in the tissues. Unless this primary lodgement of microbes succeeds, no infection ensues. The characteristic local reaction to a primary lodgement is acute inflammation, which is characterized, in particular, by a leakiness of the small blood vessels. It is generally held that this increased permeability of the vessel walls contributes to antimicrobial defence, because it allows the exudation into the infected tissues of antimicrobial proteins of the blood plasma, which kill the invaders, and of blood white cells, the phagocytes, which first ingest and then digest the invaders.

Using the skin of the guinea-pig as the test tissue, Miles and his colleagues first established that the acute inflammatory reaction to the primary lodgement occurred in two phases; an immediate phase of increased vascular permeability, with a slight and transient exudation of plasma proteins and, after some hours, a phase of greater protein exudation and of migration of phagocytes from the blood. The increased vascular permeability of inflammation was then thought to be induced by histamine, a substance discovered by Henry Dale and George Barger in 1911, but it soon became evident from a study of microbial, as well as of thermal and other forms of non-microbial injury, that only the first phase was demonstrably mediated by histamine. The substances that mediated the second phase of permeability were unknown. An examination of blood proteins, however, revealed a new class of globulins, apparently enzymes, that increased permeability. They were present in an inactive but readily activable form in the blood of man and of a number of mammals and birds, and could perhaps be considered as examples of a general class of mediators operating in all acute inflammatory reactions.

It later became apparent that the permeability globulins resembled some globulins discovered in mammalian blood by Werle and colleagues in Germany, in an investigation of substances from blood and pancreas that lowered blood pressure. It is now clear that the globulin permeability factors are part of a system present in animal plasma whereby a number of precursors are activated in series, resulting in proteolytic enzymes that finally attack a serum protein to release small molecular substances known as kinins. It is the kinins which have the exceedingly potent action on blood pressure and vascular permeability. The permeability globulins arise early in this sequence of activation of the kinin system. Although the kinin system is now known to be activated in a number of natural inflammatory conditions in man and animal, its role as a general participant in inflammation is as yet far from established.

Besides these efforts to identify the mediators of the two permeability phases of inflammation, attempts were made to measure the defensive value of the two responses. The method adopted was to modify the responses by substances with a known action on the tissues or the animal as a whole. Local adrenalin, for example, constricts the blood vessels, thus shutting off the supply of blood to the part. In doing so, it increases the infectivity of bacteria injected into the same region from ten to a million times, depending upon the kind of microbe tested. Another substance, which inhibited anti-microbial substances of the blood and the capacity of phagocytes to migrate towards the infecting organism, also increased infectivity to this degree. Again, transient shock, in which there is partial collapse of the circulatory system of the skin and therefore a diminution of blood supply, allows the infecting bacteria a much better chance of getting a foothold and multiplying than they would have in perfectly healthy tissues. The interesting feature of the action of these and other modifiers, however, was that if they were used when the lodge-ment of bacteria was four or more hours old they had no effect on the subsequent course of infection. In other words, there was an early period in the primary lodgement when the local defences that had been disturbed by these modifiers had a decisive effect in determining whether the lodgement failed or succeeded. But whether it failed or succeeded, it was clear that a large proportion of the lodgement was killed during these first few decisive hours; and this occurred in spite of a very small exudation of the presumed microbi-cidal substances from the plasma and in the absence of emigration of any defensive leukocytes.

The resistance to the primary lodgement can be raised by specific immunization, though this is mainly effective only against the organism immunized against. The non-specific resistance of microbes to the primary lodgement of microbes can also be aug-mented by a variety of treatments, including antimicrobial drugs. Even the presence of an active infection in another part of the body will increase resistance to a new invasion. But except for anti-microbial drug therapy, none is sufficiently understood for exploita-tion in man. In time however it may be possible to exploit this augmentation in the prophylaxis and therapy of infection. In the meantime, the magnitude of the early kill and the speed with which the local decision occurs serve to emphasize the importance — sometimes the vital importance — of starting antibiotic and antitoxic therapy of an infection at the earliest possible moment.

The precise mechanism of this early kill of invaders remains to be determined; but the resistance to infection that it confers is largely independent of the kind of immunity induced by immunization with vaccines or antitoxins, for it is non-specific, and active against a wide variety of infective microbes.

The nucleus of the present department of microbiology is the Guinness-Lister Unit, established in 1953 through the generosity of Arthur Guinness Son and Company. Under the direction of Dr Bruce Stocker, this unit played a predominant role in the development of microbial genetics in the U.K. The study of heredity in higher animals established the concept of the gene as the unit in the chromosome that determines the possession of a given character in living organisms and which is itself reproduced so that the particular character is handed on to the progeny. Nevertheless, the study of bacteria and viruses has led to many further advances in this field.

Professor Joshua Lederberg and his student Norton Zinder, in the University of Wisconsin, devised an ingenious technique for transferring genes from one bacterium to another, a procedure they called 'transduction'. In this process, the donor bacterium is infected with a bacterial virus (a bacteriophage) which enters the bacterium, multiplies there and causes it to burst. About a hundred virus particles are liberated, and some of them contain fragments of the bacterial chromosome, that is, a number of the bacterial genes. When these virus particles are brought into contact with a genetically different recipient bacterium, they in turn enter it and the bacterial genes they are carrying may enter the recipient's chromosomes and endow its descendants with characters derived from the donor bacterium. Much of the work on transduction was carried out with species of *Salmonella*, a bacterial genus that includes the typhoid bacillus and other microbes causing enteric disease.

Before Bruce Stocker came to the Institute he was a guest in Lederberg's laboratory, where he suggested that the motility possessed by some salmonellas was a genetic character readily susceptible to direct observation. Most members of the Salmonella bacteria are equipped with one or more flagella, which are extremely thin appendages responsible for motility. Stocker and his hosts showed that the genetic character of motility could indeed be conferred by transduction. When phage was grown on a flagellated donor strain of Salmonella and used to infect non-flagellated organisms, some of the descendants produced flagella and were motile. The new character was retained in subsequent generations, which meant that the transferred gene was being reproduced in the recipient bacterium and transmitted to its offspring.

The inheritance of motility by salmonellas was studied by Stocker in the Guinness-Lister Unit with remarkable success. Amongst the Unit's discoveries was that of 'unilinear inheritance'. There was a suspicion that some bacteria made motile by transduction were not breeding true but were producing mainly non-motile descendants. The puzzle was unravelled by microscopic studies of the behaviour of individual motile cells, when each was allowed to produce a number of descendants. Sometimes the transduced gene for motility was not integrated into the chromosome of the recipient bacterium, but nevertheless persisted in the cell without being reproduced. As a consequence it could be transmitted to only one of the two daughter cells formed when the microbe divided. In all subsequent divisions only a single descendant then received the gene, rather like the heir to an entailed estate.

Another type of inheritance not under the control of chromosomal genes was encountered in a flagellated bacterium, whose offspring were themselves unable to make new flagella but inherited those of their parents. When such a bacterium divided into two, each of its daughter cells acquired about half the parental flagella, and the process was repeated at subsequent divisions until most of the progeny had no flagella and were therefore non-motile. A few cells carried one of the ancestral flagella each and were motile. From this point the inheritance was unilinear, the solitary flagellum being handed on to only one descendant in later generations, the rest being non-motile. This again resembles the inheritance of an entailed estate; but here, as Stocker put it, only one heir can go canoeing because he inherits a paddle, whereas in abortive transduction of motility, he inherits a factory for making paddles.

It was long believed that there was no process in bacteria entailing any fusion of cells or parts of cells, and therefore none of the exchange or redistribution of genes that characterizes sexual reproduction in other organisms. In 1948, however, Tatum and Lederberg discovered a kind of sexual process in the bacterium *Escherichia coli* by which one-way gene transfer occurred from the donor to the recipient during conjugation. Stocker's team found in Salmonella a similar type of hybridization also brought about by what appeared to be a transient pairing of bacteria. Some salmonella strains produce antibiotics named 'colicins' which kill certain types of colon bacillus.

This is because these strains carry a specialized group of genes named 'colicin factors'. These factors were known to be transmitted from donor to recipient, but a visitor in the Unit, Haruo Ozeki, discovered that the donor's chromosome proper was also transferred to the recipient. At least twenty minutes' contact was required. A character was thus transferred from the donor to the recipient and a hybrid produced by a new method, the application of which, soon after, led to the mapping of the whole of the Salmonella chromosome.

In 1963 a new professorial Chair was established in the Institute, the Guinness Chair of Microbiology, of which Stocker was the first holder. When he took up a post at Stanford University in 1965, he was succeeded by Guy Meynell and, at the same time, a department of microbiology was brought into being which included not only the Guinness Unit but other microbiologists of the Institute's staff.

Bacterial genetics together with work on the dynamics of microbial infection continued to be major departmental interests. Much of the genetic work concerned bacterial 'plasmids' of which the colicin factors were now seen to be but one example. By examining the way in which colicin factors were transferred, Meynell, in collaboration with Alan Lawn of the department of electron microscopy, identified a new type of bacterial appendage (a 'sex pilus') involved in conjugation. These sex pili subsequently proved to be of great value in classifying various bacterial plasmids, including those responsible for the present-day resistance, to antibiotics and other antibacterial drugs, of many bacteria that cause intestinal infections.

Bacterial and bacteriophage genetics have proved to be a powerful tool for the analysis of many bacteriological problems. Perhaps one of these unexpected applications has been that certain combinations of phages enabled Meynell and his colleagues to measure how fast bacteria divide inside infected animals. Formerly, the difficulty was that only the net result of bacterial division and of killing by the host defences had been measurable. But the new method measured divisions alone and established that *Salmonella typhimurium*, an important intestinal pathogen in man, divided only every twelve hours in mice compared to every thirty minutes in broth.

This account of some of the advances in bacterial genetics made in the Guinness-Lister Unit does scant justice to the ingenuity and the labour with which this knowledge has been acquired. One index is the stock collection of the Unit, which now possesses more than 2,000

8

bacterial mutants, each distinguished by a particular combination of genes and characters; these include motility, the capacity to produce colicins or a particular antigen, susceptibility to one or another of different types of the bacteriophages which attack them, and resistance to particular antibiotics. Bacteria such as these are the raw material for every kind of genetic and physiological investigation.

Current research within the department continues to be concerned with a wide range of material, extending from pure bacterial genetics, morphological studies of sex pili, the growth of bacteriophage and the synthesis of colicins by bacteria, to the immunochemistry of *Mycoplasma*.

Physiologists, biochemists and biophysicists as well as bacteriologists are interested in the structure of cells and its relation to function. The cells making up the tissues of animals are separated from each other by an envelope or membrane, and they contain some distinct structures, such as the nucleus containing the genetic material, and other smaller bodies called mitochondria. When the cells are disrupted by grinding or by freezing and thawing, these small bodies may retain their structure and, being different from each other in size and shape, can be separated by differential contrifuging.

In this way much knowledge has been gained of the chemical composition and biochemical activities of the mitochondria and other parts of the cell. In the biochemical department, investigations of this kind were begun by Marjorie Macfarlane in 1948; later, when she was joined in 1954 by G. M. Gray, they made extensive studies of the fatty components of animal and bacterial cells, in the course of which a number of new fatty substances containing phosphorus or sugars were isolated and identified. Gray and his colleagues are now examining the membranes which contain these phospholipids and glycolipids, and other lipo-protein structures, for these membranes regulate the permeability of cells, and are therefore of great importance in regulating their activities.

In any attempts however to correlate structure with function, the old adage 'seeing is believing' is very pertinent. The minute internal structures of animal cells and of bacteria are below the limits of visibility of the ordinary light microscope. In 1964 the Institute received a generous grant of £35,000 from the Trustees of the Fleming Memorial Fund for Medical Research. This enabled it to instal a Phillips EM200 Electron Microscope, in a suite of rooms at Chelsea specially converted for the purpose. Dr A. M. Lawn, a physiologist at the Royal Veterinary College, was appointed to take charge of the Electron Microscopy Unit, which forms a most valuable addition to the resources of the Institute. Dr Lawn himself is investigating changes in the ultramicroscopic structure of the mouse uterus during early ovo-implantation, and other physiological studies. He has also undertaken for his colleagues in other departments a diversity of enquiries which range from the pili of bacteria to the attempted visualization of a giant molecule, the alpha-macroglobulin of human plasma.

The structure of macromolecules and of the way in which they are built up in the living organism can also be explored by enzymic studies, such as those made by W. J. Whelan and his team in the biochemistry department on the biosynthesis of starch and glycogen. Whelan graduated from the famous carbohydrate school at the University of Birmingham under W. N. Haworth and later colla- borated with Professor Stanley Peat at Bangor in studies of the breakdown of starch, the giant molecule that constitutes the plants' major store of carbohydrate food. He joined the staff of the Lister Institute in 1956, and first investigated two types of enzymes con- cerned in the metabolism of starch. One type was the amylases that break starch down into smaller units; the other was an enzyme in the potato called a transferase, which rearranges the position of the glucose units in the starch molecule.

This work led Whelan and his team to a close study of glycogen, the animal counterpart of starch, which is stored in liver and muscle. The enzyme transferase was found in muscle, where it plays an important part in the breakdown of glycogen to glucose. It is now known that a certain human disease in which glycogen breakdown is impaired is due to the lack of this enzyme. A detailed study of the complex array of amylases and of the enzymes called glucosidases in muscle was made. One of them, an alpha-glucosidase, is of particular interest to clinicians, for its absence from heart muscle results in the death within a few months of any child born with a congenital absence of the enzyme. Studies such as those of Whelan are impor- tant for the understanding of congenital disorders in carbohydrate metabolism, for knowing the precise nature of the biochemical defect is the first step towards its cure or amelioration.

Whelan resigned from the Institute staff in 1964 to become

Professor of Biochemistry at the Royal Free Hospital Medical School.

The seventy-fifth anniversary of the foundation of the Lister Institute was celebrated on Wednesday, November 9, 1966. It was a day of historical and scientific exhibits, made for a distinguished gathering of guests, scientific and other, from overseas and the United Kingdom; and of a public anniversary lecture given by Lord Florey, O.M., at the Royal College of Physicians. Among the messages from leading research centres in Europe and North America, it was gratifying to receive congratulations, not only from the Institut Pasteur in Paris, whose existence had stimulated the founders of the Lister Institute in 1891, but from the Robert Koch Institut in Berlin and the Gamaleya Institute of Epidemiology and Microbiology in Moscow; both these sister institutes, like the Lister, reached a flourishing age of seventy-five in 1966.

Since its foundation, the Institute has had the support of many distinguished men who have given their services on the Governing Body and on the Council. The first three Chairmen of the Governing Body, Lord Lister, Sir Henry Roscoe and Sir David Bruce, had been concerned in its foundation. Bruce was succeeded by William Bulloch. In 1942 Sir Henry Dale took office as Chairman and nineteen years later, Sir Charles Dodds began a nine years' term of service. He was succeeded in 1968 by Sir Lindor Brown. Sir Hugh Beaver held office as Treasurer from 1958 until 1966, when he was succeeded by Mr Paul Channon.

The Governing Body has the formidable task of deciding broadly on the scientific and production policy of the Institute and of reconciling this policy with the funds available. In taking this responsibility, the chairmen and the varying members of the Governing Body — bankers and businessmen, administrators and scientists — have given unstintedly not only time for deliberations, but active help in arranging the Institute's affairs. The Institute has particular reason to be grateful for their success in obtaining financial support for its activities.

The authors have told the story of the founding of the Lister Institute of Preventive Medicine, and of the problems and personalities of those early days and the succeeding years, and of some of its contributions to medical research in Great Britain. The rest is to be found in its scientific contributions over the last seventy-five years, and in the long roll of distinguished scientists who spent some part of their lives in the laboratories at Chelsea and Elstree. The history tells only a little about the administrative and technical staff. Many of these have been outstanding and often racy characters and the Institute owes much to them all.

In these years, the Lister Institute has achieved international distinction in a wide variety of scientific activities and as a post-graduate school of the University of London. In essence it has always been a collection of individualists, with their quirks and different approaches to research, under a direction flexible enough for research to be chosen *ad hominem* and new adventures welcomed. The balance of different disciplines is rewarding in providing opportunities for fruitful collaboration in ideas and methods.

Since 1900 the Institute has maintained itself as a private research organization on income from endowments and from the sale of vaccines and antisera. In this sense, like its great exemplar the Pasteur Institute, it is a survival from the past, when such an arrangement was common, though it has survived with increasing difficulty in the last decade, as developing countries began producing on their own, and as competition became increasingly keen at home and abroad. The Institute is justifiably proud of its achievements for British science, and of remaining in existence as a corporate body through its own financial efforts. It receives public money from research councils and other government bodies for specified pieces of research work; but it receives none as a school of the University of London, because its teaching is informal and restricted to post-graduate students and those, mainly from overseas, being trained in the production of antisera and vaccines. It has however benefited greatly by the generosity of private persons and charitable foundations.

The Lister Institute was once unique in this country, but establishments set up since that time have evolved a very similar pattern of work. It differs however from most in its independence and in the degree to which it combines research and technology. These are differences which are strongly believed to be worth preserving.

The Institute has achieved much as a small establishment; but with the increasing complexity of medical research it must continually provide for new skills, new instruments, even new disciplines. Building has begun at both Elstree and Chelsea for this purpose. At

Chelsea, a new wing on the old studio site will house, among other things, a department of experimental immunology. The Wolfson Foundation, the most recent of many generous benefactors, has given £300,000 towards this wing; it will contain a lecture theatre which is a gift from one of the Institute's earliest benefactors, the Grocers' Company.

It would be presumptuous further to forecast the future of the Lister Institute, in view of its tradition of going where the ideas of its scientists lead. Given the financial means of survival, its course will be constrained only by the founders' directive 'to study, investigate, discover and improve the means of preventing and curing disease of man and animals'.

Appendix

Appendix

CHAIRMEN OF THE GOVERNING BODY

1898–1903	Rt. Hon. Lord Lister, P.C., O.M., F.R.S. (President 1904–1911)
1904–1912	Rt. Hon. Sir Henry E. Roscoe, P.C., D.C.L., F.R.S.
1913–1914	Sir John Rose Bradford, K.C.M.G., M.D., F.R.S.
1915	Rt. Hon. Sir Henry E. Roscoe, P.C., D.C.L., F.R.S.
1915–1931	Gen. Sir David Bruce, A.M.S., C.B., D.Sc., LL.D., F.R.S.
1932–1940	Professor William Bulloch, M.D., LL.D., F.R.S.
1941–1942	Rt. Hon. Lord Moyne, P.C., D.S.O.
1942–1961	Sir Henry H. Dale, O.M., G.B.E., M.D., F.R.C.P., F.R.S.
1961–1968	Sir Charles Dodds, M.V.O., M.D., D.Sc., F.R.C.P., F.R.S.
1968–1970	Sir Lindor Brown, C.B.E., F.R.C.P., F.R.S.
1970–	Professor Albert Neuberger, M.D., F.R.C.P., F.R.S.

DIRECTORS

1893–1896	Sir Marc Armand Ruffer, M.A., M.D.
1896–1903	Allen MacFadyen, M.D., B.Sc.
1903–1930	Professor Sir Charles J. Martin, C.M.G., M.B., D.Sc., F.R.S.
1931–1942	Professor Sir John C. G. Ledingham, C.M.G., M.B., D.Sc., LL.B., F.R.S.
1943–1952	Sir Alan N. Drury, C.B.E., M.A., M.D., F.R.C.P., F.R.S.
1952–	Professor Sir A. Ashley Miles, C.B.E., M.D., F.C.Path., F.R.C.P., F.R.S.

The following is a list of scientists and administrative staff who worked at the Lister Institute between 1898 and 1966, for periods ranging from a few weeks to many years. It has been compiled from records which, especially in the earlier years, were not always complete; we hope that errors of commission and omission are few.

The countries cited indicate only the provenance of visitors, and not necessarily their nationality. We have also noted those who at some period in their career became Nobel Laureates and Fellows of the Royal Society. The asterisk indicates workers directly supported by the Medical Research Council.

8*

Y. B. Abdoosh (Egypt) 1936
M. Abdullah (Pakistan) 1957–63
E. P. Adams 1965–
Jean Addey 1951–54
N. Ahad (Burma) 1955
R. T. Ahmed (Egypt) 1966
A. W. Alcock, F.R.S. 1907–08
R. A. Alexander (South Africa) 1931
Joan Allen 1960–63
P. Z. Allen (U.S.A.) 1959–60
C. R. Amies 1932–45
D. Aminoff (Israel) 1947–50, 1955
A. J. Anderson 1909
L. P. Andral (Ethiopia) 1959
C. T. Andrew 1909
F. W. Andrewes, F.R.S. 1917
S. Andrews 1925
E. F. Annison 1948–51
F. N. Appleyard 1928
C. L. Arcus 1939–42
R. Arevalo (San Salvador) 1957
J. A. Arkwright, F.R.S. 1906–44
H. W. Armit 1905–13
W. D. Armstrong (U.S.A.) 1939
H. R. F. Arnstein* 1949–51
L. Aschoff 1902
Elizabeth Asheshov 1954–58
I. N. Asheshov* 1954–59
T. Ashiotis (Cyprus) 1965
W. P. Aston 1966–
E. E. Atkin 1912–26
E. L. Atkinson 1910
W. R. Aykroyd 1929–32
Laura Ayres (Portugal) 1961

J. S. D. Bacon* 1941–43
A. W. Bacot 1911–22
J. Baddiley, F.R.S. 1950–54
H. Bad el Din (Egypt) 1959
A. G. Bagshaw 1909
W. R. Bailey (U.S.A.) 1964
F. A. Bainbridge, F.R.S. 1908–11
Mrs K. M. Balfour 1924–26, 1930–31
Betty Balfour* 1948
J. G. Balteanu (Roumania) 1925–27
M. P. Banks 1961–
G. Barger, F.R.S.* 1917–18
J. E. Barnard, F.R.S. 1898–1904
Rosamund (Pilgrim) Barnes* 1918–19, 1938–47
Jean Barnett 1936–37
J. O. W. Barratt 1902–16, 1920–42
Mary Barratt 1914–15
Dr Barton 1900
E. F. Bashford 1920
C. Basile 1922
P. C. Basu (India) 1964
H. R. Bateman 1908–09
Marion Battie 1929
H. Bayon 1907–8, 1912–13
Anne Beattie 1963–64
Margaret Beech 1956
S. P. Bedson, F.R.S. 1914–17, 1921–26
Capt. Bell 1917
F. Bergel, F.R.S. 1937–39
Helen Bernstein 1956–58
Doreen Bertinshaw* 1949
A. C. Bescoby 1921
S. S. Bhatnagar, F.R.S. (Pakistan) 1934–36

B. J. Bines 1959–62
Catherine Bingham (U.S.A.) 1963
G. G. Birch 1961
G. W. G. Bird (India) 1957–58
Janet Bishop 1954–55
J. B. Blaikie 1901
R. G. Blaker (U.S.A.) 1959
Margaret Blewett 1952
W. A. Blyth 1956–
Stina Bobeck (Sweden) 1959
D. R. Body (New Zealand) 1965–66
Birgitte Bohn (Denmark) 1959
T. J. Bokenham 1900
P. F. L. Boreham 1965
W. C. Bosanquet 1909–14
Barbara Boughton* 1948–49
A. E. Boycott, F.R.S. 1905–07
J. E. M. Boyd 1920
E. Boyland 1928–31
F. Bozok (Turkey) 1955–56
Mary Bracewell* 1929–31
W. L. Braddon 1913–14
J. Rose Bradford, F.R.S. 1920
C. J. B. Bradish 1944–48
C. H. B. Bradley 1908–10
Dr Brickdale 1902–03
Ann Brimacombe 1960–62
Caroline Bronne 1966
R. St. John Brooks* 1911–46
Inna Brovsin 1936
A. H. Brown 1924–25
Janet Brown 1928
J. W. Brown 1912
M. Ord Brown 1911
Lucy Bryce (Australia) 1926
Dorothy Buchanan (U.S.A.) 1954–55
J. G. Buchanan 1953–55
Emma Buckley (Australia) 1916
Wendy Bull 1966
R. C. Burbank 1938–42
Maisie Burbury 1922, 1925
J. F. Burke (U.S.A.) 1955–57
F. M. Burnet, F.R.S., Nobel Laureate 1926–28

T. Camera (Guinea) 1963
Dr Campbell (Canada) 1928
Janet Campbell 1957–58
Mabel Campbell 1920
J. Cann 1965
A. J. Canny 1929–30
Dorothy Card 1951–57
H. R. Carne (Australia) 1934–35
J. G. Carr 1938–40
Marjorie Carr* 1922–26
E. A. Caspary 1951–58
A. Castellani 1902, 1909, 1913
E. P. Cathcart, F.R.S. 1904–05
Dorothy Cayley 1918
D. S. Chandrasekhar (India) 1960
M. Chasmi (Iran) 1956
Harriette Chick 1905–45
H. Chojnowski (Poland) 1959
S. R. Christophers, F.R.S. 1913
B. Cinader 1945–56
A. Ciuca (Roumania) 1927–29
M. J. Clancy 1958–60
B. Clapham 1943
A. Clarke (Lebanon) 1963

Jane Clausen 1949–52
S. Cmelik (Yugoslavia) 1957
J. Cohen 1942
Anne Cole 1942
L. H. Collier 1948–
Dorothy Collison 1929–30
D. Combiesco (Roumania) 1925
S. J. B. Connell* 1924
Kathleen Cook 1952–55
P. T. L. Cook 1962
E. A. Cooper 1910–15
G. Cooper 1912
G. N. Cooper 1898–1931
Dr Cope 1910
S. Monckton Copeman, F.R.S. 1900, 1902–03
M. Coplans 1914
Alice Copping 1929–30, 1932–49
R. F. Cordova, 1915–17
Capt. Corfield 1916
J. T. Cornelius (India) 1926–29
Dr Cossery (Egypt)
R. Côté 1955–58
R. A. Coulson 1943–44
S. T. Cowan 1947
Miss Crabtree 1935
J. P. Craig (U.S.A.) 1959
J. A. Cranston 1931
J. Anderson Craw 1904–05
Margaret Crawford 1929–34
J. M. Creeth 1961–
W. C. Crimmin 1956–57
Clarice Crocker (South Africa) 1955
J. Crookston (Canada) 1956
J. W. Cropper 1912–16
Patricia Crowe 1948–49
M. J. Crumpton 1951–53
S. L. Cummins 1914
H. Cumpston 1907–08
J. D. Cunningham 1910–13
A. C. Cunliffe 1957
Miss Curwen 1909
Margery Cutting 1942–43
Mme J. Czarkowska-Gladney (Poland) 1931–1932
Nina Czeczowiczka 1953–54

H. D. Dakin, F.R.S. 1902–06
H. H. Dale, F.R.S., Nobel Laureate* 1917–18
Elsie Dalyell (Australia) 1914–22
O. C. C. Damant 1907–09
S. Danish (Egypt) 1962
A. T. Dann 1935–37
J. H. Darbyshire 1959
Naomi Datta 1951–52
C. G. Daubney 1926–29
Alice Davey 1918–19
H. David (Sweden) 1921
S. Davidovici (Israel) 1956
Mr Davies 1911–12
D. A. L. Davies 1950–53
Mary Dawbarn (Australia) 1933
G. Dean 1898–1908
H. R. Dean 1910–12
Marion Delf 1917–19
J. P. Dempster 1957
Marjorie Dennison 1929–37
D. Denny-Brown 1934
M. Derechin (Argentina) 1958–60

Sara Derechin (Argentina) 1958
S. Dharmaraka (Thailand) 1955
Miss Dixon 1922
Barbara Dod 1965–
H. Dogal (Turkey) 1965
D. E. Dolby 1939–40, 1951–
Jean Dolby* 1958–
A. S. R. Donald* 1965–
Joy Donegani* 1949
Miss Dorman 1920
S. R. Douglas, F.R.S. 1905–06
E. Downing 1935–38
D. Doyle 1960
W. T. Drabble 1964–65
A. N. Drury, F.R.S. 1943–52
J. M. Dubert (France) 1955–56
S. Dubiski (Poland) 1959
Eugenie Dubnau (U.S.A.) 1962–63
J. P. Duguid 1959
H. L. Duke 1910, 1920
J. S. Dunkerley 1910–12
J. Dunstone (Australia) 1963
E. S. Duthie 1946–48

G. H. Eagles* 1926–47
N. D. Easterbrook 1957
Janice Edgar 1958–59
A. Edwards 1958
J. T. Edwards 1930–33
Susan Edwards 1966–
L. G. Egyud 1960–63
J. M. Elder (Canada) 1955–56
Dr Elders 1911
Margaret Eldridge 1937
P. Ellinger (Germany) 1934–52
D. Ellis 1966–
L. A. Elson 1933–34
Alexandra Emanuelowa 1946–49
Dagny Erikson* 1934–35
A. H. Esterabady (Iran) 1962
P. R. Evans 1938
Shirley Evans 1952–66
R. J. Ewart 1913–15
J. W. H. Eyre 1906–07

M. Fagerhol (Norway) 1965
R. W. Fairbrother 1928–30
H. Fairley (Australia) 1920
G. Favilli (Italy) 1934–35
H. Feier (Germany) 1958
Dr Fein (U.S.S.R.) 1909
J. G. Feinberg (U.S.A.) 1947–54
A. Felix, F.R.S. 1929–46, 1954–55
Honor Fell, F.R.S. 1929–33
E. H. Fenwick 1921–22
C. Ferreora Crespo (Portugal) 1964
Miss Field 1917
P. Fildes, F.R.S.* 1947–49
M. H. Finkelstein 1933–34
M. H. Finlayson 1935
E. H. Fischer (U.S.A.) 1963
J. L. Fitton 1957
Margaret (Boas) Fixsen 1922–31
Fernie Fletcher 1913–19
J. Fonseca da Cunha (Brazil) 1959
T. M. Fortescue-Brickdale 1902–03
A. G. R. Foulerton 1898
F. K. Fox 1922–59

Dr Foy 1911
Elizabeth Fraser * 1960–65
F. R. Fraser 1924
Mavis Freeman (Australia) 1935–36
D. French (U.S.A.) 1962
A. A. Frohlich* 1959–60
W. B. Fry 1909
C. Funk 1911–14
G. Furness* 1960–62
K. Furuhjelm (Finland) 1965

Y.E.S. Gabr (Egypt) 1951–54
Mary Gaffikin 1930–33
J. S. Gale 1957
Jennifer Gallai-Hatchard 1964–
M. Garay 1956–60
Doris Gardiner 1918
June Gavin* 1961–
P. Gemski (U.S.A.) 1965
Eva Gerhard (Austria) 1938
Mlle M. M. Gex (France) 1959
J. Gheorghin (Roumania) 1926
Marian Gibbons 1953–54
R. A. Gibbons 1950–54
Patricia Gibson 1957
E. S. Gilbert 1908
Carolyn Giles* 1956–
W. A. Gillespie 1939
Lillis (MacGregor) Gillies 1958–59
G. P. Gladstone* 1947–48
Gertrude Glock 1943
T. H. Gloster 1910–11, 1920
Philomena Glover 1958
K. Goadby 1917
D. G. Godfrey 1966–
Noreen Goggin 1966–
M. A. Gohar (Egypt) 1929, 1932
Vidya Gokhale 1966
H. Goldblatt 1922–24
K. L. G. Goldsmith* 1960–
I. J. Goldsteine (U.S.A.) 1960
Dr Golliveri (India) 1924
Sheila Gompertz 1962–64
H. W. Goodwin 1924
R. M. Gordon 1928
P. A. Gorer, F.R.S. 1935–41
S. Govindarajan (India) 1957
A. N. Goyle (India) 1923–25
Doris Graetz 1931–32
Jean Graff* 1953–55
Doris Graham* 1960–65
N. C. Graham 1930
G. A. Grant (Canada) 1934–36, 1938
Nicolle Grasset (France) 1961
J. P. G. Gratia (Belgium) 1961
L. Gravel (Canada) 1938
Dr Gray 1913
A. R. Gray (Nigeria) 1959, 1960, 1963
G. M. A. Gray 1955–
A. B. Green 1904–35
M. Greenwood 1909–20
E. C. Grey 1913–14
F. Griffiths 1911
Ewa Grochowska (Poland) 1966
Mr Groom 1910
Anna Grove-White* 1950
R. Grubb (Sweden) 1949–50
J. M. Gulland, F.R.S. 1931–35

Z. Gunja-Smith 1960, 1962–63, 1965–66
S. Guptarak (Thailand) 1959
M. Gutstein (Germany) 1935–38
K. K. Gyi (Burma) 1964

E. Hackel (U.S.A.)* 1957–58
H. D. Hacker (Fed. Malay States) 1921
J. S. Haldane, F.R.S. 1907–9, 1919
C. W. Hale 1941, 1944
Kathleen Hall 1936–44
H. Hamer (Canada) 1961
A. E. Hamerton 1908–09
G. Hamoir (Belgium) 1949
Y. Hamon (France) 1957
Florence Hamper* 1960–62
R. E. Handschumacher (U.S.A.) 1954–55
F. S. Hansman 1924–25
S. Haq (Pakistan) 1956–58
A. Harden, F.R.S., Nobel Laureate 1898–1930
V. J. Harding 1912
Dorothy Hare 1937
T. Hare 1928–29
G. J. Harrap 1963–66
Gillian Harris 1950–52
P. Hartley, F.R.S. 1907, 1913–19, 1950–53
P. E. Hartman (U.S.A.) 1963
A. W. M. Harvey 1914–15, 1921
M. A. Haseeb (Sudan) 1959
F. Hassan (Egypt) 1964
M. A. Hassanein (Egypt) 1928–30
S. Hata 1921
G. B. Hay 1965–
Noreen Haysom* 1948–50
O. W. Heal 1957
S. G. Hedin 1901–05
F. Hemmi 1922
Hilda Hempl 1917
F. Henaff (France) 1956
D. W. Henderson F.R.S. 1932–39, 1940–44
  (Ministry of Supply), 1946
J. M. Hendersson (India) 1930
F. R. Henley 1915, 1920–30
Capt. Henry 1918
D. Herbert* 1947–49
R. T. Hewlett 1898–1901
Ruth van Heyningen 1943–44
O. Hildesheim 1903–04
K. J. Himmelspach (Germany) 1962
H. G. Hind* 1939–41
Miss Hindmarsh (Australia) 1924
A. S. Hirst 1914
L. F. Hirst (Ceylon) 1933
R. Hodges 1954–55
Dorothy Hoffert 1925–26
Margaret Holden 1943–44
Kathleen Hole 1912–14
Helene Holt* 1949–51
J C. Holt 1966–
Annie Homer 1913–21
C. Hong Min (Southern Korea) 1959
F. L. Hopwood 1940
J. H. Horne 1926–28
A. A. Horner 1958–59
E. C. Hort 1911–17
Jean Horton 1952–57
A. C. Houston, F.R.S. 1905
G. A. Howard* 1947–48
Sheila Howarth 1959–60

E. Hoyle* 1928–30
Dr Hucker (U.S.A.) 1928
C. B. Huggins (U.S.A.) 1931
R. C. Hughes 1958–59
Mrs S. Hughes 1936–37
Margaret Hume* 1916–1961
J. H. Humphrey, F.R.S. 1941–42
F. E. Humphreys* 1929–31
Frances Hunter 1966–
E. Weston Hurst 1929–33, 1934–36
M. Huseini (Egypt) 1931
J. C. D. Hutchinson 1933–35

H. M. Ibrahim (Egypt) 1928
Elizabeth Ikin* 1948–60
Major Inglis 1920
W. W. Ingram 1914–15
C. Ionescu-Mihaesti (Roumania) 1925
S. Iseki (Japan) 1957

Hester Jackson 1931–33
Anni Jacob (Germany) 1938–39
Helga Jahn (Germany) 1939–40
P. K. Jain (India) 1965
A. T. James 1948–50
P. V. James* 1947–48
S. P. James, F.R.S. 1907
G. A. Jamieson 1953–55
F. Janssens (Belgium) 1910
Barbara Jaroszynska-Weinberger (Poland) 1966
Rosamund Jefferis* 1948
Mary Jennens* 1948–49
Louis Jenner 1898–1903
E. Jennings 1913
C. M. Jephcott (Canada) 1932–33
A. J. Jex-Blake 1908–09
O. Jøgensen (Denmark) 1959
Z. E. Jolles (Italy) 1939–41
J. L. Jona 1913–14
D. Jones 1958
G. Jones 1957
J. M. Jones 1966–
Margaret Jones 1946
R. O. Jones 1933–35
S. W. Johnson* 1930, 1941–48
Mary Johnston 1923–25
Ruth Jordan* 1948
Yvonne Joyeux (France) 1962
J. M. Joys 1958–60
N. Julga (Turkey) 1957

M. M. A. Kader (Egypt) 1946–49
S. Kakehi 1915–16
D. Kalic 1927
S. Kanai (Japan) 1921–22
C. Kaplan 1954–66
J. Karrs-Sypesteyn (Netherlands) 1965
H. Katagiri (Japan) 1925–27
F. Kauffman (Denmark) 1948
Dr Kaul (India) 1931
D. Kay* 1948
H. D. Kay, F.R.S. 1922–24
R. A. Kekwick, F.R.S. 1938–
Marianne Kelemen 1964
A. M. Kellas 1919
C. H. Kellaway, F.R.S. 1920
Mary Kelleher 1951–52
A. E. Kellie 1934–39

E. L. Kennaway, F.R.S. 1908–09
Shirley Kent 1950
J. Keppie 1941–47
D. Kerridge 1957–59
Z. Khaled (Egypt) 1921, 1923–24
D. H. King 1941–42
E. J. King (Canada) 1929
H. K. King 1941–43
Mr Kirkpatrick 1912
R. G. Kirton 1898–99
Emmy Klieneberger-Nobel 1934–62
Dr Knight 1898
B. C. J. G. Knight 1939–43
C. G. Knight 1963–65
Ellen Knight 1932–40
E. F. Knight 1925
F. Knight 1954
Harriet Knight 1924
K. Knox (Australia) 1952–54
C. A. Kofoid (U.S.A.) 1910
W. Köhler (Germany) 1958
Alice Kohn-Speyer 1926–30, 1933–34
A. H. Kordi (Egypt) 1932
V. Korenchevsky* 1920–44
A. E. Kortekangas (Finland) 1960
E. J. Koscielak (Poland) 1961
Marjorie Krauss (U.S.A.) 1956
K. S. Krikorian (Israel) 1923
A. E. Kulkarni (India) 1962
K. U. Kulkarni (India) 1960
Dr Kumagava (Japan) 1910
P. Kumar (India) 1965
N. B. Kuppurajan (India) 1961

C. H. Lack 1946–48
L. Lack 1898–1902
G. Lamb 1910
Lisa (Lorenz) Lamb 1948–55
A. Lambrechts (Belgium) 1937
W. F. Lanchester 1910, 1912–14
W. Landauer (U.S.A.) 1933–34
Janet Lane-Claypon 1908–12
Sheila Lanham 1956–
E. R. Lankester, F.R.S. 1910
G. Lapage 1913–14
V. Lapiccirella (Italy) 1932
M. Laskowski (Poland) 1936–38
A. Latham 1900
H. Laurell (Sweden) 1945–46
N. Laurie 1932–33
Elisabeth Lavington 1933
Kathleen Law (Australia) 1935–36
Sylvia Lawler* 1947–49
A. M. Lawn 1966–
A. Lawson 1898–99
Valerie Lawton 1955–57
C. Leaf 1902–03
J. B. Leathes, F.R.S. 1901–08
K. Lebech (Sweden) 1958
J. C. G. Ledingham, F.R.S. 1906–43
E. Y. C. Lee 1963–64
Frances Lee-Jones 1955–61
Joan Leigh-Clare* 1926–28
Ruth Lemcke 1959–
P. E. Lemoine (Belgium) 1962
A. Lennerstrand (Sweden) 1939
Margit Lennerstrand (Sweden) 1939
Susan Leong (Hong Kong) 1966

Elizabeth Lepper 1920–30
J. T. W. Leslie 1909
J. Lewin (France) 1965
M. J. Lewis 1964
P. Lhoas (Belgium) 1961
E. G. T. Liddell, F.R.S. 1918
T. Lino (Japan) 1959
K. B. Linton 1953–54
L. Linzell 1920
I. A. F. Lister-Cheese 1958–60
W. G. Liston 1910–11, 1920
Marjorie Little 1920
Blodwen Lloyd 1931
E. J. H. Lloyd 1961–
Olive Lodge 1915–18
F. Lopez Bueno (Spain) 1964–65
Z. Lorkiewicz (Poland) 1958–59
Eileen Lovett 1966
Miss Lowe* 1922
Eva Lubrzynska 1913–14
N. S. Lucas 1925–36
Ethel Luce* 1921–24
T. Lumsden 1922–29, 1934–37
A. Lundsgaard (Denmark) 1965
R. W. S. Lyons 1905
Katharine (Tansley) Lythgoe 1934–35
J. W. Lyttleton 1948–51

G. H. K. Macalister 1910–12
A. B. Macallum, F.R.S. 1913–15
Rachel McAnally 1934–37
R. McCanison 1910
E. F. McCarthy 1944–49
P. B. McCay (U.S.A.) 1961, 1962
D. McClean 1927–61
Alfred MacConkey 1902–26
J. F. McCrea (Australia) 1949–51
E. A. McCulloch (Canada)* 1949
H. D. McCulloch 1908
J. McCunn 1927
M. W. McDonough 1959–65
E. I. McDougall 1943
Allan Macfadyen 1898–1906
A. S. McFarlane 1935–44
Marjorie Macfarlane 1927–64
W. S. McGillivray 1924–25
Helen Mackay 1920–22
M. D. McKay 1909
Margaret Mackay* 1943–
D. F. Mackenzie 1911
A. McKenzie 1901–02
P. L. McKinlay 1930
R. R. McLaughlin 1930–31, 1934
H. Maclean 1910–13
Ida (Smedley) Maclean 1910–43
Mary Maclean 1930–32
A. P. MacLennan 1951–54
L. D. Macleod 1936–38
Morna MacLeod 1929–31
J. V. McLoughlin 1954–57
Marion MacOwan 1932
T. F. Macrae 1932–46
J. L. Madinaveitia 1938–39
T. P. Magill (U.S.A.) 1959
N. Mahony 1965–66
W. Mair 1914–16
H. B. Maitland 1925–27
Mary (Cowan) Maitland 1921–24, 1928–29

P. H. Mäkelä (Finland) 1963–64
M. Malkani (India) 1929–30
M. H. Malkinson 1966
R. J. Manning 1925
W. H. Manwaring 1910–11
S. S. Marennikova (U.S.S.R.) 1962
Helene de Margerie (France) 1956–59
G. V. Marinetti (U.S.A.) 1966
Ann Marr 1966
W. E. Marshall 1906–07
A. J. P. Martin, F.R.S., Nobel Laureate* 1949
C. H. Martin 1912
C. J. Martin, F.R.S. 1903–30, 1943
M. Martin 1922
N. Martin 1948–49
N. H. Martin 1951–
I. F. G. Martinez 1912–14
Marjorie Martland 1922–29
J. Mas (Spain) 1960
Brenda Mason 1958–
F. Massari (Egypt) 1950–52
P. Mathews 1959
A. P. Mathias 1951–54
J. Matsui 1915–16
T. Matsumoto (Formosa) 1928
P. Mattern (Senegal) 1965
Joan Mattingly 1955
Miss M. Maughan 1925–26
B. Maupin (France) 1956
A. Mavrogordato 1907–10
W. d'A. Maycock 1946
T. H. Mead 1932–35
P. D. Meers 1960
E. Megrail (U.S.A.) 1927
B. Melen (Sweden) 1955
K. Meyer (France) 1935–36
G. G. Meynell 1960–
J. G. Michael (U.S.A.) 1965
Miss Michaelis 1913
F. W. Michel (U.S.A.) 1963
Miss D. Mickerts (Austria) 1965
L. R. Micklem 1958
A. A. Miles, F.R.S. 1952–
P. J. Mill 1954–57
Delphine Miller 1966
J. K. Miller 1962–64
J. A. Mills 1960
E. A. Minchin, F.R.S. 1906–15
D. T. Mitchell (S. Africa) 1923
M. Miura 1921–22
B. M. Mizen (Turkey) 1963
G. Modiano (Italy) 1959–60, 1960–61
Dr Mohammed (Egypt) 1925–26
J. Mohn (U.S.A.) 1958
E. H. Molesworth 1910
J. F. Moloney* 1963
A. Moore 1900–02
P. T. Moore 1946
Phyllis Moores* 1956–57
J. Moor-Jankowski (U.S.A.) 1959, 1962
H. de R. Morgan 1902–15
K. Morgan 1962
W. T. J. Morgan, F.R.S. 1926–66
C. J. O. R. Morris 1933–36
G. H. Morris 1899–1900
L. Morris 1924
Capt. Morrison 1914
W. Mosimann (Switzerland) 1949–50

Appendix   237

A. E. Mourant, F.R.S.* 1947–65
Anna Muhlenbach 1910–11
B. M. Mukherji (India) 1963
H. G. S. Murray 1961–

D. N. Nabarro 1911
H. Naganishi (Japan) 1924–26
M. Naidoff (U.S.A.) 1963
B. P. B. Naidu 1922
K. Nain (India) 1923–25
Margaret Nance (Australia)* 1949–53
R. Narayanan* 1964
Dr Nasution (Java) 1959
A. Natarajan (India) 1961
M. J. Naumovic (Yugoslavia) 1957
H. Neimark (U.S.A.) 1964
A. Neuberger, F.R.S.* 1941–42
M. Neustat (U.S.S.R.) 1934
J. Newsome 1966
R. W. Nichol 1954
W. Nicoll 1910–12
N. Nielson 1937
S. B. Nilsson (Sweden) 1965
Y. S. Nimbkar (India) 1960
Janet Niven 1932
Jean Noades* 1958–66
L. Noon 1906, 1908
Dorothy Norris 1911–15, 1921
R. V. Norris 1910–13
J. Novotny (Czechoslovakia) 1964
Hilary Nunn* 1964–
L. C. A. Nunn 1936–40
Riitta Nurkka (Finland) 1965
Miss Nutt 1922

R. A. O'Brien 1910–11
J. O'Dea (Australia) 1952–54
Dr Onodera 1915
Dr Orr 1928
G. Owen 1953–55
P. A. Owren 1947–48
H. Ozeki 1958–60
E. Ozlüarda (Turkey) 1962

R. H. Pain 1962
A. Paine 1903–04
S. G. Paine 1910–11
H. A. Painter 1945–50
R. H. Painter 1956–57
T. J. Painter 1960–64
W. E. Parish 1964–
F. Parkes-Weber 1913
Dorothy Parkin* 1951–59
F. W. Parrish 1957–59
Mrs Parsons 1912
P. Parthasarathy (India) 1922
S. M. Partridge 1939–42
Lavinia Patterson 1930–32
V. N. Patwardhan (India) 1934–35
S. G. Pavlidis (Greece) 1956
A. V. Payne 1966
I. J. Payne 1960
J. H. Pearce 1955–57
Margaret Pearce 1930–32
Ursula Pearce 1963–65
J. D. Pearson 1953
W. J. Penfold 1909–16

J. R. Penney 1941–47
L. Penrose, F.R.S. 1931
H. R. Perkins 1947–50
C. J. Perret 1954–57
H. Perrot (France) 1956–57
Edith Perry* 1929–35
E. A. Peters 1900, 1901
G. F. Petrie 1901–39, 1941–43
Toby Phillips 1966–
Margaret Pickersgill* 1923–24, 1931
A. E. Pierce 1950–53
Regina Pietruszko 1960–61
Margaret Pile 1948–51
Jane Pincent* 1947–49
Dr Piper 1930
Ruth Pitt 1928–40
M. D. Pittam 1956–64
Helen Pixell 1911–13
C. A. Placido de Sousa 1963–66
P. Plackett (Australia) 1962
P. Plieger (Netherlands) 1961
Mrs Plimmer 1918
H. G. Plimmer 1902–04, 1906, 1908
R. H. A. Plimmer 1903
L. Poleff (Morocco) 1958
M. R. Pollock, F.R.S.* 1947–49
Vanda Pond 1944–48
Annie Ponsford 1932–34
G. Pontier (Italy) 1957
K. Porchinski (Austria) 1956
Agnes Porter 1911
A. M. Porter 1956
P. Poszwinski (Poland) 1962
F. Pötsch (Austria) 1955–56
R. Pournaki (Iran) 1957
D. J. Pratt-Johnson (South Africa) 1921–22
Evangeline Price 1919
Barbara Prideaux 1961–
H. Priestley 1912–13
J. Priestley 1898–99
G. Prodi (Italy) 1956
T. F. G. Prunty 1933–35
A. J. Pusztai (Hungary) 1958–63
Szuzsanna Pusztai (Hungary) 1966

C. Quadling 1931–56
M. Y. Qureshi 1964

R. R. Race. F.R.S.* 1947–
M. R. Radovanovic (Yugoslavia) 1962
J. J. Rae (Canada) 1934–35
A. Rafyi 1947
S. S. Randall 1934–37
R. F. Rao (India) 1955
H. S. Raper, F.R.S. 1905–08
L. H. Rasch (Germany) 1955
O. D. Ratnoff (U.S.A.) 1962
N. Raw 1920
W. Ray 1912
J. M. Reckler (U.S.A.) 1966
B. R. Record 1939–41, 1945–47
P. Reeve* 1959–
Y. Rege 1962–63
W. S. Reich (France) 1939
D. Reid 1907–09
C. Renner 1900
Mabel Rhodes* 1912–49

Elsie Richardson 1945–46
D. P. Rimal (India) 1963
Margaret Rissik 1963
Jane Ritchie 1963
R. J. Roantree (U.S.A.) 1964
D. S. Roberts 1963–64
Margaret Roberts 1938
A. W. Robertson 1908
Muriel Robertson, F.R.S. 1909–61
Mr Robinson 1909
L. C. Robinson 1959–66
R. Robison, F.R.S. 1913–41
J. F. Robyt (U.S.A.) 1964
Andrée Roche 1931
Jean Roche 1931
L. Roden (Sweden) 1961
G. J. Roderick 1960–
J. Rodican 1954–60
R. Roger 1918–19
H. J. Rogers 1940–47
Joan Rogers 1959
L. Rogers 1908
Elzbieta Romanowska (Poland) 1962
J. M. Rondle* 1952–54
Margaret Roscoe* 1925–33
J. Rose Bradford 1920
Adèle Rosenheim 1930–38
Alison Ross 1939–42
E. H. Ross 1912–16
H. C. Ross 1912–16
M. A. Ross 1940
E. R. Rost 1914
Margaret Rowatt 1950–56
S. Rowland 1898–1917
Dr Rozansky (Israel) 1958
J. Rücher (Yugoslavia)
G. Rummelsbrug 1950
Bertha Runge 1919
M. Ruszkiewicz 1954–57
T. S. Rutherfoord 1914–15
Sheila Rutherford 1920
H. N. Rydon* 1947

A. B. Sabin (U.S.A.) 1934–35
J. Sachs 1966–
W. Sackman (Switzerland) 1957
M. M. El. Sadr (Egypt) 1938–41
M. H. Salaman 1935–39
A. Salter 1899–1900
A. Sampaio (Portugal) 1962, 1963
Georgina Sampson 1961–64
Myra Sampson (U.S.A.) 1932–33
K. E. Sanderson (U.S.A.) 1965
Ruth Sanger* 1947–
Dr el Sarky (Egypt) 1964
M. Sato 1920–21
M. W. Schachter 1953–55
H. Schmidt 1913–15
Marjorie Schultess-Young 1927–28
H. L. Schütze 1913–46
Miss Schwab 1915
J. H. Schwab (U.S.A.) 1961
A. M. Scott (Nigeria) 1956
F. Scott 1903
Major Seddon 1920
J. Ségal (France) 1922
H. Seidelin 1911

S. Seidl (Germany) 1965
C. G. Seligman, F.R.S. 1916
K. C. Sellers 1942
Marjorie Semple 1923
B. Sevgen (Turkey) 1955
J. Sevi 1922
B. Seydian (Iran) 1958
H. Seyfried (Poland) 1963
Dr Sezginman (Turkey) 1964
F. Sgambati (Italy) 1957
A. W. Shaafsma (South Africa) 1956
Rosa Shalit 1932
Constance Shaw* 1948–
Patricia Sheehan 1953–54
W. Shepherd 1964
J. A. H. Sherwin 1913–14
H. L. Shipp 1928–29
G. Shwarztzman (U.S.S.R.) 1922
Elsie Silk 1964–65
B. T. Simpson (U.S.A.) 1929
Ruth Skelton 1917–18
E. B. Slack 1944–46
K. N. Slessor (Canada) 1964
A. B. Smallman 1904
Alice Henderson Smith 1919
Anne Smith 1966–
D. D. Smith 1958
E. E. Smith 1960–63
Edna Smith 1926–28
G. H. Smith 1947–49
G. W. Smith 1910
Greig Smith 1922
Hannah Henderson Smith* 1919–50
J. Henderson Smith 1908–16
K. A. Smith 1946–49
Sylvia Smith 1958–63
Joan Sneath* 1954–55
G. A. Snow 1938–45
Katharine Soames* 1922–30
H. S. Sodhi (Burma) 1957
Dr Soemiatno (Indonesia) 1958
T. Soodsakoran (Thailand) 1963
Elizabeth Sparrow 1956–57
J. Spasojevic (Yugoslavia) 1957
Janet Spencer 1965
Shirley Spooner 1945–48
N. R. Srbije (Yugoslavia) 1957
M. V. Stack 1946–48
Ann Staley* 1966
A. F. B. Standfast 1928, 1946–
Winifred Stanier 1950
Anne-Marie Staub* (France) 1947–48
R. de S. Stawell (Australia) 1908
Dorothy Steabben 1922–45
Marguerit Steiger (Switzerland) 1939
J. S. Stephens 1927–28
Dr Stern 1926
Miss Sternberg 1910
F. H. Stewart 1920–21
B. A. D. Stocker, F.R.S. 1953–65
Jane Stocker* 1958–59
G. Stone 1961–64
T. V. Subbaiah (India) 1963
K. V. Subbarao (India) 1964
Dr Sulcz (Germany) 1920
W. St. C. Symmers 1898
R. L. M. Synge, F.R.S., Nobel Laureate 1944–48

G. Szabo (Hungary) 1964
L. Szabo (France) 1953–55

G. Talbot 1920
B. Tanko (Hungary) 1933–35
Dr Tarapurvalla 1912
H. L. A. Tarr 1935
Janice Taverne* 1962–
C. Taxner (Hungary) 1934–35
S. el Tayeb (Egypt) 1966
Angela Taylor 1965–
Pamela Taylor 1960–64
Alice Tazelaar 1937–41
Mary Tazelaar 1925
H. Tebbutt 1912–13
J. S. Tew 1898
E. M. Thain 1950–55
A. C. Thaysen 1914–17
J. Thomas 1957–58
Lisel Thomas 1956–59
Aileen Thompson 1955–56
Cecily Thompson 1919
Joan Thompson* 1950–53
J. D. Thomson 1906–08, 1912–16
Doraine Thow 1954–56
T. Thunberg (Sweden) 1901
F. Tidswell 1913
G. L. Timms (Kenya) 1965
Patricia Tippett* 1958–
T. Toda (Japan) 1923–24
A. R. Todd, F.R.S., Nobel Laureate 1937–38
C. Todd, F.R.S. 1901–04
P. K. Topa (Pakistan) 1963
Doris Toten 1938–41
Frances Tozer 1917–20
J. Triginer (Spain) 1960
Mr Trotter 1909
M. Tsurumi 1916–17
P. Tuchinda (Thailand) 1959
N. Tulga (Turkey) 1957
P. Tulkens (Belgium) 1965
W. J. Tulloch 1918
S. Tuncman 1954
Miss Turner 1915
G. S. Turner 1962–66
Patricia Turner 1955–57
H. M. Tyler 1958–60

G. Uhlenbruck (Germany) 1960–61
A. Umnova (U.S.S.R.) 1959

J. Valladares 1912
L. Vallet 1950–
B. R. Varella (Spain) 1947
Dr Vickers 1911
A. M. Vilches (U.S.A.) 1960
J. L. V. Villamarin (Spain) 1965
W. A. Vincent 1961–65
H. Violle 1914
C. J. Virden 1935
A. Visentini 1912
Maija Vitolins 1962
F. Vivanco (Spain) 1936–37
N. Vorias (Greece) 1965

Marion Waddell 1944–46
Martha Wadja 1963–64

S. D. Wainwright* 1948–49
Jean Walby 1950–52
H. Waldmann 1937
Gwen Walker 1956–59
Marian Waller (U.S.A.) 1961, 1962
S. Walpole 1905–09
Joan Walsh 1966
P. W. Walton 1959–62
A. Wander (Germany) 1958
Denise Ward 1966–
R. O. Ward 1909
S. A. Warsi (Pakistan) 1956–57
J. W. Washbourne 1899
T. Watabiki 1916
Winifred Watkins, F.R.S. 1950–
Capt. Watson (Canada) 1920
Miss W. A. F. Webber (Uganda) 1959
Dr Weber 1913
L. Meyer Wedell 1909
H. Weil-Malherbe 1940
B. G. F. Weitz 1947–66
F. R. Wells 1963–
Mrs Werner 1913
E. D. Wesley 1964–
A. L. de Wesselow 1914–15
C. West 1944
L. W. Wheeldon 1959
W. J. Whelan 1956–64
Doreen Whitaker* 1948
A. L. White 1899–1949
J. D. White 1910–11
P. Bruce White, F.R.S. 1924–27
R. G. White 1925–26
S. A. White 1931–
T. White 1940
A. White-Robertson 1908
J. T. Wigham 1906
D. L. Wilhelm (Australia) 1953–59
R. G. Wilkinson 1964–66
Dr Williams 1898
T. Williams 1966
Gillian Williamson 1966–
Miss I. J. F. Williamson 1929
Dr Wilson 1920
Dagmar Wilson 1942–45
Florence Wilson 1911–12
Mr Wingate 1912
Joyce Witt 1943
Ruth Wittler (U.S.A.) 1949–51, 1960
P. Wolf 1954–56
P. W. Wolf 1959
Frances (Chick) Wood 1912–15
H. M. Woodcock* 1906–18, 1925–28
Hilda Woods 1919
A. N. Worden 1939–40
Constance (Edgar) Work 1935–41
T. S. Work 1937–38
C. C. Worrill 1957
G. P. Wright 1931
O. K. Wright 1920–22

S. Yabe 1922
K. Yamakami 1920
Dr Young 1924
E. G. Young (Canada) 1939
W. J. Young 1901–13
G. Udny Yule, F.R.S. 1912–14
H. S. Yusef (India) 1934–35

Miss E. Zachari (Indonesia) 1962
K. Zakrzewski 1947
S. M. Zan (Burma) 1964

Diane Ziderman 1965–
S. S. Zilva* 1914–50
M. Zorriassatein (Persia) 1945–46

Index

Index

Accessory food factors, 145; *see* Vitamins

Accessory Food Factors Committee, 128, 152–7

Acton Castle, smallpox vaccine at, 86

Addison, Lt. Col., 129

Admiralty Committee on Diving, 107–12

Adrenaline, 60, 220

Agglutinating sera in diagnosis, 124

Agglutination, of bacteria, 125; red blood cells, 193–6

Aykroyd, W. R., 144

Albumin fraction of blood, 203

Alcoholic fermentation, 113–9

Allen & Hanbury, 39

Amies, C. R., 134, 175

Amino acids, in blood group substances, 195; in proteins, 198

Anaerobic infections, *see* tetanus, gas gangrene

Anderson, Sir John, *see* Waverley, Viscount

Aneurin, *see* Vitamin B

Animals, licence for experiments on, 29–34

Anniversary, 75th, of Lister Institute, 226

Anopheles, see mosquitoes

Antibodies, 21; protein nature, 91, 202; *see* antisera, antitoxins

Antigens, 21; bacterial, 136–8; blood group, 193; chemical nature, 167–70, 194–7

Antihaemophilic factor, 203–4

Antisera, 22; production, 84–5, 184–5; in precipitin tests, 207

Antitoxins, 21; *see* diphtheria, gas gangrene, tetanus

Antivivisectionists, opposition by, 29, 43–6

Arkwright, J., 73, 134–7, 142

Ascorbic acid, *see* Vitamin C

Asquith, H. H., 43

Atkin, E. E., 78

Australian Army Medical Corps, 68–9

Australia, Martin in, 64–6

Bacot, A., 78, 100–1, 134–5

Bacteria, freezing and grinding, 57–73; generation time, 223; genetics, 221–3; L-forms, 138–40; pure cultures, 19; variation, 136–8

Bacterial Vaccine Laboratory, *see* Lister Institute

Bacteriology, clinical, 56; Department, *see* Lister Institute industrial, 56

Bacteriophage, 221

Baddiley, J., 166

Barnard, J. E., 36, 58